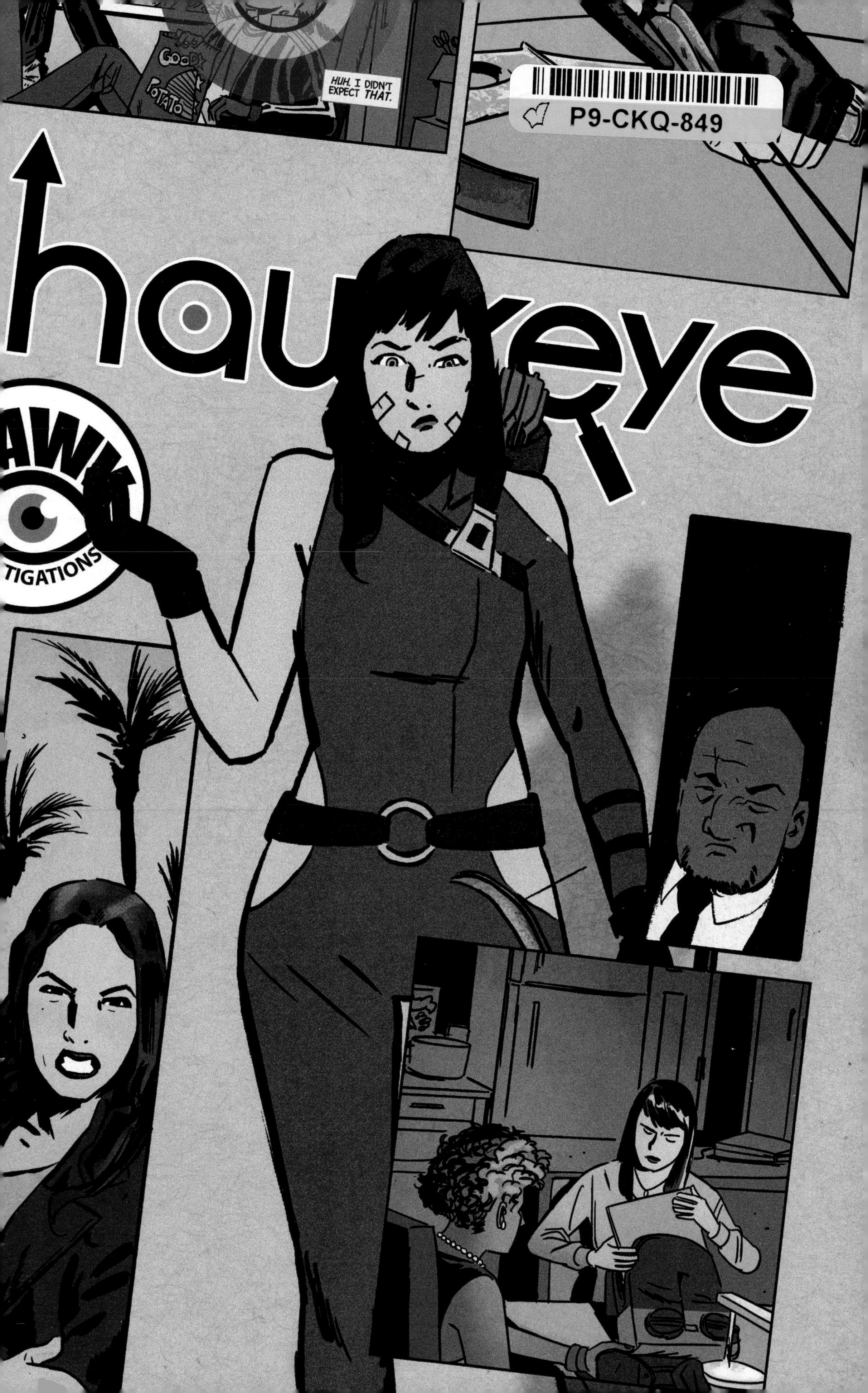
HUH, I DIDN'T EXPECT THAT.
hawkeye
AWK
TIGATIONS

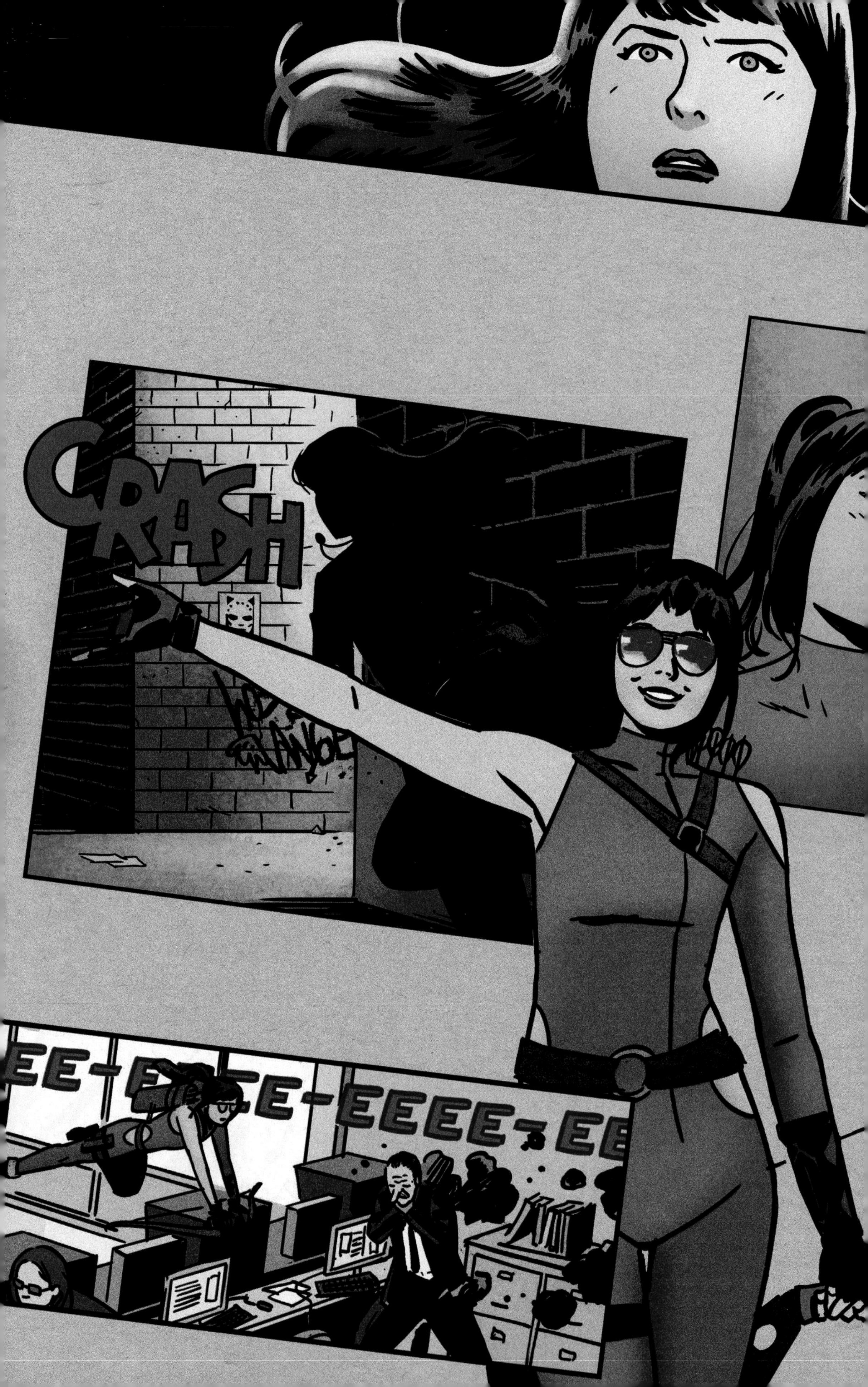
CRASH
EE-E E-EEEE-EE

hawkeye
anchor points

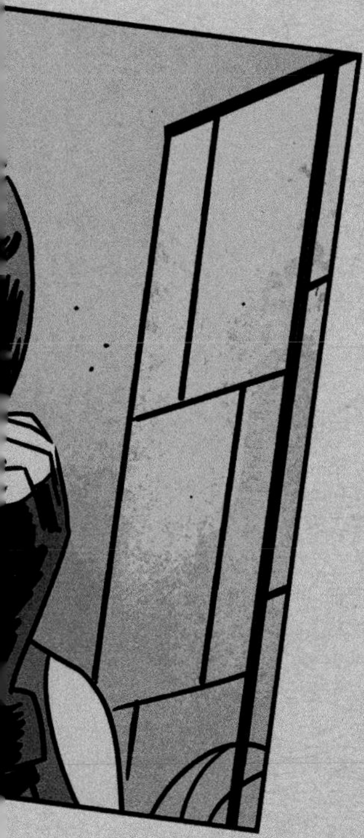

Kelly Thompson
writer

Leonardo Romero (#1-4)
& **Michael Walsh** (#5-6)
artists

Jordie Bellaire
color artist

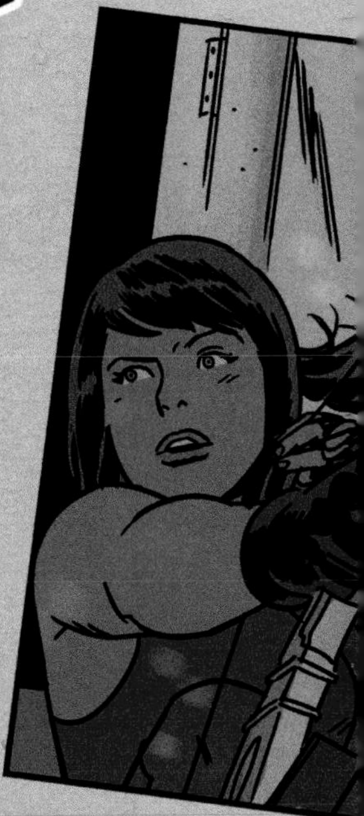

VC's Joe Sabino
letterer

Julian Totino Tedesco
cover art

Charles Beacham
& **Sana Amanat**
editors

collection editor **Jennifer Grünwald** • assistant editor **Caitlin O'Connell**
associate managing editor **Kateri Woody** • editor, special projects **Mark D. Beazley**
vp production & special projects **Jeff Youngquist** • svp print, sales & marketing **David Gabriel**
book designer **Jay Bowen**

editor in chief **Axel Alonso** • chief creative officer **Joe Quesada**
president **Dan Buckley** • executive producer **Alan Fine**

HAWKEYE: KATE BISHOP VOL. 1 — ANCHOR POINTS. Contains material originally published in magazine form as HAWKEYE #1-6. First printing 2017. ISBN# 978-1-302-90514-9. Published by MARVEL WORLDWIDE, INC., a subsidiary of MARVEL ENTERTAINMENT, LLC. OFFICE OF PUBLICATION: 135 West 50th Street, New York, NY 10020. **Printed in the U.S.A.** DAN BUCKLEY, President, Marvel Entertainment; JOE QUESADA, Chief Creative Officer; TOM BREVOORT, SVP of Publishing; DAVID BOGART, SVP of Business Affairs & Operations, Publishing & Partnership; C.B. CEBULSKI, VP of Brand Management & Development, Asia; DAVID GABRIEL, SVP of Sales & Marketing, Publishing; JEFF YOUNGQUIST, VP of Production & Special Projects; DAN CARR, Executive Director of Publishing Technology; ALEX MORALES, Director of Publishing Operations; SUSAN CRESPI, Production Manager; STAN LEE, Chairman Emeritus. For information regarding advertising in Marvel Comics or on Marvel.com, please contact Vit DeBellis, Integrated Sales Manager, at vdebellis@marvel.com. For Marvel subscription inquiries, please call 888-511-5480. **Manufactured between 4/7/2017 and 5/9/2017 by QUAD/GRAPHICS WASECA, WASECA, MN, USA.**

10 9 8 7 6 5 4 3 2 1

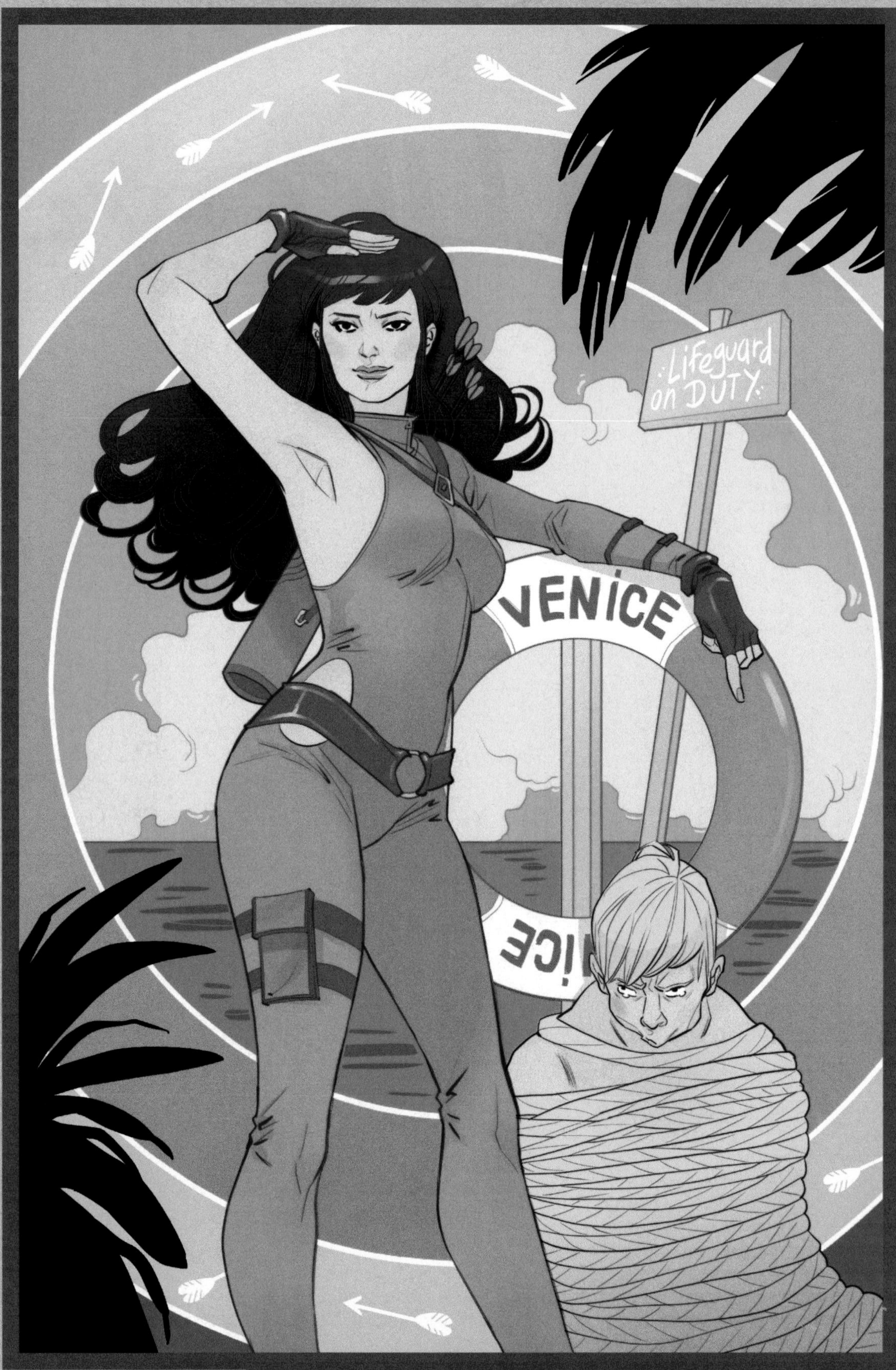
Lifeguard
on DUTY
VENICE

#1 variant by
Marguerite Sauvage

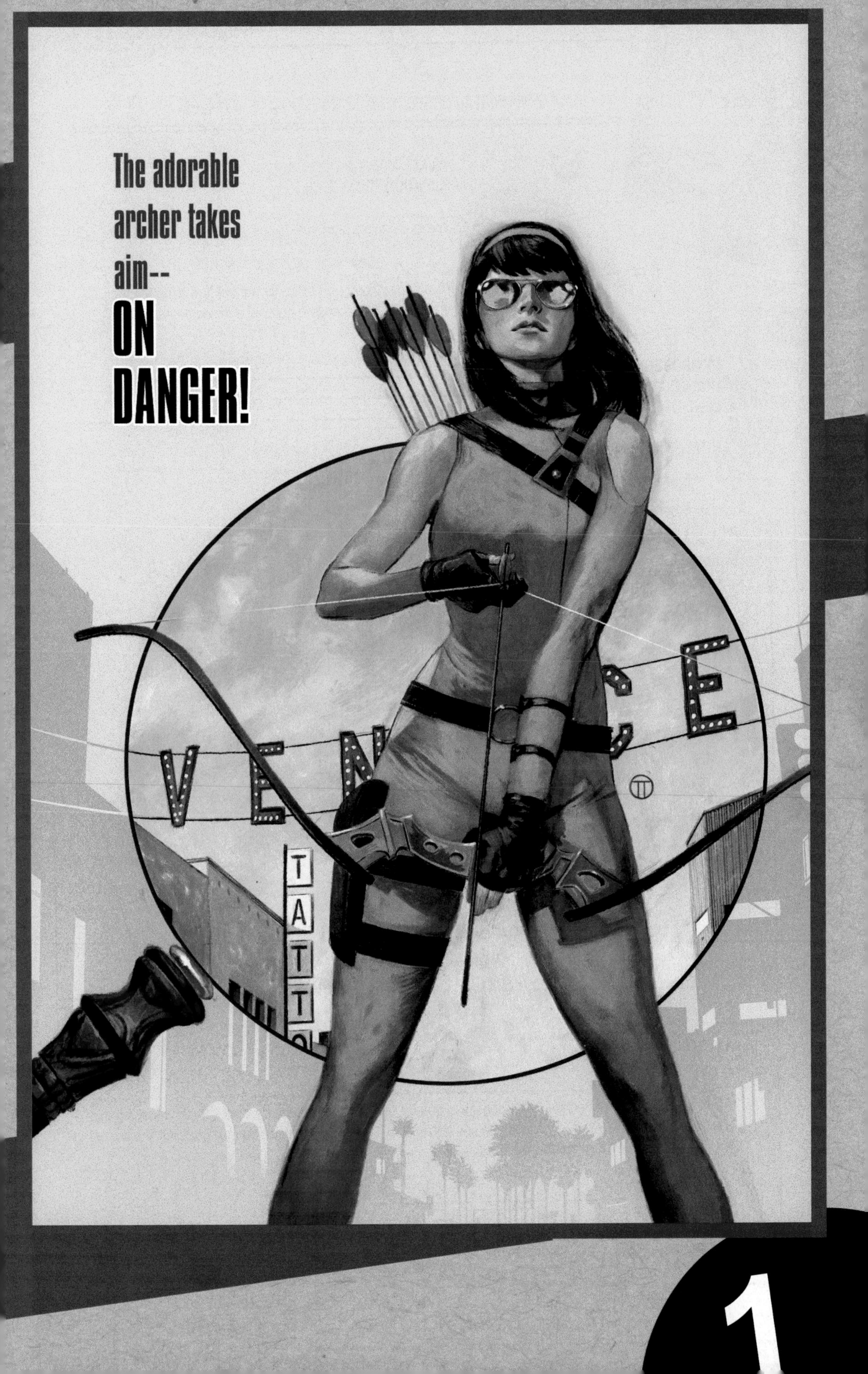
The adorable archer takes aim--
ON DANGER!
1

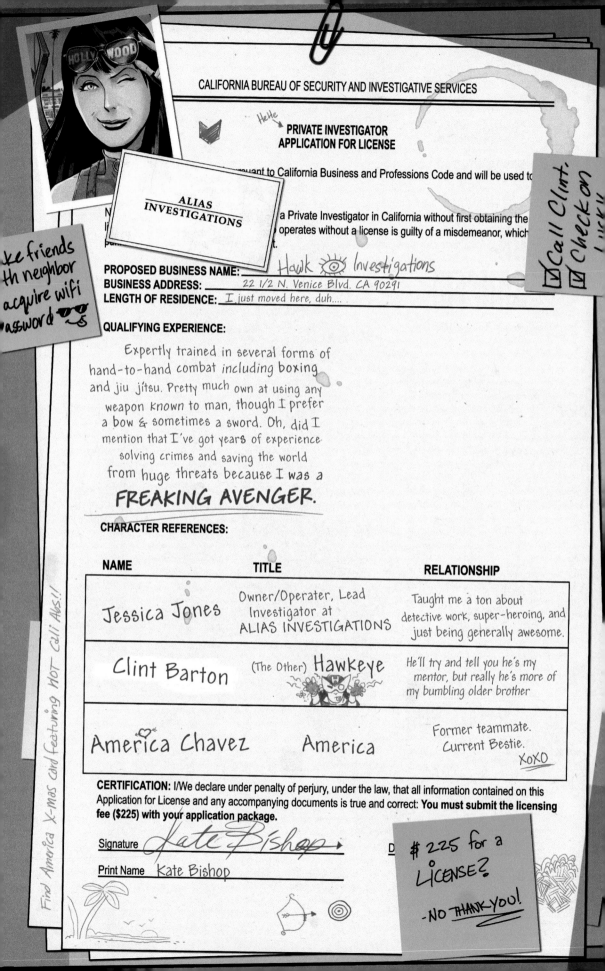

CALIFORNIA BUREAU OF SECURITY AND INVESTIGATIVE SERVICES

HeHe

**PRIVATE INVESTIGATOR
APPLICATION FOR LICENSE**

...suant to California Business and Professions Code and will be used to...

...a Private Investigator in California without first obtaining the...
...operates without a license is guilty of a misdemeanor, which...

ALIAS INVESTIGATIONS

☑ Call Clint.
☑ Check on Lucky!!

PROPOSED BUSINESS NAME: Hawk 👁 Investigations
BUSINESS ADDRESS: 22 1/2 N. Venice Blvd. CA 90291
LENGTH OF RESIDENCE: I just moved here, duh....

...ke friends
th neighbor
acquire wifi
*assword 🕶

Find America X-mas card featuring HOT Cali Abs!!

QUALIFYING EXPERIENCE:

Expertly trained in several forms of hand-to-hand combat including boxing and jiu jitsu. Pretty much own at using any weapon known to man, though I prefer a bow & sometimes a sword. Oh, did I mention that I've got years of experience solving crimes and saving the world from huge threats because I was a

FREAKING AVENGER.

CHARACTER REFERENCES:

NAME	TITLE	RELATIONSHIP
Jessica Jones	Owner/Operater, Lead Investigator at ALIAS INVESTIGATIONS	Taught me a ton about detective work, super-heroing, and just being generally awesome.
Clint Barton	(The Other) Hawkeye	He'll try and tell you he's my mentor, but really he's more of my bumbling older brother
America Chavez	America	Former teammate. Current Bestie. XOXO

CERTIFICATION: I/We declare under penalty of perjury, under the law, that all information contained on this Application for License and any accompanying documents is true and correct: **You must submit the licensing fee ($225) with your application package.**

Signature *Kate Bishop*

Print Name Kate Bishop

$ 225 for a
LICENSE?

- NO THANK YOU!

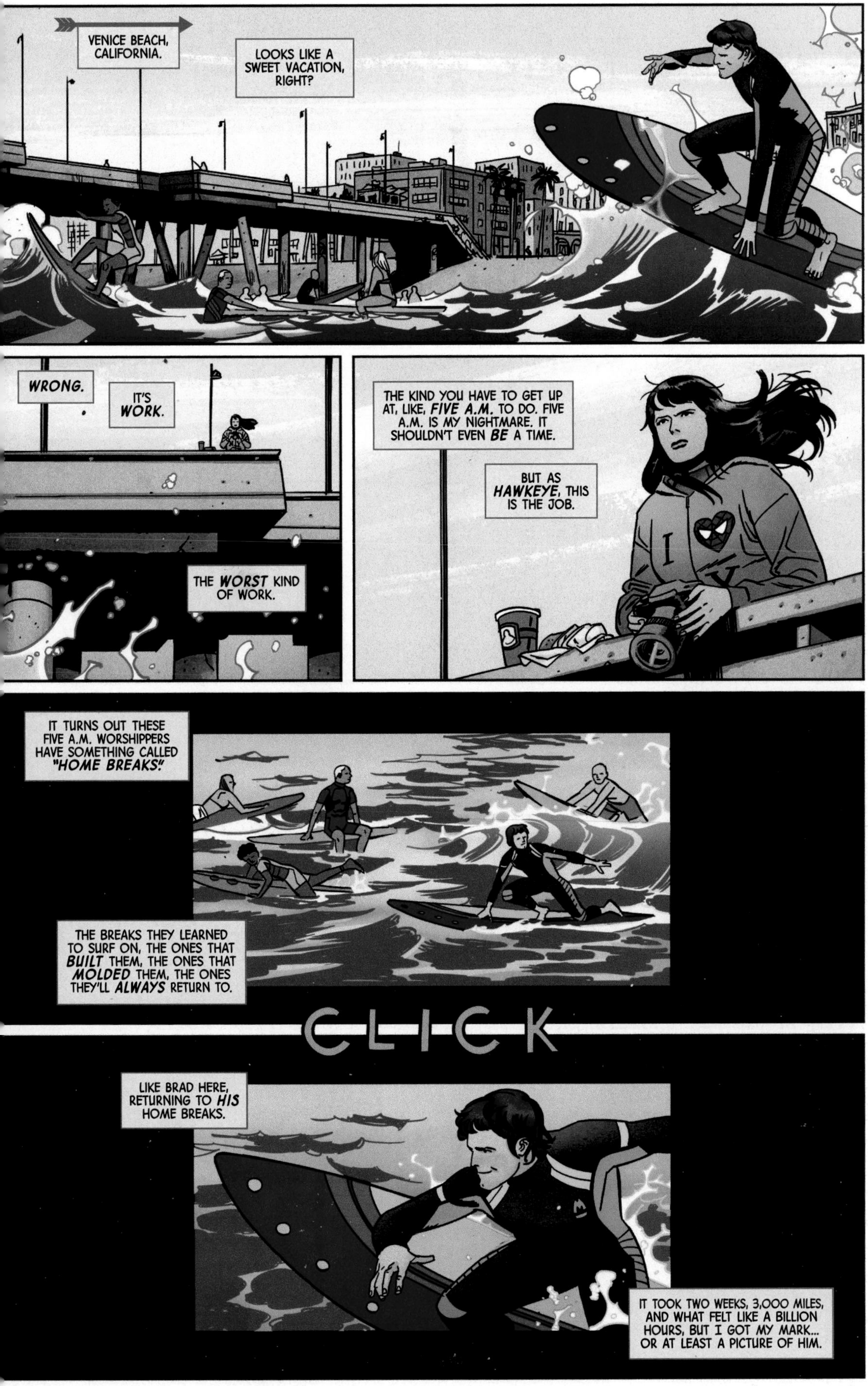
VENICE BEACH, CALIFORNIA.
LOOKS LIKE A SWEET VACATION, RIGHT?
WRONG.
IT'S WORK.
THE WORST KIND OF WORK.
THE KIND YOU HAVE TO GET UP AT, LIKE, FIVE A.M. TO DO. FIVE A.M. IS MY NIGHTMARE. IT SHOULDN'T EVEN BE A TIME.
BUT AS HAWKEYE, THIS IS THE JOB.
IT TURNS OUT THESE FIVE A.M. WORSHIPPERS HAVE SOMETHING CALLED "HOME BREAKS."
THE BREAKS THEY LEARNED TO SURF ON, THE ONES THAT BUILT THEM, THE ONES THAT MOLDED THEM, THE ONES THEY'LL ALWAYS RETURN TO.
CLICK
LIKE BRAD HERE, RETURNING TO HIS HOME BREAKS.
IT TOOK TWO WEEKS, 3,000 MILES, AND WHAT FELT LIKE A BILLION HOURS, BUT I GOT MY MARK... OR AT LEAST A PICTURE OF HIM.

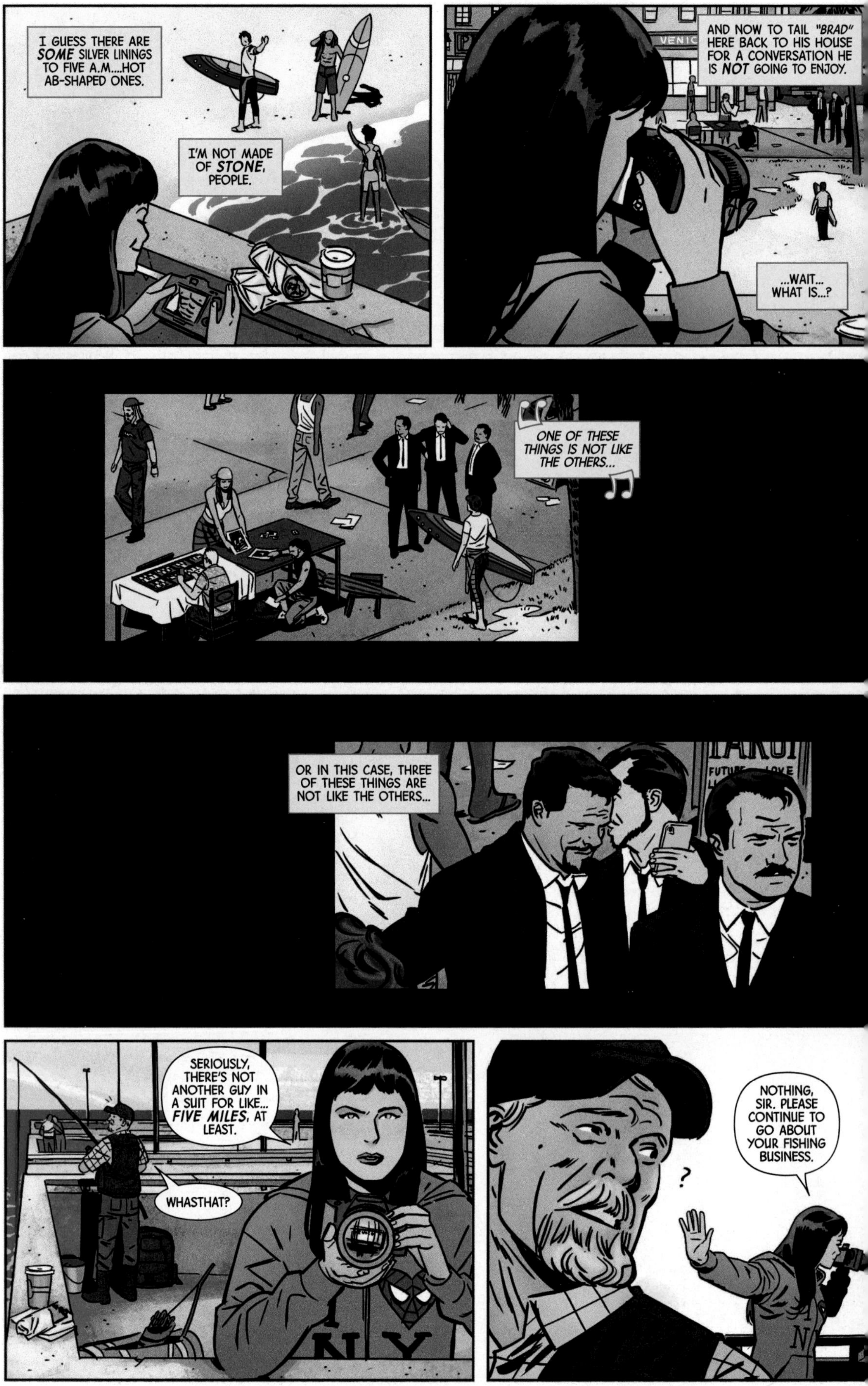
I GUESS THERE ARE SOME SILVER LININGS TO FIVE A.M....HOT AB-SHAPED ONES.
I'M NOT MADE OF STONE, PEOPLE.
AND NOW TO TAIL "BRAD" HERE BACK TO HIS HOUSE FOR A CONVERSATION HE IS NOT GOING TO ENJOY.
...WAIT... WHAT IS...?
ONE OF THESE THINGS IS NOT LIKE THE OTHERS...
OR IN THIS CASE, THREE OF THESE THINGS ARE NOT LIKE THE OTHERS...
SERIOUSLY, THERE'S NOT ANOTHER GUY IN A SUIT FOR LIKE... FIVE MILES, AT LEAST.
WHASTHAT?
?
NOTHING, SIR. PLEASE CONTINUE TO GO ABOUT YOUR FISHING BUSINESS.

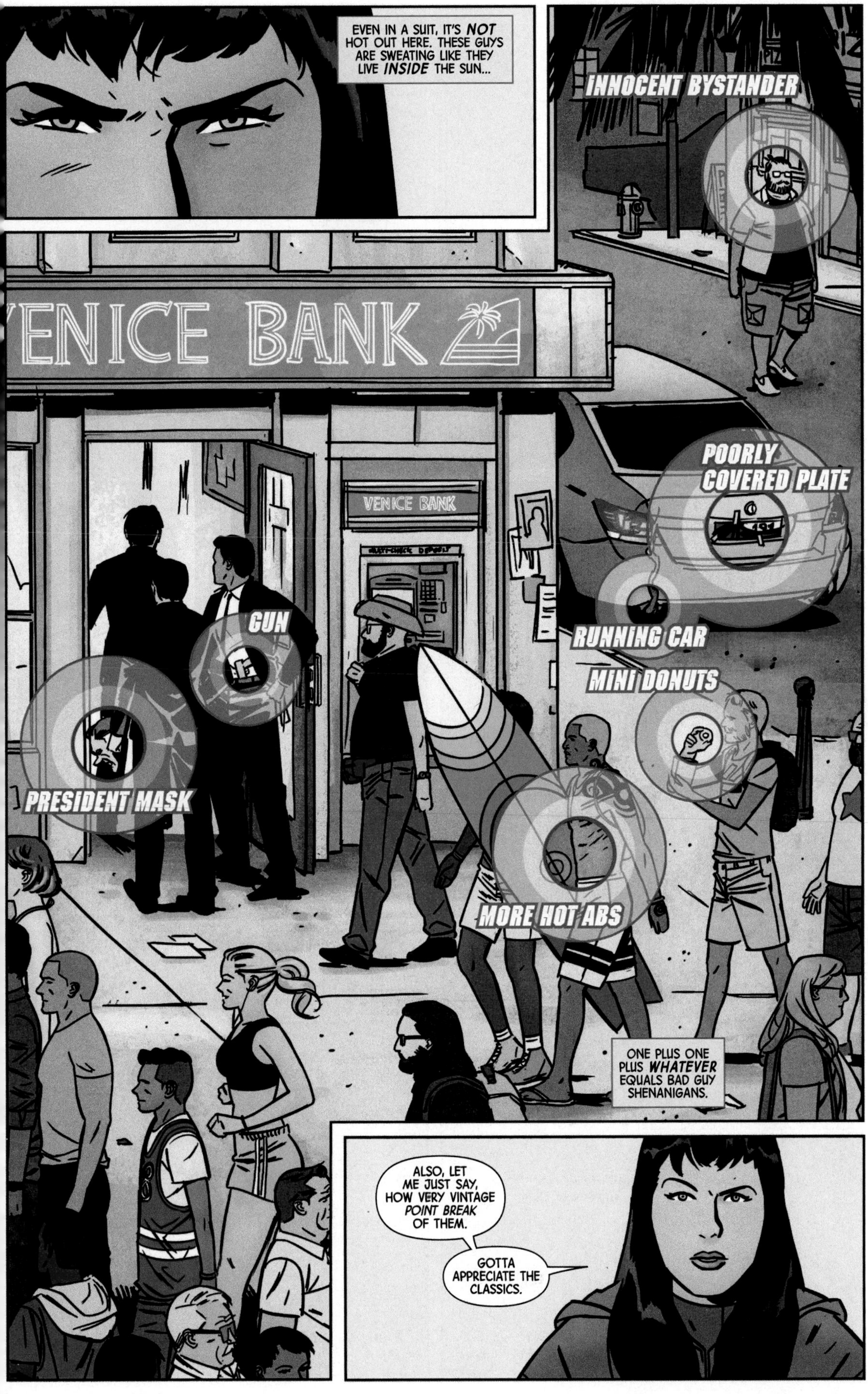
EVEN IN A SUIT, IT'S NOT HOT OUT HERE. THESE GUYS ARE SWEATING LIKE THEY LIVE INSIDE THE SUN...
INNOCENT BYSTANDER
VENICE BANK
VENICE BANK
POORLY COVERED PLATE
GUN
RUNNING CAR
MINI DONUTS
PRESIDENT MASK
MORE HOT ABS
ONE PLUS ONE PLUS WHATEVER EQUALS BAD GUY SHENANIGANS.
ALSO, LET ME JUST SAY, HOW VERY VINTAGE POINT BREAK OF THEM.
GOTTA APPRECIATE THE CLASSICS.

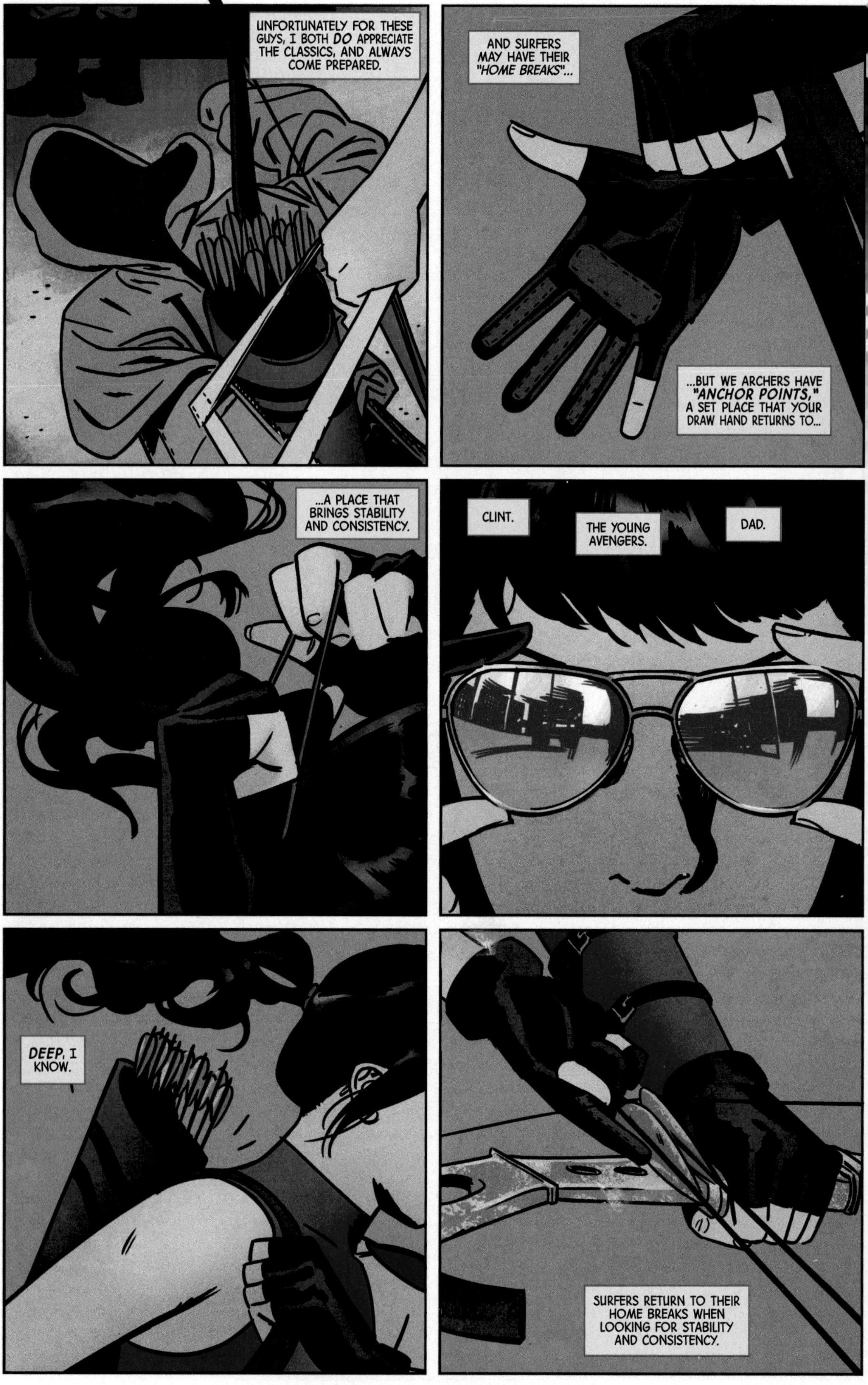
UNFORTUNATELY FOR THESE GUYS, I BOTH *DO* APPRECIATE THE CLASSICS, AND ALWAYS COME PREPARED.
AND SURFERS MAY HAVE THEIR "*HOME BREAKS*"...
...BUT WE ARCHERS HAVE "*ANCHOR POINTS,*" A SET PLACE THAT YOUR DRAW HAND RETURNS TO...
...A PLACE THAT BRINGS STABILITY AND CONSISTENCY.
CLINT.
THE YOUNG AVENGERS.
DAD.
DEEP, I KNOW.
SURFERS RETURN TO THEIR HOME BREAKS WHEN LOOKING FOR STABILITY AND CONSISTENCY.

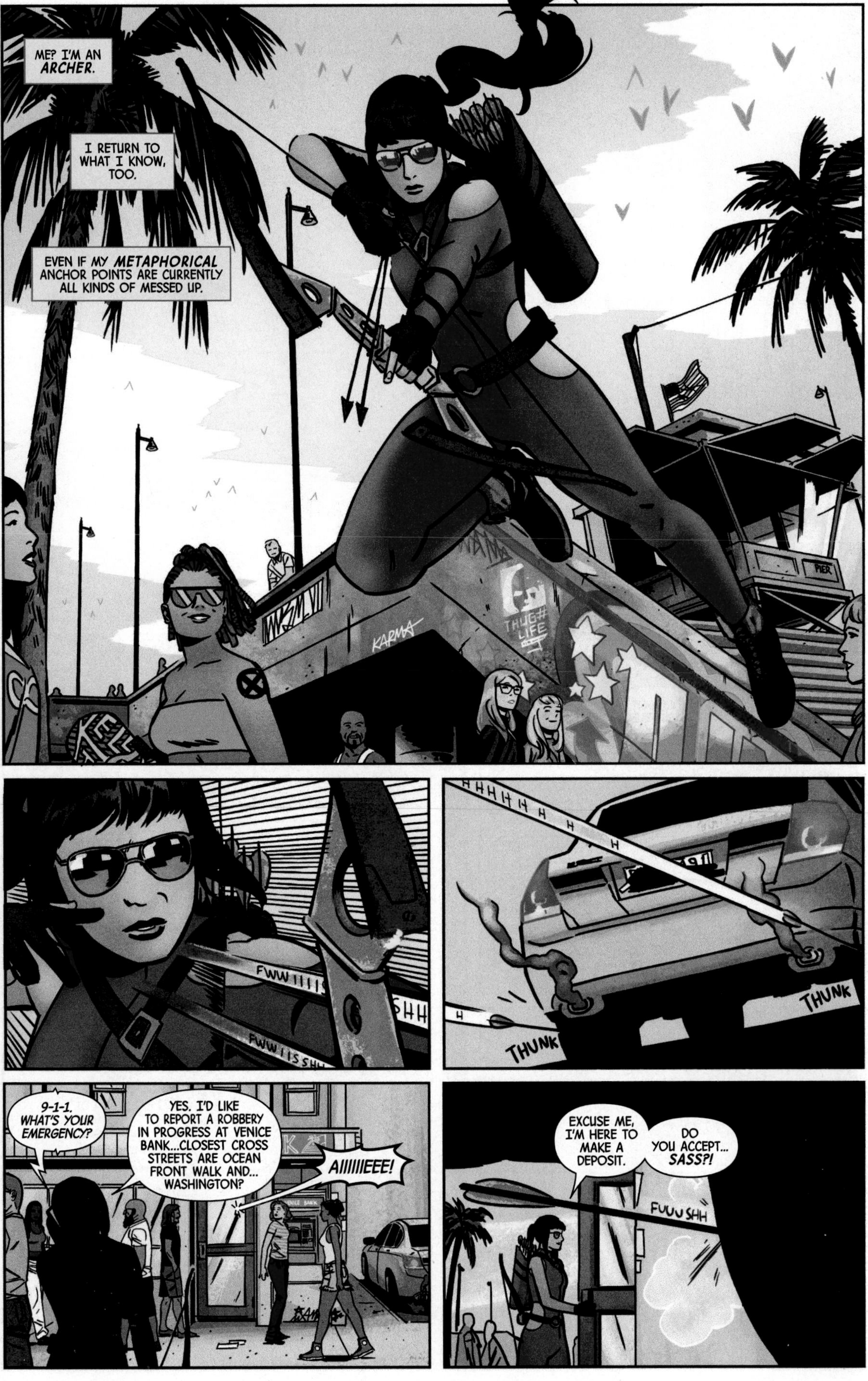
ME? I'M AN ARCHER.
I RETURN TO WHAT I KNOW, TOO.
EVEN IF MY METAPHORICAL ANCHOR POINTS ARE CURRENTLY ALL KINDS OF MESSED UP.
KARMA
THUG LIFE
PIER
FWWIIIISSHH
FWWIISSHH
THUNK
THUNK
9-1-1. WHAT'S YOUR EMERGENCY?
YES. I'D LIKE TO REPORT A ROBBERY IN PROGRESS AT VENICE BANK...CLOSEST CROSS STREETS ARE OCEAN FRONT WALK AND... WASHINGTON?
AIIIIIIEEE!
EXCUSE ME, I'M HERE TO MAKE A DEPOSIT.
DO YOU ACCEPT... SASS?!
FUUUSHH

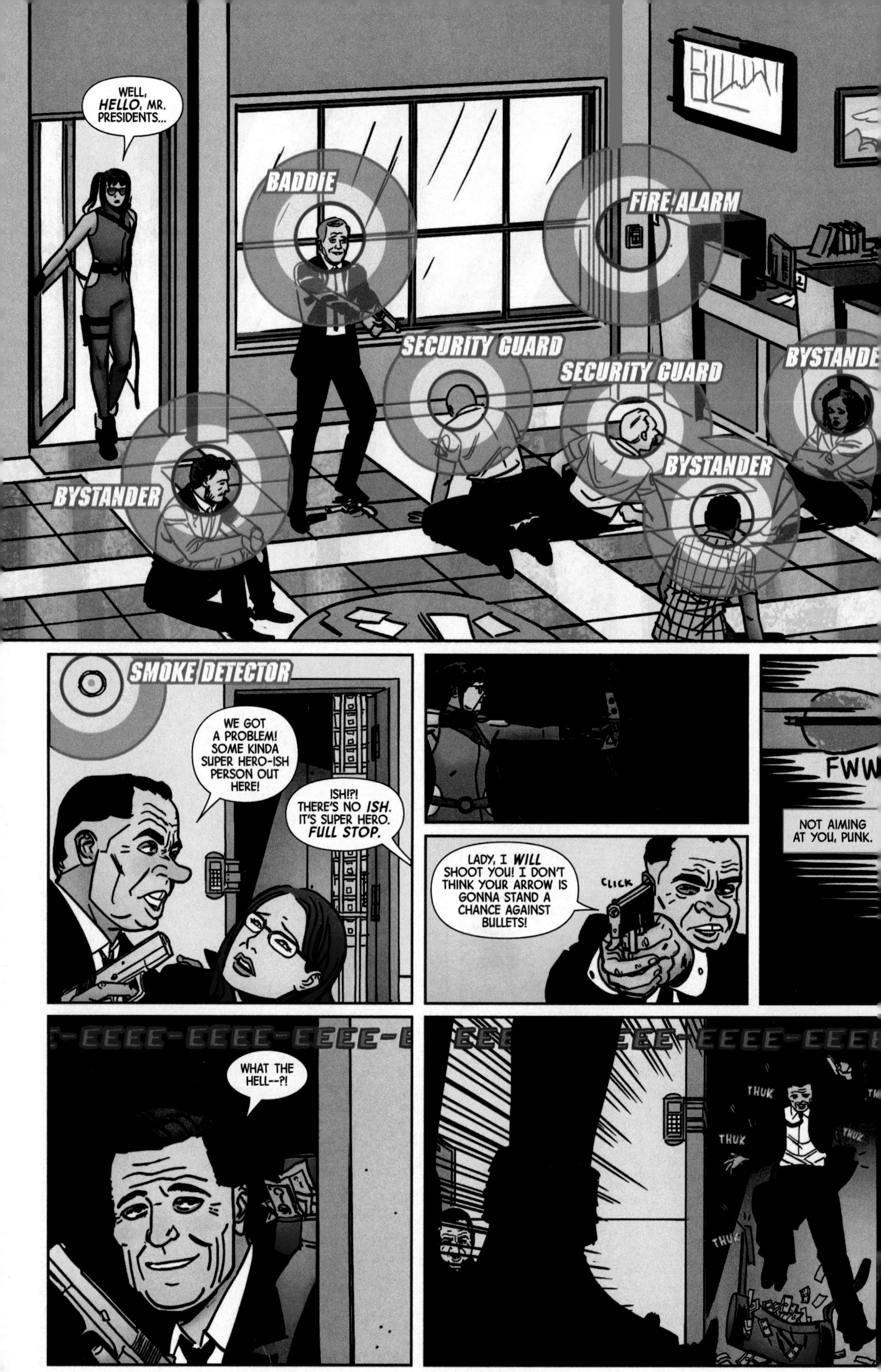
WELL, *HELLO*, MR. PRESIDENTS...
BADDIE
FIRE ALARM
SECURITY GUARD
SECURITY GUARD
BYSTANDE
BYSTANDER
BYSTANDER
SMOKE DETECTOR
WE GOT A PROBLEM! SOME KINDA SUPER HERO-ISH PERSON OUT HERE!
ISH!?! THERE'S NO *ISH*. IT'S SUPER HERO. *FULL STOP.*
LADY, I *WILL* SHOOT YOU! I DON'T THINK YOUR ARROW IS GONNA STAND A CHANCE AGAINST BULLETS!
CLICK
FWW
NOT AIMING AT YOU, PUNK.
E-EEEE-EEEE-EEEE-E
WHAT THE HELL--?!
EEEE-EEEE-EEEE
THUK
THUK
THUK
THUK

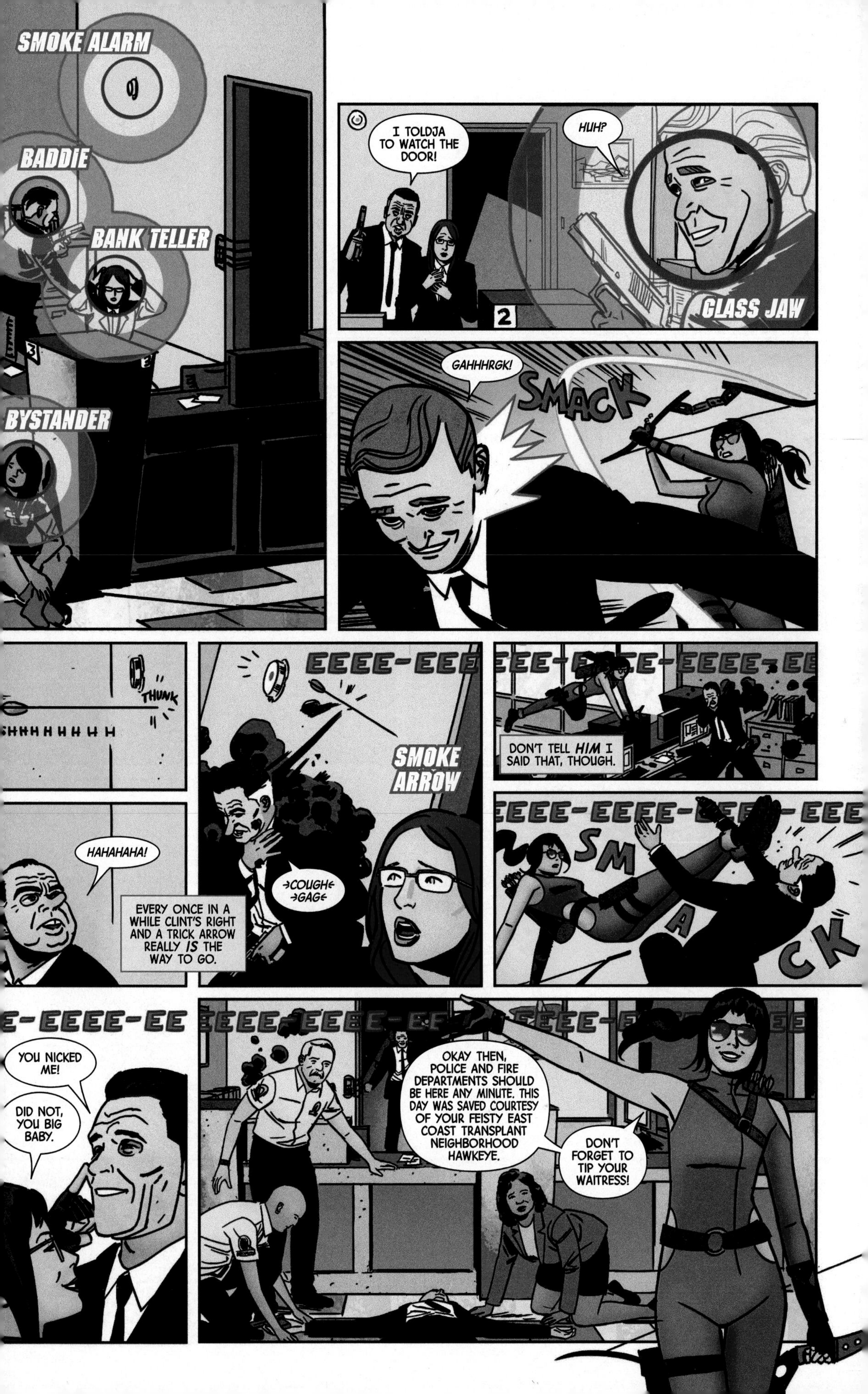
SMOKE ALARM
BADDIE
BANK TELLER
BYSTANDER
I TOLDJA TO WATCH THE DOOR!
HUH?
GLASS JAW
GAHHHRGK!
SMACK
THUNK
SMOKE ARROW
EEEE-EEE
→COUGH← →GAG←
HAHAHAHA!
EVERY ONCE IN A WHILE CLINT'S RIGHT AND A TRICK ARROW REALLY *IS* THE WAY TO GO.
DON'T TELL *HIM* I SAID THAT, THOUGH.
SMACK
YOU NICKED ME!
DID NOT, YOU BIG BABY.
OKAY THEN, POLICE AND FIRE DEPARTMENTS SHOULD BE HERE ANY MINUTE. THIS DAY WAS SAVED COURTESY OF YOUR FEISTY EAST COAST TRANSPLANT NEIGHBORHOOD HAWKEYE.
DON'T FORGET TO TIP YOUR WAITRESS!

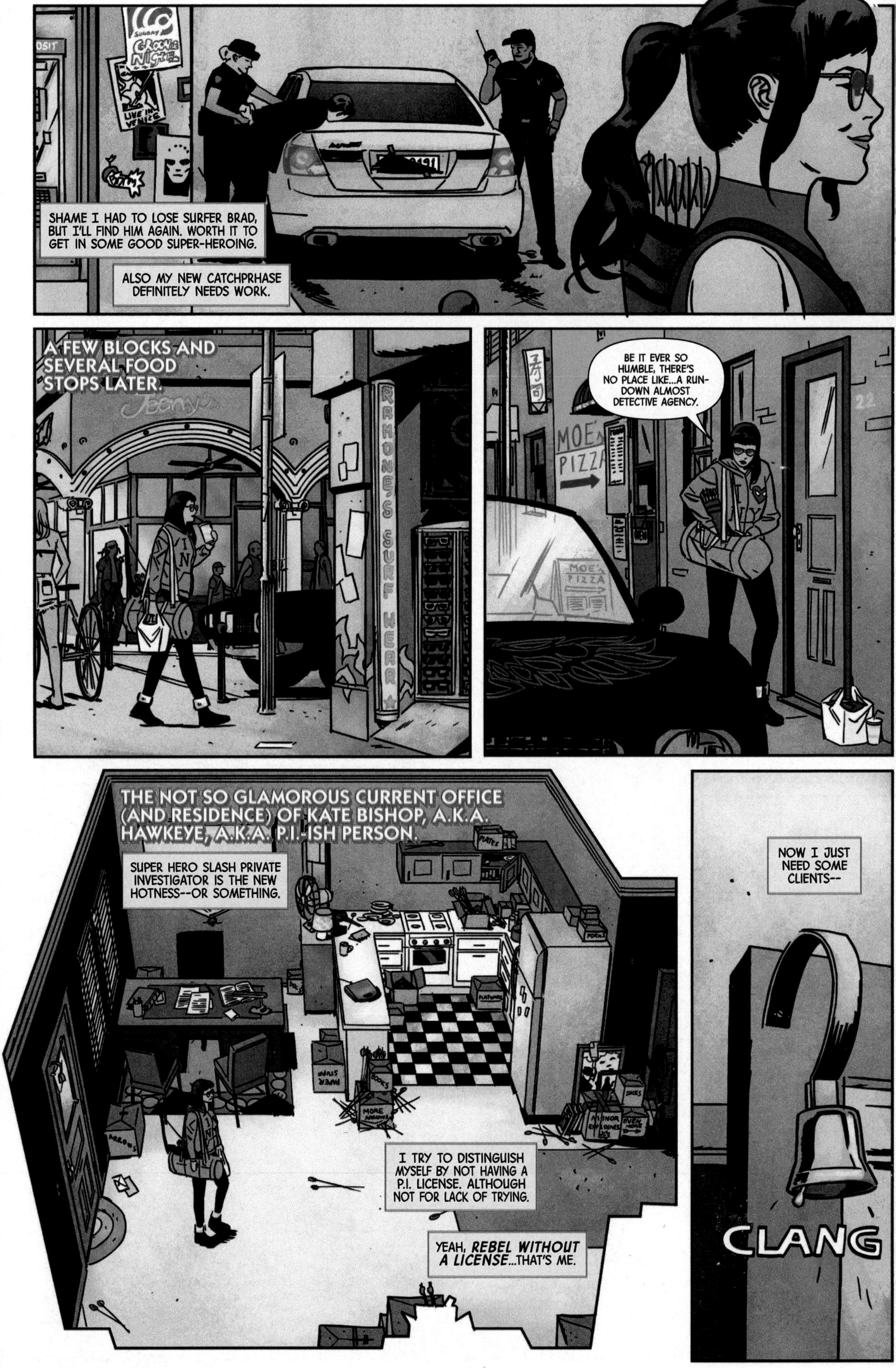
SHAME I HAD TO LOSE SURFER BRAD, BUT I'LL FIND HIM AGAIN. WORTH IT TO GET IN SOME GOOD SUPER-HEROING.
ALSO MY NEW CATCHPHRASE DEFINITELY NEEDS WORK.
A FEW BLOCKS AND SEVERAL FOOD STOPS LATER.
RAMONE'S SURF WEAR
BE IT EVER SO HUMBLE, THERE'S NO PLACE LIKE...A RUN-DOWN ALMOST DETECTIVE AGENCY.
MOE'S PIZZA
THE NOT SO GLAMOROUS CURRENT OFFICE (AND RESIDENCE) OF KATE BISHOP, A.K.A. HAWKEYE, A.K.A. P.I.-ISH PERSON.
SUPER HERO SLASH PRIVATE INVESTIGATOR IS THE NEW HOTNESS--OR SOMETHING.
I TRY TO DISTINGUISH MYSELF BY NOT HAVING A P.I. LICENSE. ALTHOUGH NOT FOR LACK OF TRYING.
YEAH, *REBEL WITHOUT A LICENSE*...THAT'S ME.
NOW I JUST NEED SOME CLIENTS--
CLANG

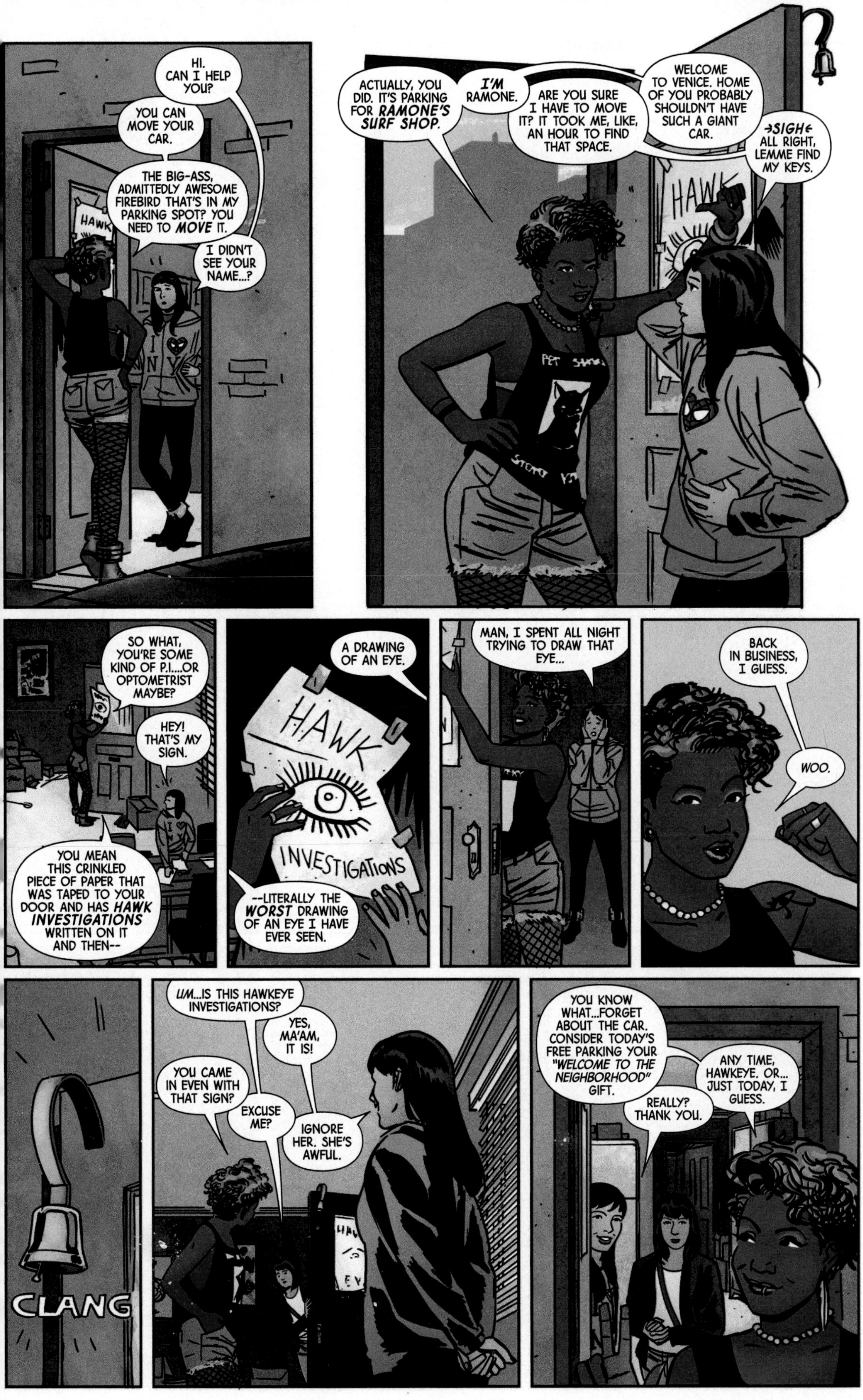
HI. CAN I HELP YOU?
YOU CAN MOVE YOUR CAR.
THE BIG-ASS, ADMITTEDLY AWESOME FIREBIRD THAT'S IN MY PARKING SPOT? YOU NEED TO MOVE IT.
I DIDN'T SEE YOUR NAME...?
HAWK
ACTUALLY, YOU DID. IT'S PARKING FOR RAMONE'S SURF SHOP.
I'M RAMONE.
ARE YOU SURE I HAVE TO MOVE IT? IT TOOK ME, LIKE, AN HOUR TO FIND THAT SPACE.
WELCOME TO VENICE. HOME OF YOU PROBABLY SHOULDN'T HAVE SUCH A GIANT CAR.
→SIGH← ALL RIGHT, LEMME FIND MY KEYS.
SO WHAT, YOU'RE SOME KIND OF P.I....OR OPTOMETRIST MAYBE?
HEY! THAT'S MY SIGN.
YOU MEAN THIS CRINKLED PIECE OF PAPER THAT WAS TAPED TO YOUR DOOR AND HAS HAWK INVESTIGATIONS WRITTEN ON IT AND THEN--
A DRAWING OF AN EYE.
HAWK
INVESTIGATIONS
--LITERALLY THE WORST DRAWING OF AN EYE I HAVE EVER SEEN.
MAN, I SPENT ALL NIGHT TRYING TO DRAW THAT EYE...
BACK IN BUSINESS, I GUESS.
WOO.
CLANG
UM...IS THIS HAWKEYE INVESTIGATIONS?
YES, MA'AM, IT IS!
YOU CAME IN EVEN WITH THAT SIGN?
EXCUSE ME?
IGNORE HER. SHE'S AWFUL.
YOU KNOW WHAT...FORGET ABOUT THE CAR. CONSIDER TODAY'S FREE PARKING YOUR "WELCOME TO THE NEIGHBORHOOD" GIFT.
REALLY? THANK YOU.
ANY TIME, HAWKEYE. OR... JUST TODAY, I GUESS.

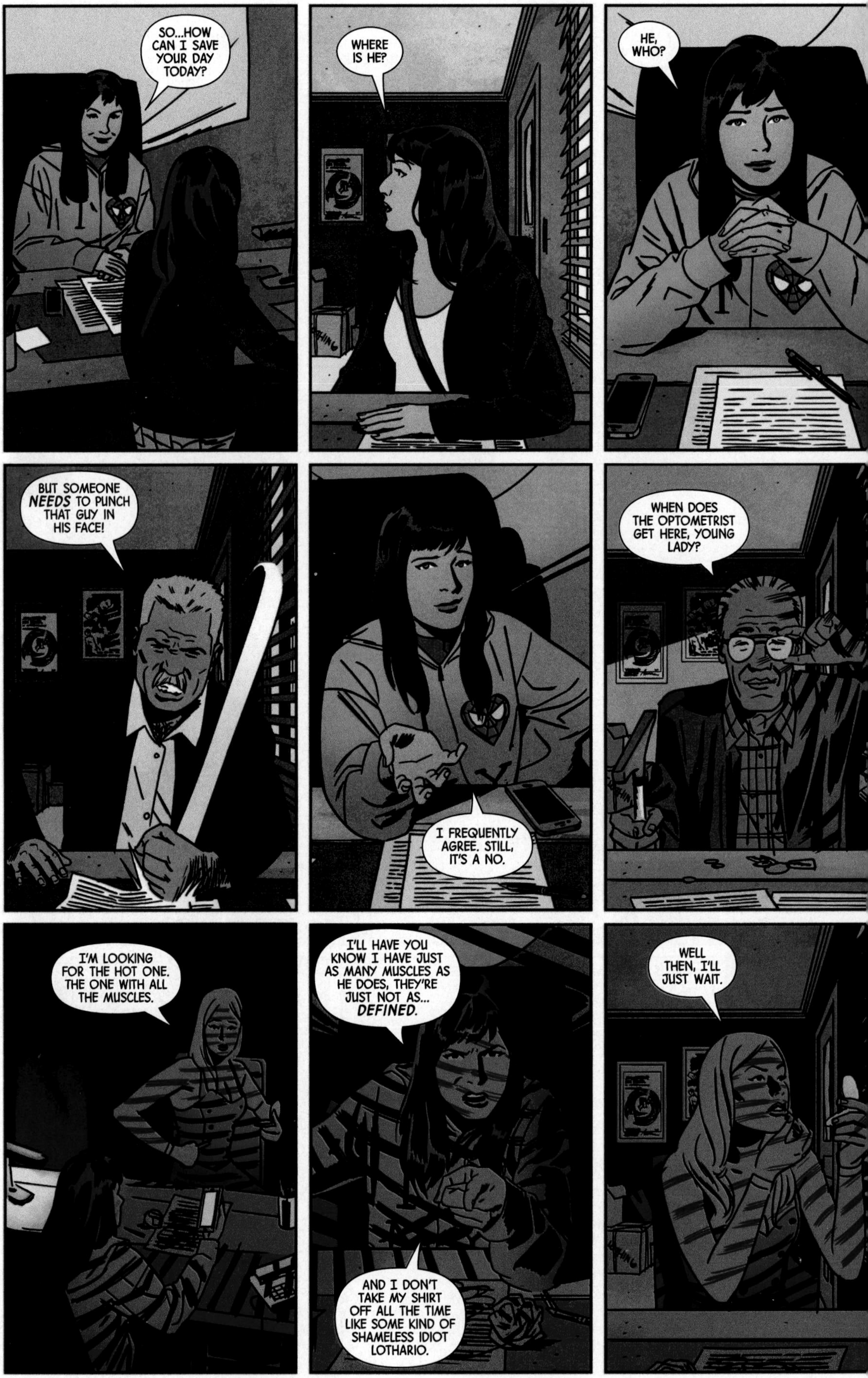
SO...HOW CAN I SAVE YOUR DAY TODAY?
WHERE IS HE?
HE, WHO?
BUT SOMEONE NEEDS TO PUNCH THAT GUY IN HIS FACE!
I FREQUENTLY AGREE. STILL, IT'S A NO.
WHEN DOES THE OPTOMETRIST GET HERE, YOUNG LADY?
I'M LOOKING FOR THE HOT ONE. THE ONE WITH ALL THE MUSCLES.
I'LL HAVE YOU KNOW I HAVE JUST AS MANY MUSCLES AS HE DOES, THEY'RE JUST NOT AS... DEFINED.
AND I DON'T TAKE MY SHIRT OFF ALL THE TIME LIKE SOME KIND OF SHAMELESS IDIOT LOTHARIO.
WELL THEN, I'LL JUST WAIT.

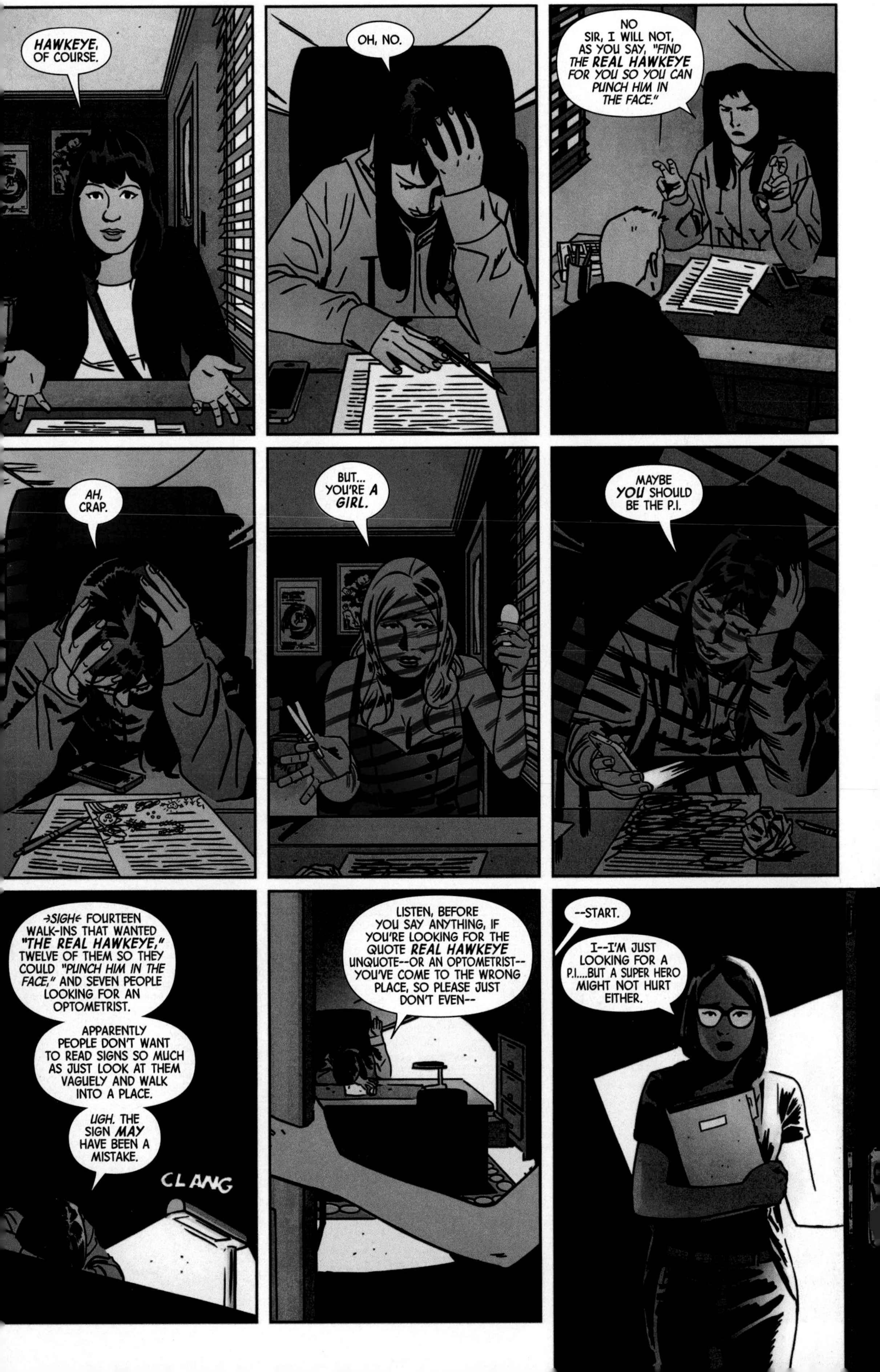
HAWKEYE, OF COURSE.
OH, NO.
NO SIR, I WILL NOT, AS YOU SAY, "FIND THE REAL HAWKEYE FOR YOU SO YOU CAN PUNCH HIM IN THE FACE."
AH, CRAP.
BUT... YOU'RE A GIRL.
MAYBE YOU SHOULD BE THE P.I.
→SIGH← FOURTEEN WALK-INS THAT WANTED "THE REAL HAWKEYE," TWELVE OF THEM SO THEY COULD "PUNCH HIM IN THE FACE," AND SEVEN PEOPLE LOOKING FOR AN OPTOMETRIST.
APPARENTLY PEOPLE DON'T WANT TO READ SIGNS SO MUCH AS JUST LOOK AT THEM VAGUELY AND WALK INTO A PLACE.
UGH. THE SIGN MAY HAVE BEEN A MISTAKE.
CLANG
LISTEN, BEFORE YOU SAY ANYTHING, IF YOU'RE LOOKING FOR THE QUOTE REAL HAWKEYE UNQUOTE--OR AN OPTOMETRIST--YOU'VE COME TO THE WRONG PLACE, SO PLEASE JUST DON'T EVEN--
--START.
I--I'M JUST LOOKING FOR A P.I....BUT A SUPER HERO MIGHT NOT HURT EITHER.

I'M A JUNIOR AT KINNEY COLLEGE... I WRITE FOR THE COLLEGE NEWSPAPER AND I ALSO WRITE A SORTA POPULAR BLOG, OR I USED TO...

YOU STOPPED BECAUSE OF THE HARASSMENT?

YEAH, I WAS FEELING SO BEAT DOWN, I JUST GAVE UP. THOUGHT MAYBE HE'D FORGET ABOUT ME, GO AWAY. I DIDN'T WRITE FOR A COUPLE MONTHS, BUT THE SECOND I STARTED WRITING AGAIN...*BAM*.

AND I JUST... I'M NOT WILLING TO LET HIM RUN MY LIFE. I'M NOT GOING TO STOP WRITING BECAUSE OF HIM, I JUST CAN'T. AT THE SAME TIME...

YOU'RE SCARED.

YEAH, SOME OF THE THINGS HE SAYS... IT'S ONLY GETTING WORSE, MORE INTENSE. WHEN IT STARTED, IT WAS JUST CALLING ME NAMES. NOW IT'S TALKING ABOUT HOW I SHOULD *DIE*...

THE SCHOOL TRIES TO HELP, THEY BAN HIM WHENEVER HE SHOWS UP, BUT THEN HE JUST COMES IN WITH A NEW EMAIL ADDRESS AND USER NAME, NEW IP ADDRESSES. I GUESS HE'S USING A PROXY SERVER OR SOMETHING. IT'S RELENTLESS.

THAT STUFF I BROUGHT...IT'S NOT ALL OF IT, BUT IT'S THE WORST OF IT, THE MOST RECENT, AND IT INCLUDES A BUNCH OF HIS LOGINS AND IPs.

SO, THE HARASSMENT IS ONLY ONLINE AT THIS POINT, RIGHT?

YES...

BUT YOU'RE WORRIED IT WILL ESCALATE?

I'M SCARED ALL THE TIME. MEETING A NEW PERSON IS TERRIFYING... OR EVEN WORSE, IMAGINING IT'S SOMEONE *ALREADY* IN MY LIFE--IT'S SILLY, I KNOW...

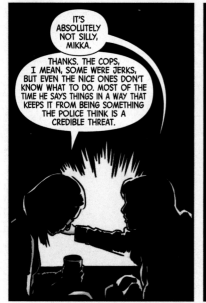

IT'S ABSOLUTELY NOT SILLY, MIKKA.

THANKS. THE COPS, I MEAN, SOME WERE JERKS, BUT EVEN THE NICE ONES DON'T KNOW WHAT TO DO. MOST OF THE TIME HE SAYS THINGS IN A WAY THAT KEEPS IT FROM BEING SOMETHING THE POLICE THINK IS A CREDIBLE THREAT.

MY GIRLFRIEND SUGGESTED I TRY A PRIVATE INVESTIGATOR. THAT IF I COULD TRACK HIM DOWN AND GET A LAWYER WE MIGHT BE ABLE TO PUT THE FEAR OF GOD INTO HIM, EVEN IF THE COPS COULDN'T PROSECUTE.

NO NEED FOR AN EXPENSIVE LAWYER, MIKKA. I'LL FIND THIS GUY AND PUT PLENTY OF FEAR INTO HIM.

WRITE DOWN YOUR CLASS SCHEDULE AND ALL THE PERTINENT INFORMATION YOU CAN THINK OF. I'LL START FIRST THING TOMORROW.

THANK YOU SO MUCH, KATE.

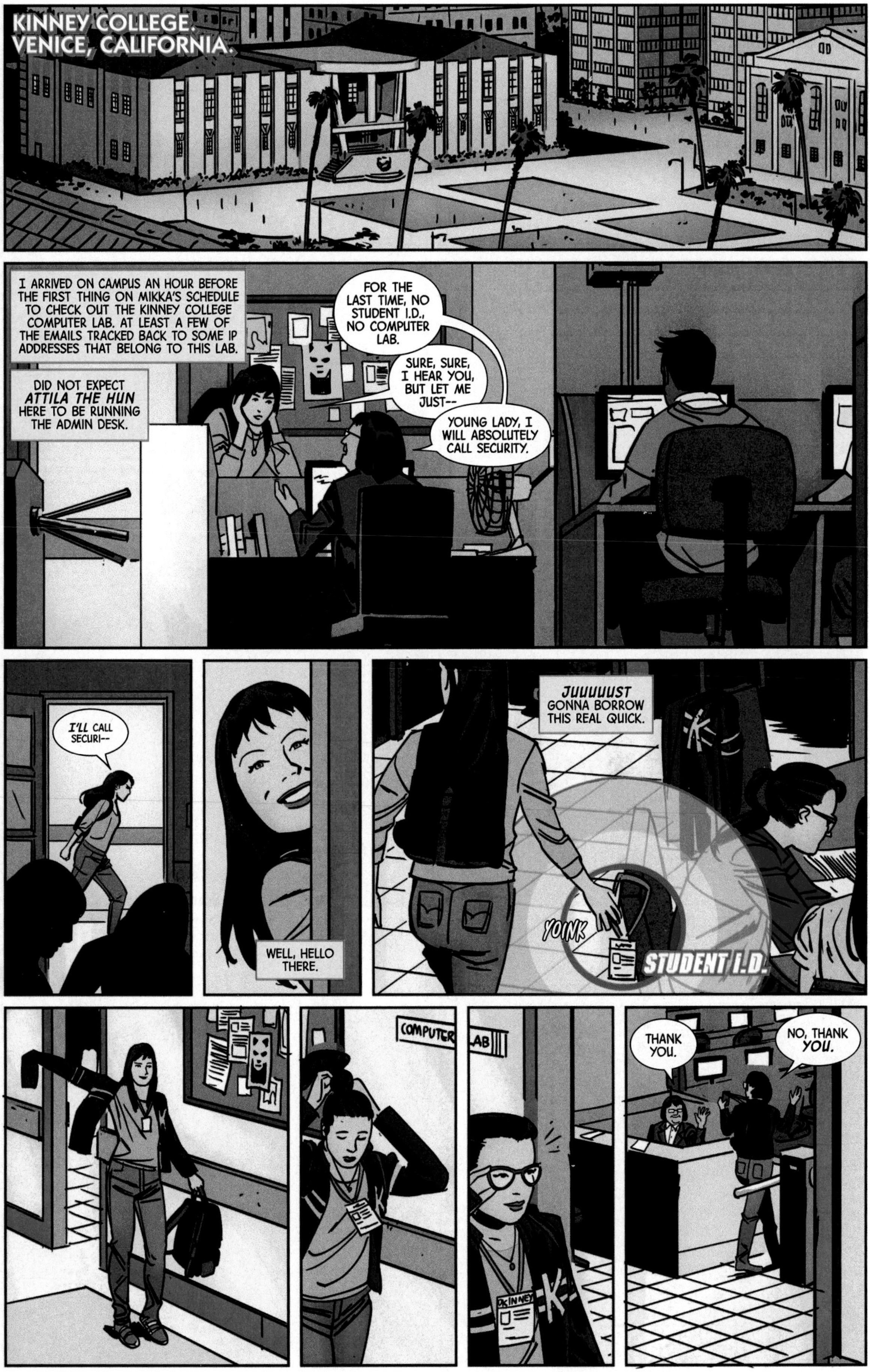
KINNEY COLLEGE. VENICE, CALIFORNIA.
I ARRIVED ON CAMPUS AN HOUR BEFORE THE FIRST THING ON MIKKA'S SCHEDULE TO CHECK OUT THE KINNEY COLLEGE COMPUTER LAB. AT LEAST A FEW OF THE EMAILS TRACKED BACK TO SOME IP ADDRESSES THAT BELONG TO THIS LAB.
DID NOT EXPECT ATTILA THE HUN HERE TO BE RUNNING THE ADMIN DESK.
FOR THE LAST TIME, NO STUDENT I.D., NO COMPUTER LAB.
SURE, SURE, I HEAR YOU, BUT LET ME JUST--
YOUNG LADY, I WILL ABSOLUTELY CALL SECURITY.
I'LL CALL SECURI--
WELL, HELLO THERE.
JUUUUUST GONNA BORROW THIS REAL QUICK.
YOINK
STUDENT I.D.
COMPUTER LAB
KINNEY
THANK YOU.
NO, THANK YOU.

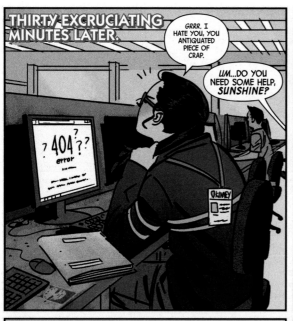

GRRR. I HATE YOU, YOU ANTIQUATED PIECE OF CRAP.

UM...DO YOU NEED SOME HELP, *SUNSHINE*?

? 404 ? ?? error

WHAT DID YOU JUST CALL ME?!

UH... SUNSHINE?

AND *WHY* WOULD YOU THINK THAT'S AN APPROPRIATE THING TO SAY TO ME?

UM...I THOUGHT IT WAS...YOUR NAME?

OH, YOU HAVE GOT TO BE KIDDING ME. SUNSHINE?!

TOTAL ROOKIE MISTAKE NOT LOOKING AT THE NAME.

UH... I...

KINNEY UNIVERSITY

Sunshine Johnson

END DATE : SEPT 2016

263748 - 8

COMPUTER LAB

RIGHT YOU ARE, YOUNG MAN... UM...YOUNG *QUINN!*

IS THAT...DID YOU *STEAL* THAT I.D.?

WHAT?! *NO WAY.* TOTALLY NOT.

BUT I *COULD* USE SOME HELP, QUINN. LOOK AT THIS. YOU KNOW ANYTHING ABOUT HIDING IP ADDRESSES?

OOF! YOU MEAN BY USING PROXY SERVERS OR VPNs?

I BARELY KNOW WHAT ANY OF THOSE WORDS MEAN, SO, PROBABLY *YES.*

SURE.

BUT CAN YOU STOP PULLING MY LANYARD?

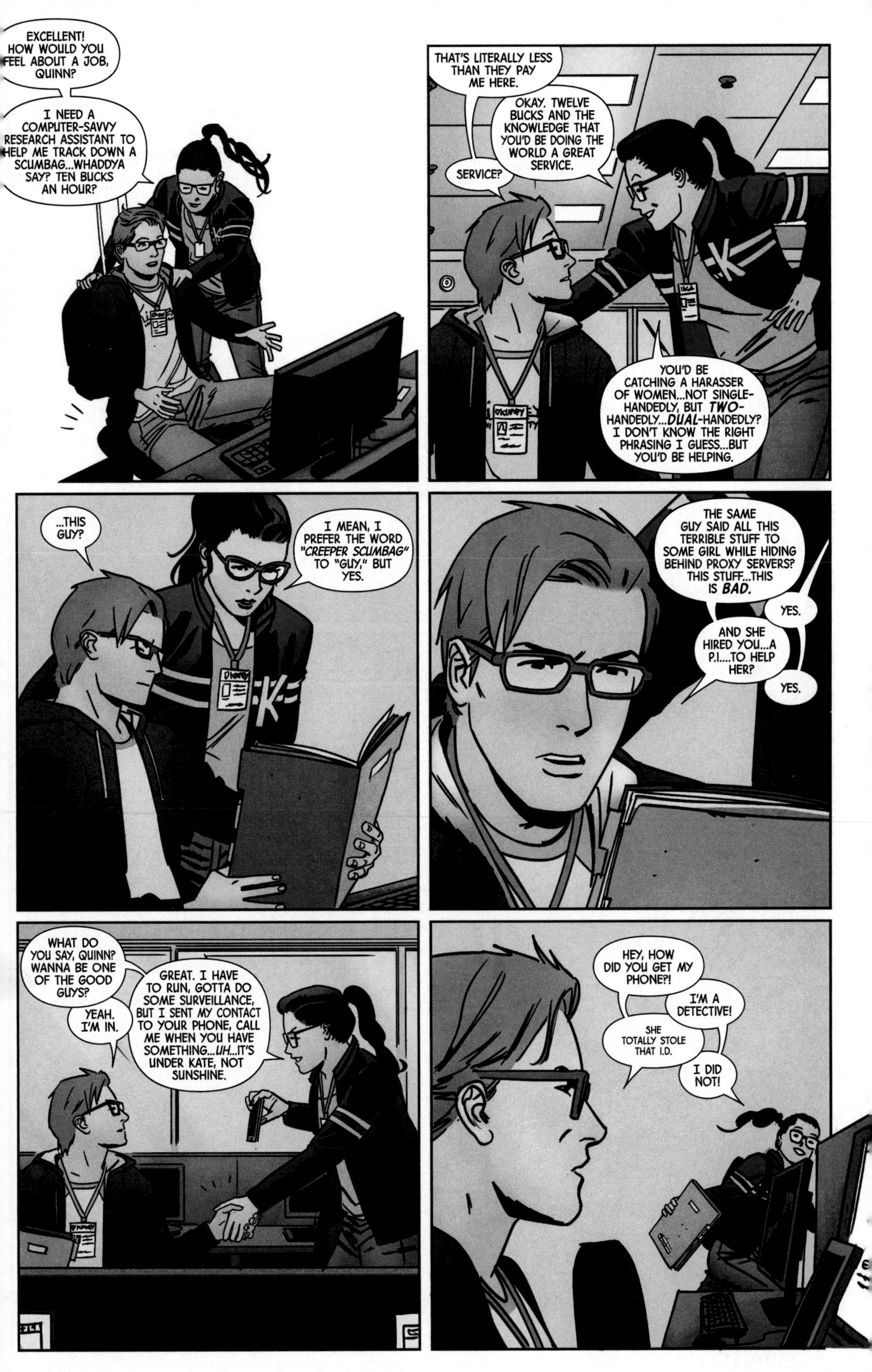
EXCELLENT! HOW WOULD YOU FEEL ABOUT A JOB, QUINN?
I NEED A COMPUTER-SAVVY RESEARCH ASSISTANT TO HELP ME TRACK DOWN A SCUMBAG...WHADDYA SAY? TEN BUCKS AN HOUR?
THAT'S LITERALLY LESS THAN THEY PAY ME HERE.
OKAY. TWELVE BUCKS AND THE KNOWLEDGE THAT YOU'D BE DOING THE WORLD A GREAT SERVICE.
SERVICE?
YOU'D BE CATCHING A HARASSER OF WOMEN...NOT SINGLE-HANDEDLY, BUT TWO-HANDEDLY...DUAL-HANDEDLY? I DON'T KNOW THE RIGHT PHRASING I GUESS...BUT YOU'D BE HELPING.
...THIS GUY?
I MEAN, I PREFER THE WORD "CREEPER SCUMBAG" TO "GUY," BUT YES.
THE SAME GUY SAID ALL THIS TERRIBLE STUFF TO SOME GIRL WHILE HIDING BEHIND PROXY SERVERS? THIS STUFF...THIS IS BAD.
YES.
AND SHE HIRED YOU...A P.I....TO HELP HER?
YES.
WHAT DO YOU SAY, QUINN? WANNA BE ONE OF THE GOOD GUYS?
YEAH. I'M IN.
GREAT. I HAVE TO RUN, GOTTA DO SOME SURVEILLANCE, BUT I SENT MY CONTACT TO YOUR PHONE, CALL ME WHEN YOU HAVE SOMETHING...UH...IT'S UNDER KATE, NOT SUNSHINE.
HEY, HOW DID YOU GET MY PHONE?!
I'M A DETECTIVE!
SHE TOTALLY STOLE THAT I.D.
I DID NOT!

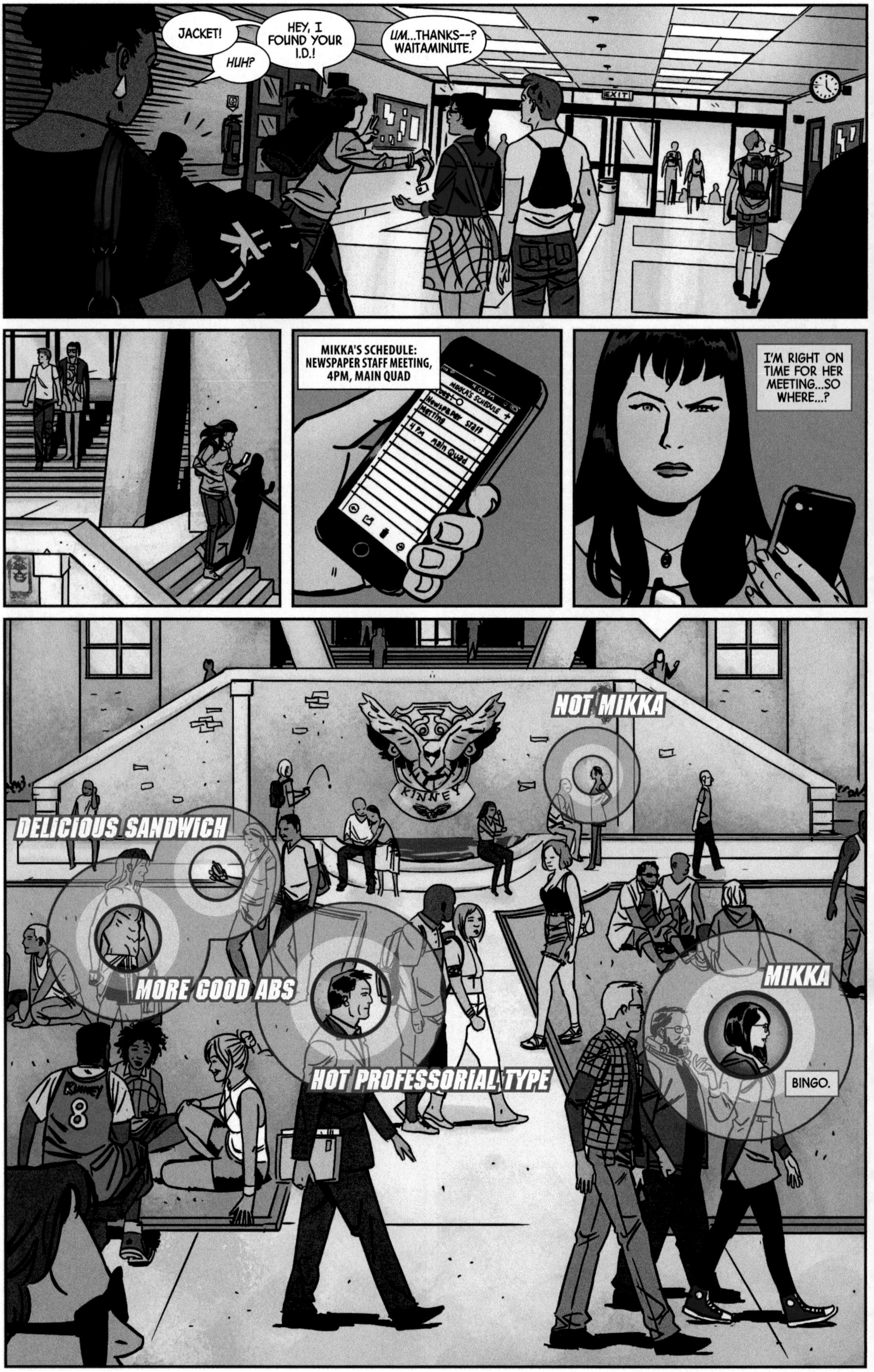
JACKET!
HUH?
HEY, I FOUND YOUR I.D.!
UM...THANKS--? WAITAMINUTE.
EXIT
MIKKA'S SCHEDULE: NEWSPAPER STAFF MEETING, 4PM, MAIN QUAD
I'M RIGHT ON TIME FOR HER MEETING...SO WHERE...?
NOT MIKKA
KINNEY
DELICIOUS SANDWICH
MORE GOOD ABS
HOT PROFESSORIAL TYPE
MIKKA
BINGO.

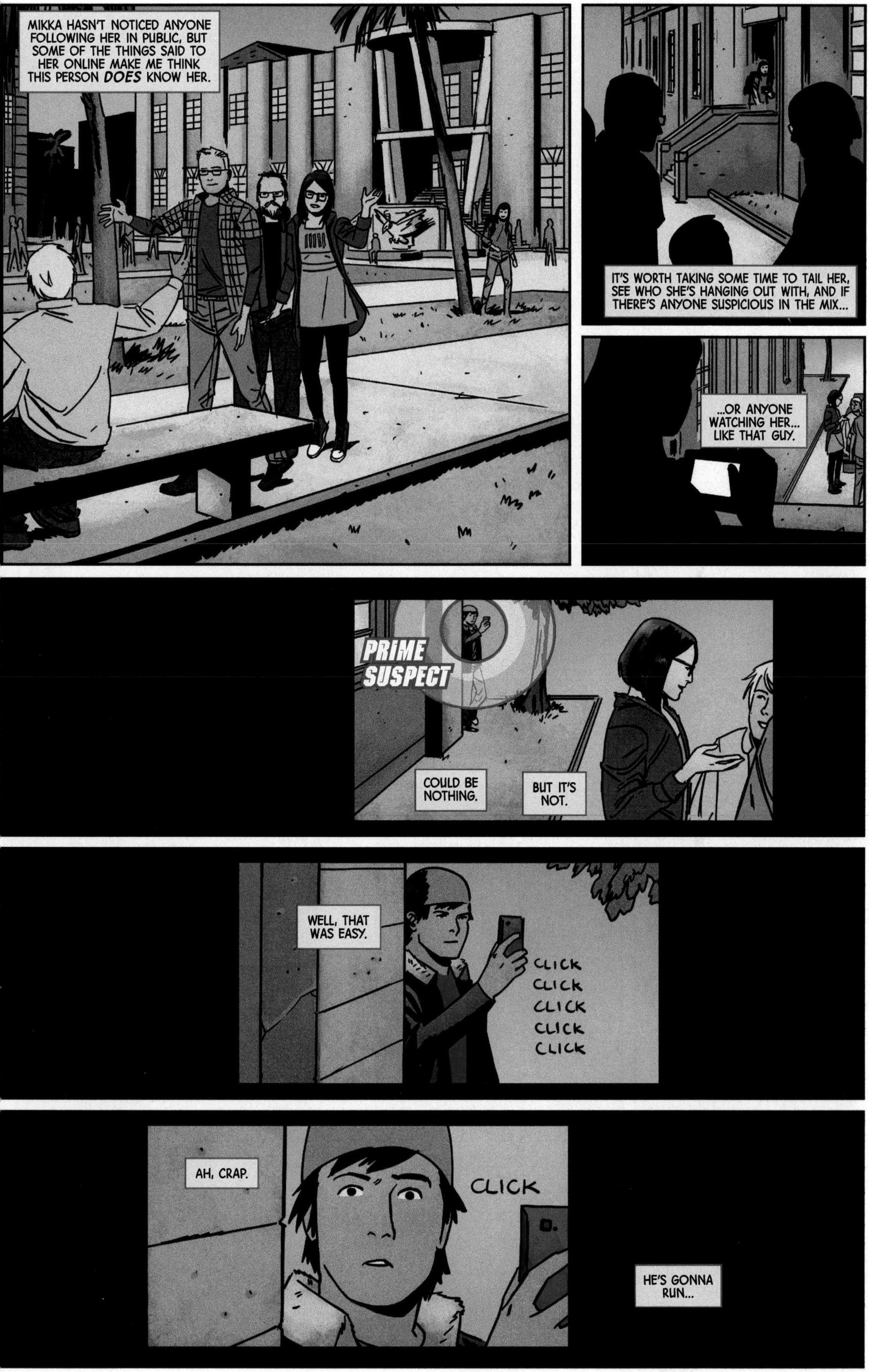
MIKKA HASN'T NOTICED ANYONE FOLLOWING HER IN PUBLIC, BUT SOME OF THE THINGS SAID TO HER ONLINE MAKE ME THINK THIS PERSON *DOES* KNOW HER.
IT'S WORTH TAKING SOME TIME TO TAIL HER, SEE WHO SHE'S HANGING OUT WITH, AND IF THERE'S ANYONE SUSPICIOUS IN THE MIX...
...OR ANYONE WATCHING HER... LIKE THAT GUY.
PRIME SUSPECT
COULD BE NOTHING.
BUT IT'S NOT.
WELL, THAT WAS EASY.
CLICK
CLICK
CLICK
CLICK
CLICK
AH, CRAP.
CLICK
HE'S GONNA RUN...

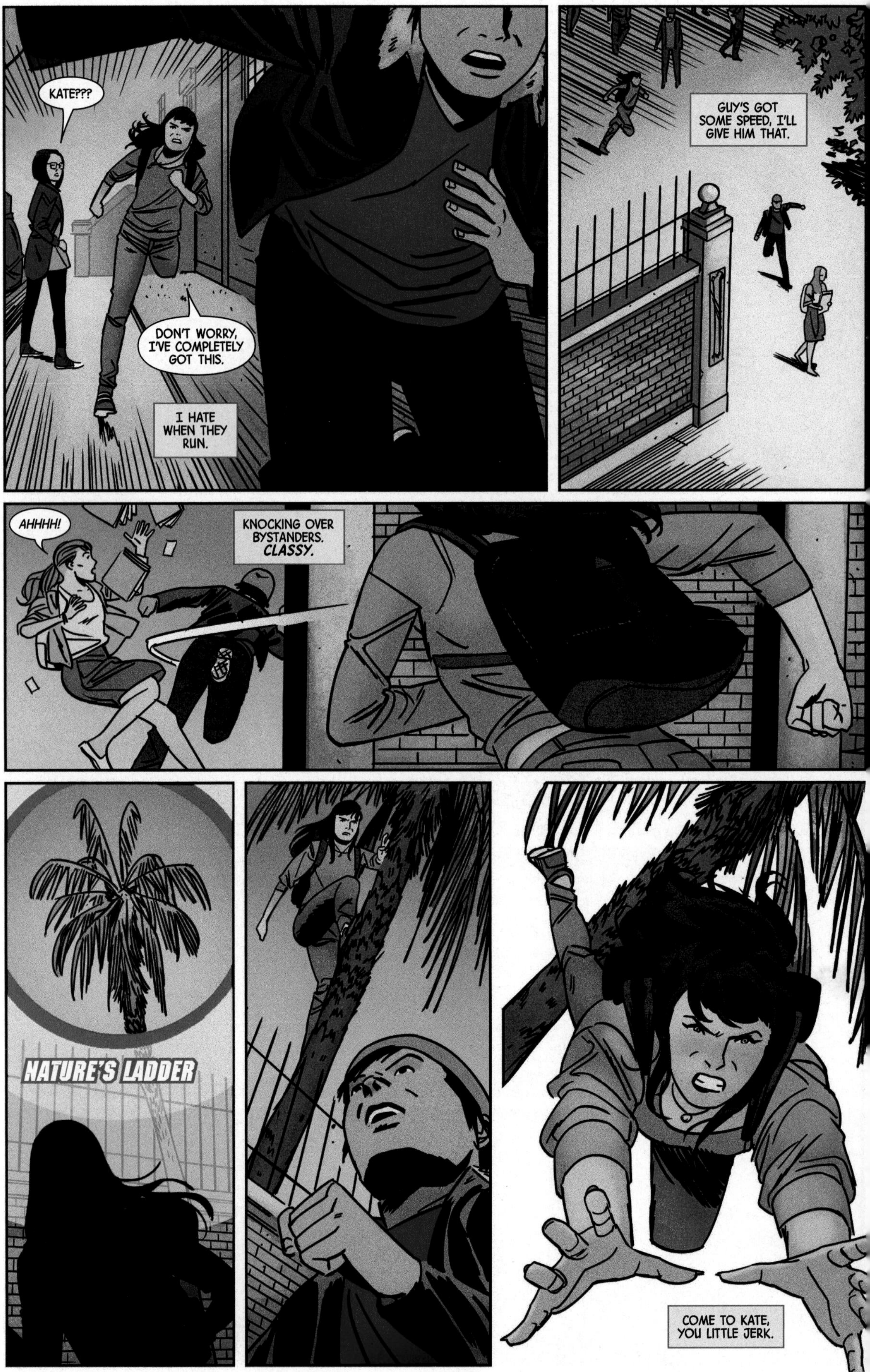

KATE???
DON'T WORRY, I'VE COMPLETELY GOT THIS.
I HATE WHEN THEY RUN.
GUY'S GOT SOME SPEED, I'LL GIVE HIM THAT.
AHHHH!
KNOCKING OVER BYSTANDERS. CLASSY.
NATURE'S LADDER
COME TO KATE, YOU LITTLE JERK.

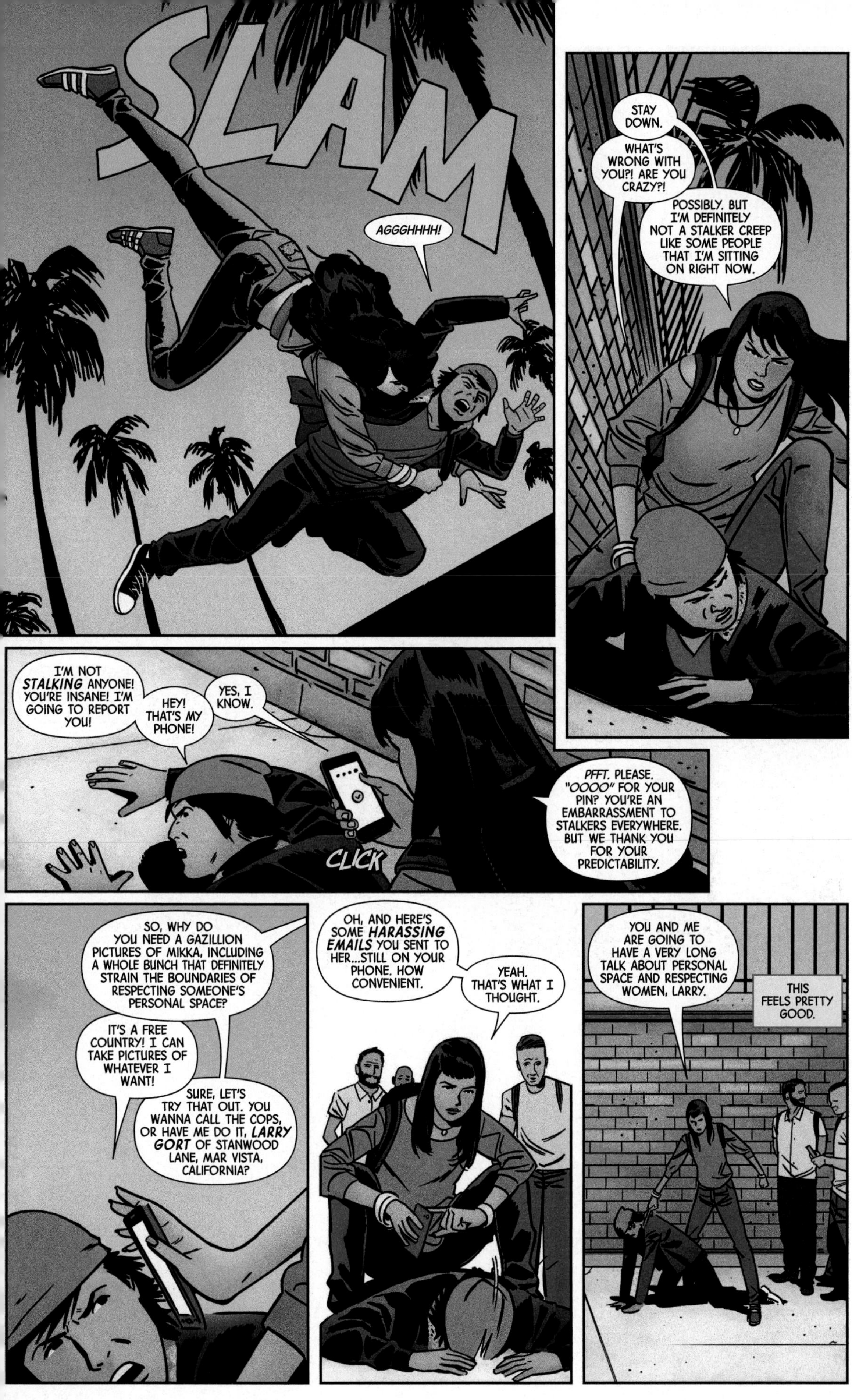
SLAM
AGGGHHHH!
STAY DOWN.
WHAT'S WRONG WITH YOU?! ARE YOU CRAZY?!
POSSIBLY. BUT I'M DEFINITELY NOT A STALKER CREEP LIKE SOME PEOPLE THAT I'M SITTING ON RIGHT NOW.
I'M NOT STALKING ANYONE! YOU'RE INSANE! I'M GOING TO REPORT YOU!
HEY! THAT'S MY PHONE!
YES, I KNOW.
CLICK
PFFT. PLEASE. "OOOO" FOR YOUR PIN? YOU'RE AN EMBARRASSMENT TO STALKERS EVERYWHERE. BUT WE THANK YOU FOR YOUR PREDICTABILITY.
SO, WHY DO YOU NEED A GAZILLION PICTURES OF MIKKA, INCLUDING A WHOLE BUNCH THAT DEFINITELY STRAIN THE BOUNDARIES OF RESPECTING SOMEONE'S PERSONAL SPACE?
IT'S A FREE COUNTRY! I CAN TAKE PICTURES OF WHATEVER I WANT!
SURE, LET'S TRY THAT OUT. YOU WANNA CALL THE COPS, OR HAVE ME DO IT, LARRY GORT OF STANWOOD LANE, MAR VISTA, CALIFORNIA?
OH, AND HERE'S SOME HARASSING EMAILS YOU SENT TO HER...STILL ON YOUR PHONE. HOW CONVENIENT.
YEAH. THAT'S WHAT I THOUGHT.
YOU AND ME ARE GOING TO HAVE A VERY LONG TALK ABOUT PERSONAL SPACE AND RESPECTING WOMEN, LARRY.
THIS FEELS PRETTY GOOD.

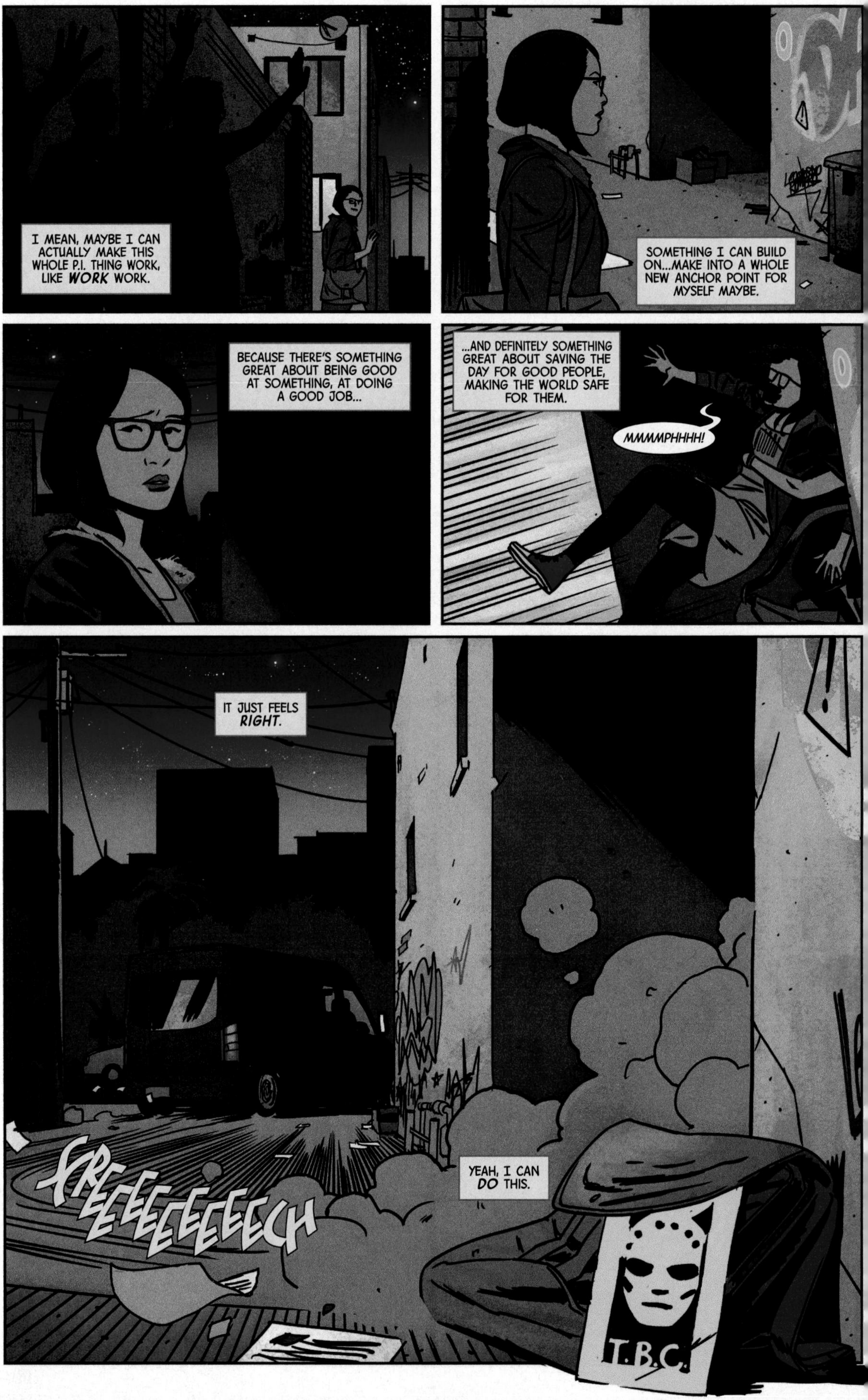

I MEAN, MAYBE I CAN ACTUALLY MAKE THIS WHOLE P.I. THING WORK, LIKE WORK WORK.
SOMETHING I CAN BUILD ON...MAKE INTO A WHOLE NEW ANCHOR POINT FOR MYSELF MAYBE.
BECAUSE THERE'S SOMETHING GREAT ABOUT BEING GOOD AT SOMETHING, AT DOING A GOOD JOB...
...AND DEFINITELY SOMETHING GREAT ABOUT SAVING THE DAY FOR GOOD PEOPLE, MAKING THE WORLD SAFE FOR THEM.
MMMMPHHHH!
IT JUST FEELS RIGHT.
SKREEEEEEEEECH
YEAH, I CAN DO THIS.
T.B.C.

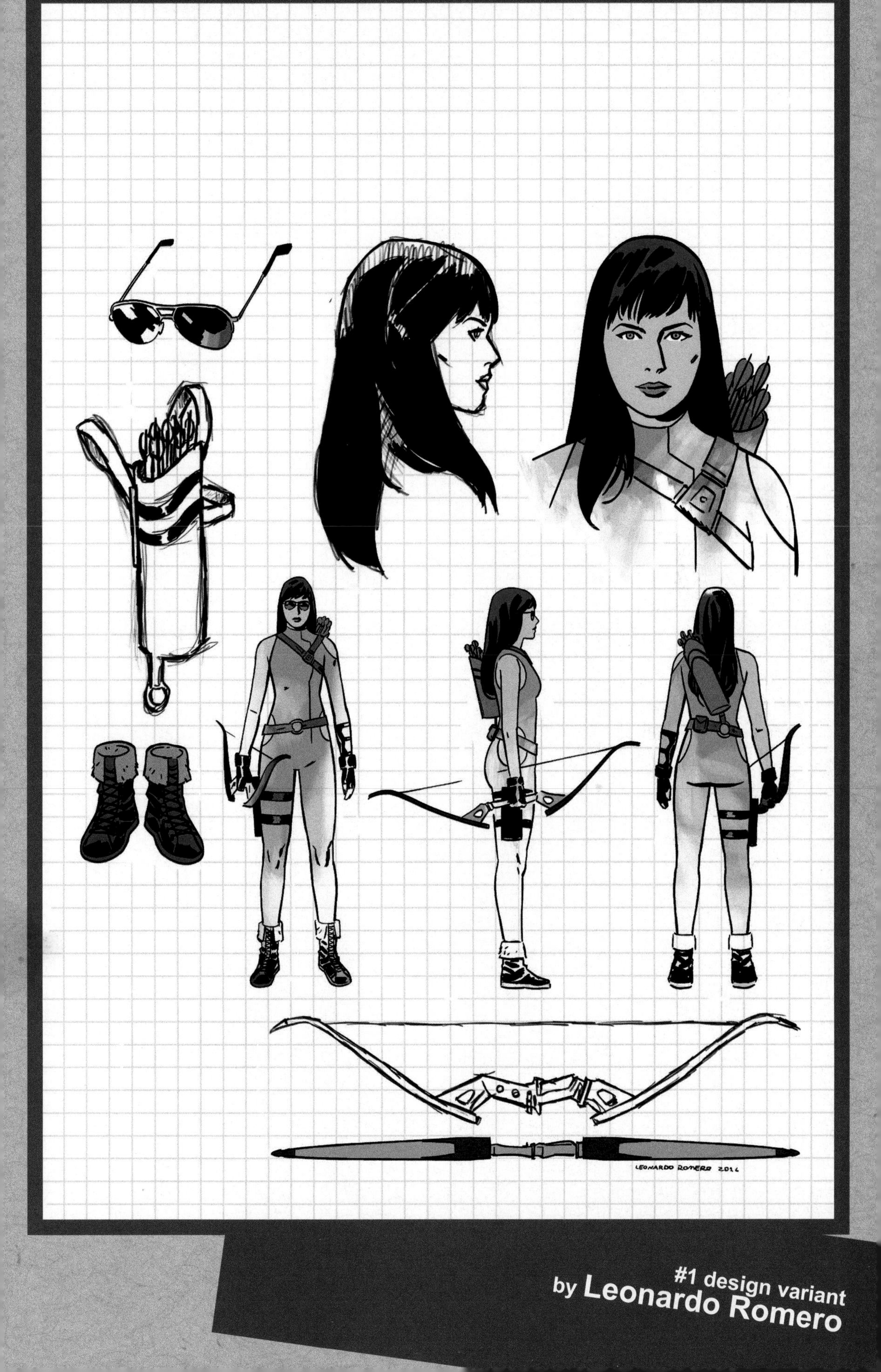
LEONARDO ROMERO 2016

#1 design variant
by Leonardo Romero

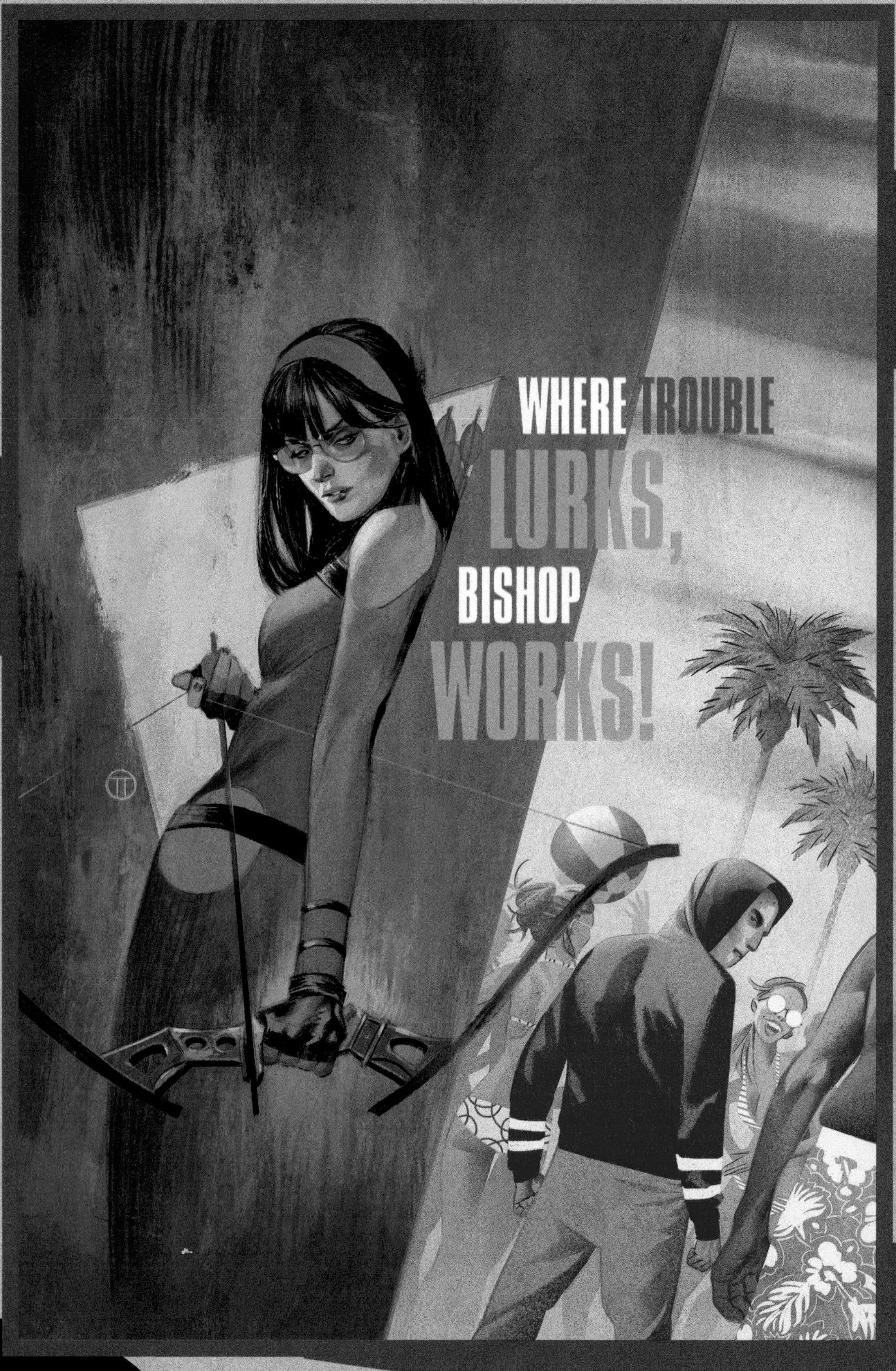
WHERE TROUBLE
LURKS,
BISHOP
WORKS!

2

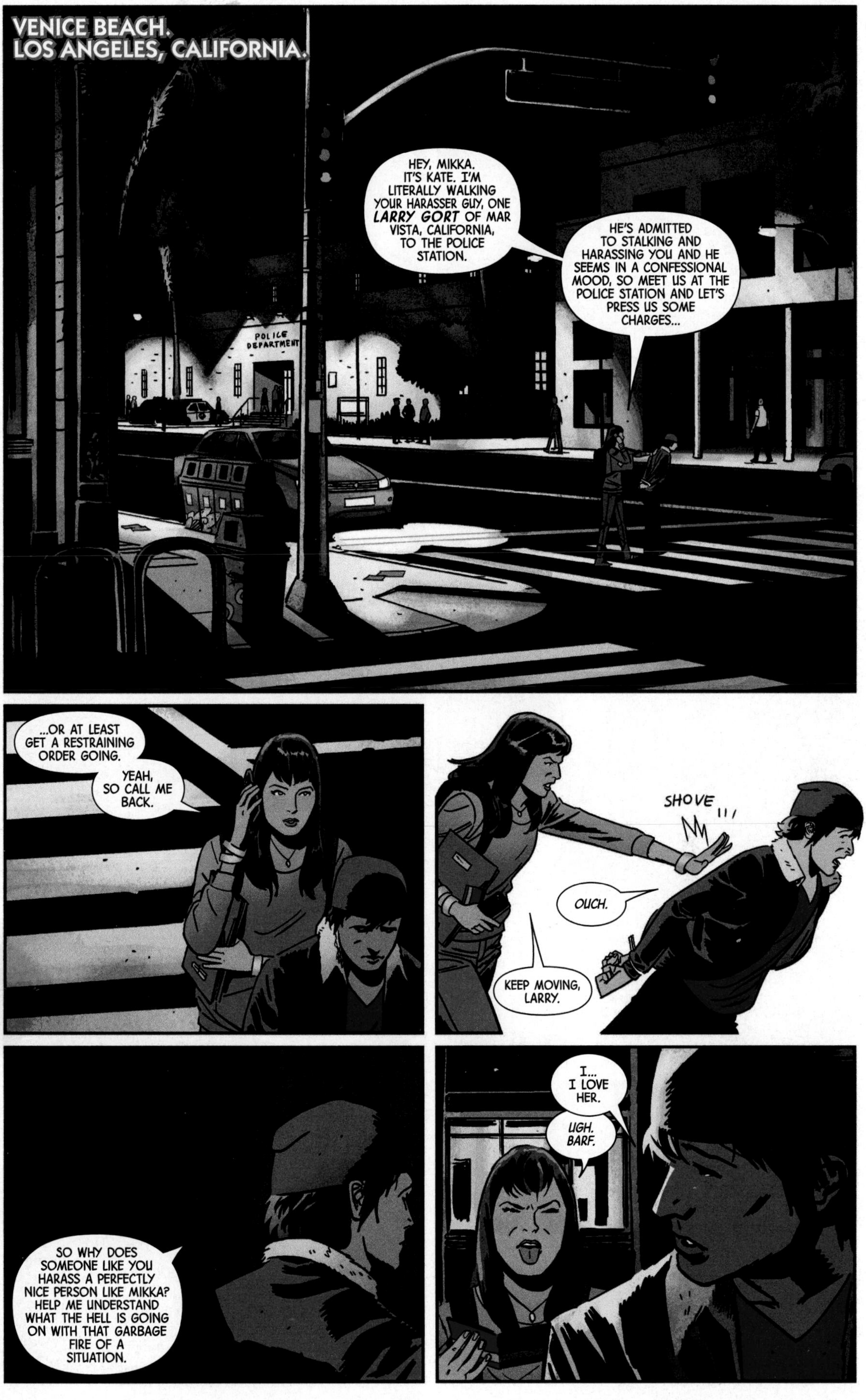
VENICE BEACH. LOS ANGELES, CALIFORNIA.
HEY, MIKKA. IT'S KATE. I'M LITERALLY WALKING YOUR HARASSER GUY, ONE LARRY GORT OF MAR VISTA, CALIFORNIA, TO THE POLICE STATION.
HE'S ADMITTED TO STALKING AND HARASSING YOU AND HE SEEMS IN A CONFESSIONAL MOOD, SO MEET US AT THE POLICE STATION AND LET'S PRESS US SOME CHARGES...
POLICE DEPARTMENT
...OR AT LEAST GET A RESTRAINING ORDER GOING.
YEAH, SO CALL ME BACK.
SHOVE
OUCH.
KEEP MOVING, LARRY.
SO WHY DOES SOMEONE LIKE YOU HARASS A PERFECTLY NICE PERSON LIKE MIKKA? HELP ME UNDERSTAND WHAT THE HELL IS GOING ON WITH THAT GARBAGE FIRE OF A SITUATION.
I... I LOVE HER.
UGH. BARF.

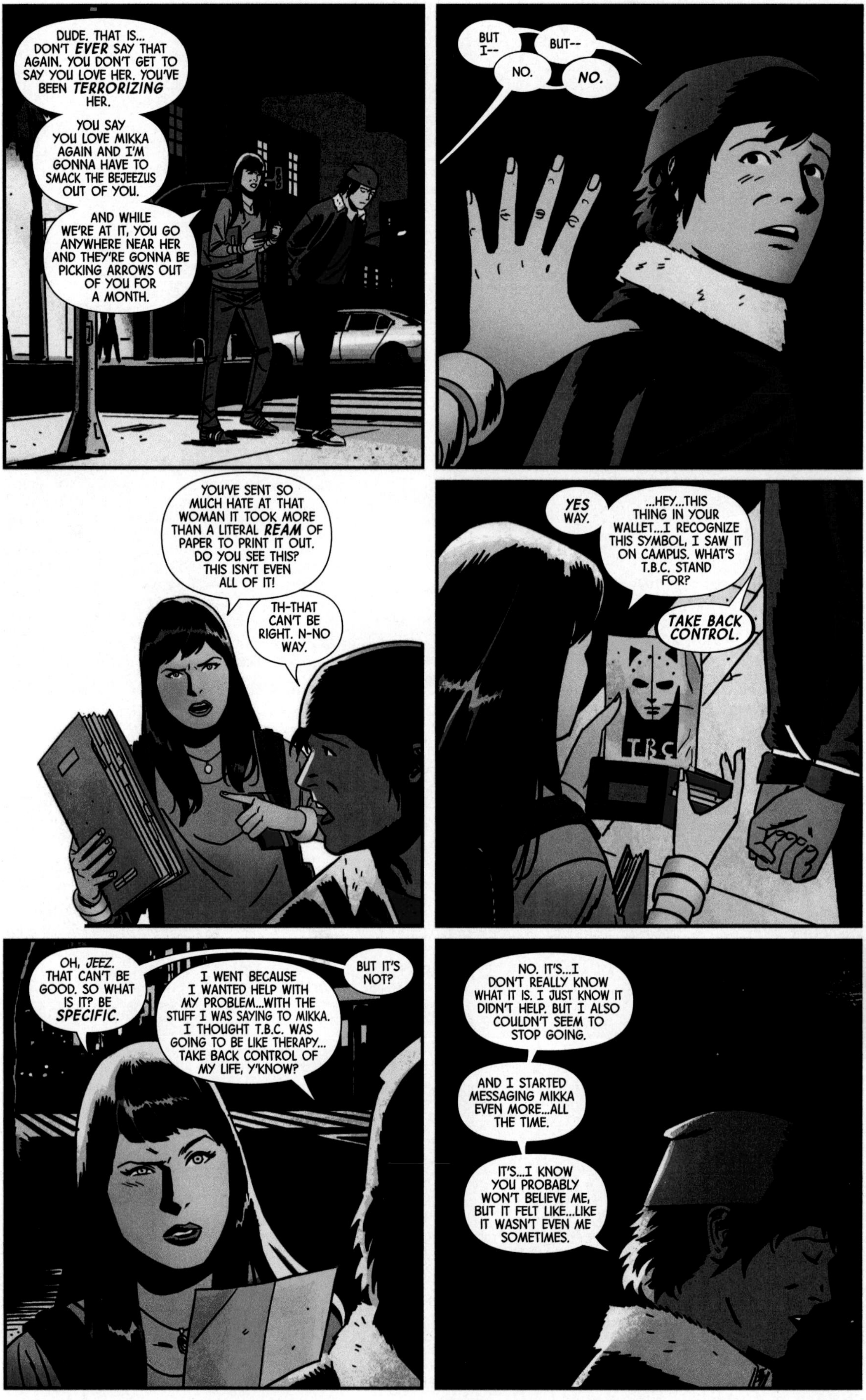

DUDE. THAT IS... DON'T EVER SAY THAT AGAIN. YOU DON'T GET TO SAY YOU LOVE HER. YOU'VE BEEN TERRORIZING HER.
YOU SAY YOU LOVE MIKKA AGAIN AND I'M GONNA HAVE TO SMACK THE BEJEEZUS OUT OF YOU.
AND WHILE WE'RE AT IT, YOU GO ANYWHERE NEAR HER AND THEY'RE GONNA BE PICKING ARROWS OUT OF YOU FOR A MONTH.
BUT I--
BUT--
NO.
NO.
YOU'VE SENT SO MUCH HATE AT THAT WOMAN IT TOOK MORE THAN A LITERAL REAM OF PAPER TO PRINT IT OUT. DO YOU SEE THIS? THIS ISN'T EVEN ALL OF IT!
TH-THAT CAN'T BE RIGHT. N-NO WAY.
YES WAY.
...HEY...THIS THING IN YOUR WALLET...I RECOGNIZE THIS SYMBOL, I SAW IT ON CAMPUS. WHAT'S T.B.C. STAND FOR?
TAKE BACK CONTROL.
T.B.C
OH, JEEZ. THAT CAN'T BE GOOD. SO WHAT IS IT? BE SPECIFIC.
I WENT BECAUSE I WANTED HELP WITH MY PROBLEM...WITH THE STUFF I WAS SAYING TO MIKKA. I THOUGHT T.B.C. WAS GOING TO BE LIKE THERAPY... TAKE BACK CONTROL OF MY LIFE, Y'KNOW?
BUT IT'S NOT?
NO. IT'S...I DON'T REALLY KNOW WHAT IT IS. I JUST KNOW IT DIDN'T HELP. BUT I ALSO COULDN'T SEEM TO STOP GOING.
AND I STARTED MESSAGING MIKKA EVEN MORE...ALL THE TIME.
IT'S...I KNOW YOU PROBABLY WON'T BELIEVE ME, BUT IT FELT LIKE...LIKE IT WASN'T EVEN ME SOMETIMES.

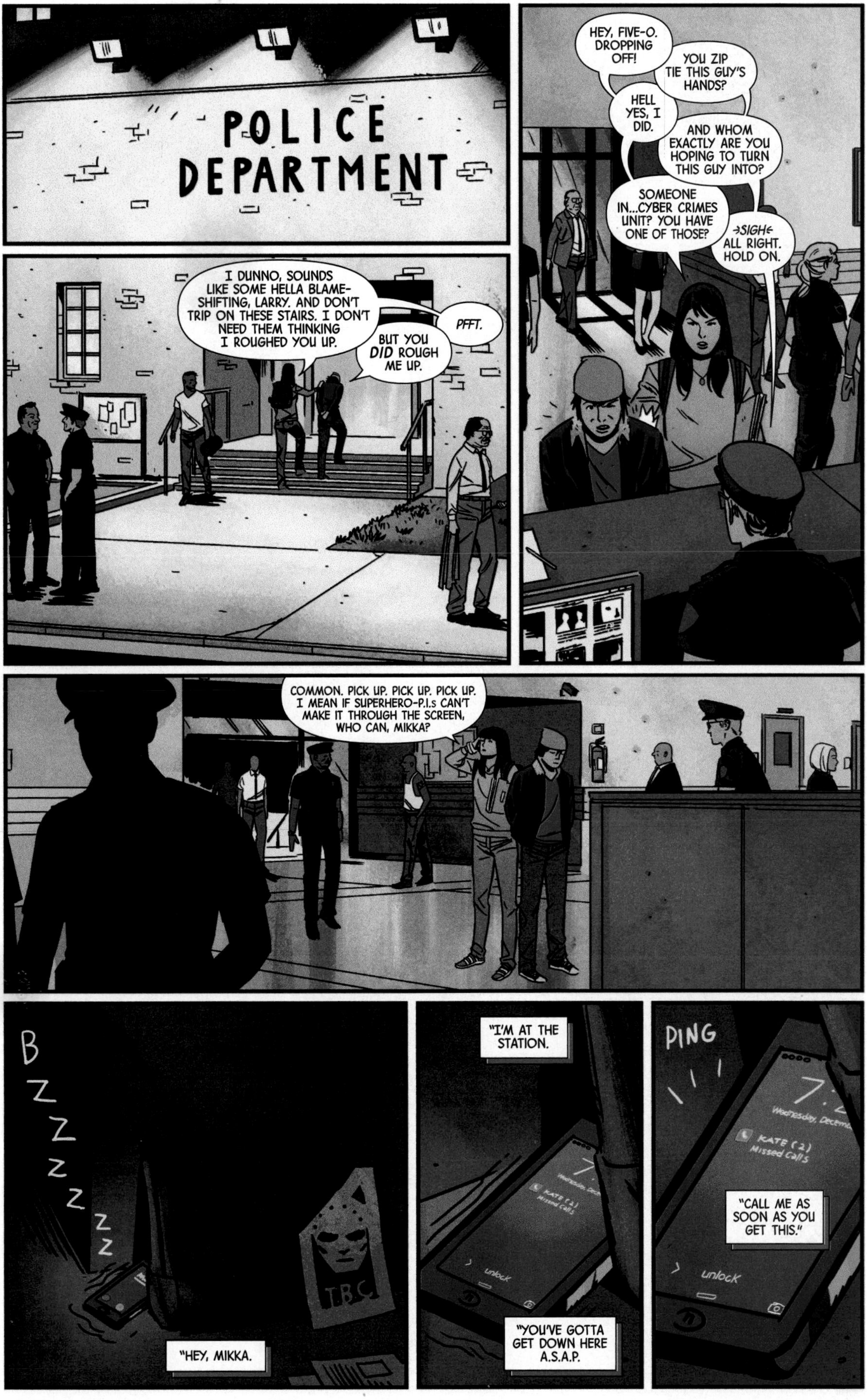
POLICE DEPARTMENT
I DUNNO, SOUNDS LIKE SOME HELLA BLAME-SHIFTING, LARRY. AND DON'T TRIP ON THESE STAIRS. I DON'T NEED THEM THINKING I ROUGHED YOU UP.
PFFT.
BUT YOU DID ROUGH ME UP.
HEY, FIVE-O. DROPPING OFF!
YOU ZIP TIE THIS GUY'S HANDS?
HELL YES, I DID.
AND WHOM EXACTLY ARE YOU HOPING TO TURN THIS GUY INTO?
SOMEONE IN...CYBER CRIMES UNIT? YOU HAVE ONE OF THOSE?
SIGH
ALL RIGHT. HOLD ON.
COMMON. PICK UP. PICK UP. PICK UP. I MEAN IF SUPERHERO-P.I.s CAN'T MAKE IT THROUGH THE SCREEN, WHO CAN, MIKKA?
BZZZZZZ
"HEY, MIKKA.
"I'M AT THE STATION.
"YOU'VE GOTTA GET DOWN HERE A.S.A.P.
PING
KATE (2) Missed Calls
unlock
"CALL ME AS SOON AS YOU GET THIS."

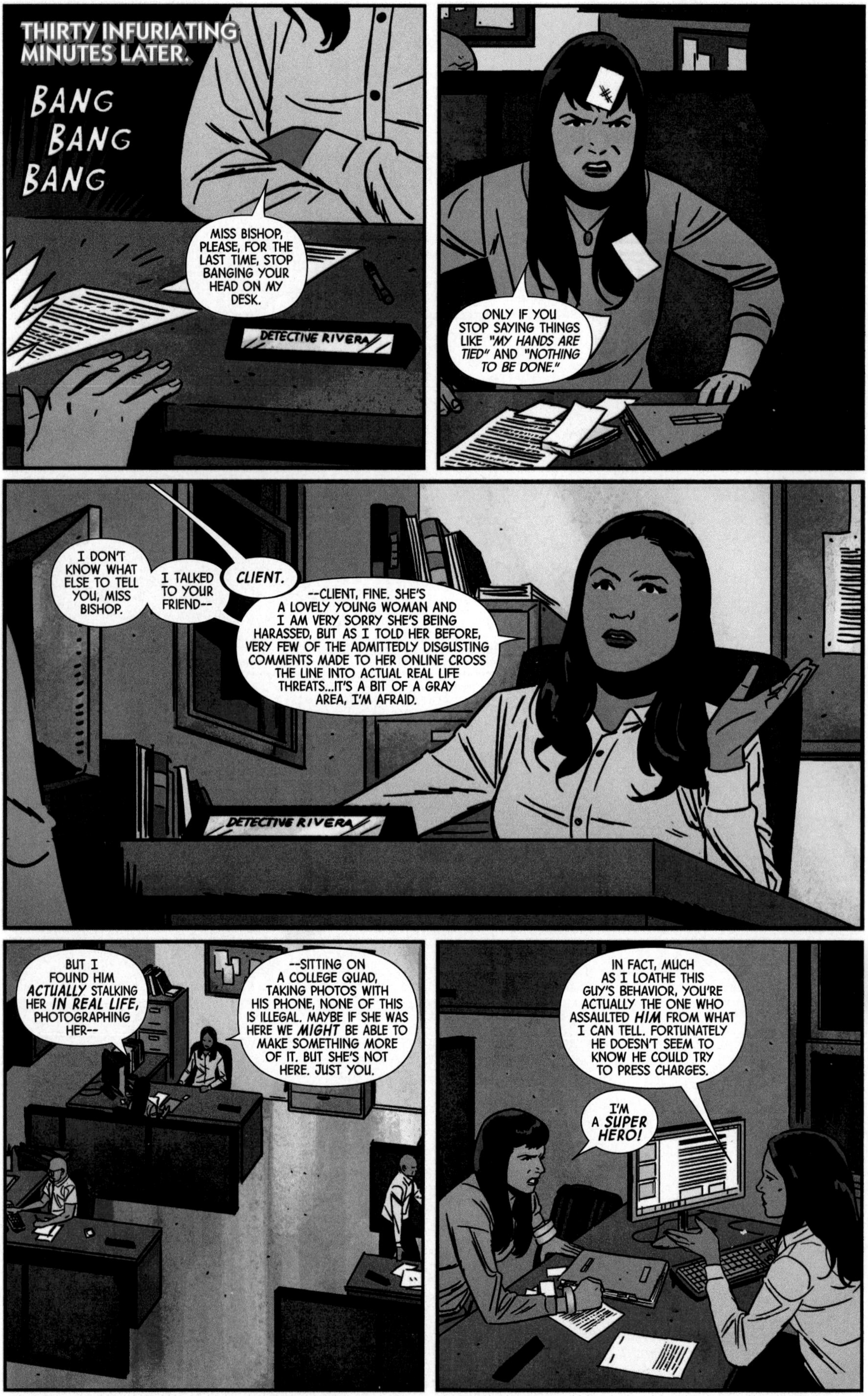
THIRTY INFURIATING MINUTES LATER.
BANG BANG BANG
MISS BISHOP, PLEASE, FOR THE LAST TIME, STOP BANGING YOUR HEAD ON MY DESK.
DETECTIVE RIVERA
ONLY IF YOU STOP SAYING THINGS LIKE "MY HANDS ARE TIED" AND "NOTHING TO BE DONE."
I DON'T KNOW WHAT ELSE TO TELL YOU, MISS BISHOP.
I TALKED TO YOUR FRIEND--
CLIENT.
--CLIENT, FINE. SHE'S A LOVELY YOUNG WOMAN AND I AM VERY SORRY SHE'S BEING HARASSED, BUT AS I TOLD HER BEFORE, VERY FEW OF THE ADMITTEDLY DISGUSTING COMMENTS MADE TO HER ONLINE CROSS THE LINE INTO ACTUAL REAL LIFE THREATS...IT'S A BIT OF A GRAY AREA, I'M AFRAID.
DETECTIVE RIVERA
BUT I FOUND HIM ACTUALLY STALKING HER IN REAL LIFE, PHOTOGRAPHING HER--
--SITTING ON A COLLEGE QUAD, TAKING PHOTOS WITH HIS PHONE, NONE OF THIS IS ILLEGAL. MAYBE IF SHE WAS HERE WE MIGHT BE ABLE TO MAKE SOMETHING MORE OF IT. BUT SHE'S NOT HERE. JUST YOU.
IN FACT, MUCH AS I LOATHE THIS GUY'S BEHAVIOR, YOU'RE ACTUALLY THE ONE WHO ASSAULTED HIM FROM WHAT I CAN TELL. FORTUNATELY HE DOESN'T SEEM TO KNOW HE COULD TRY TO PRESS CHARGES.
I'M A SUPER HERO!

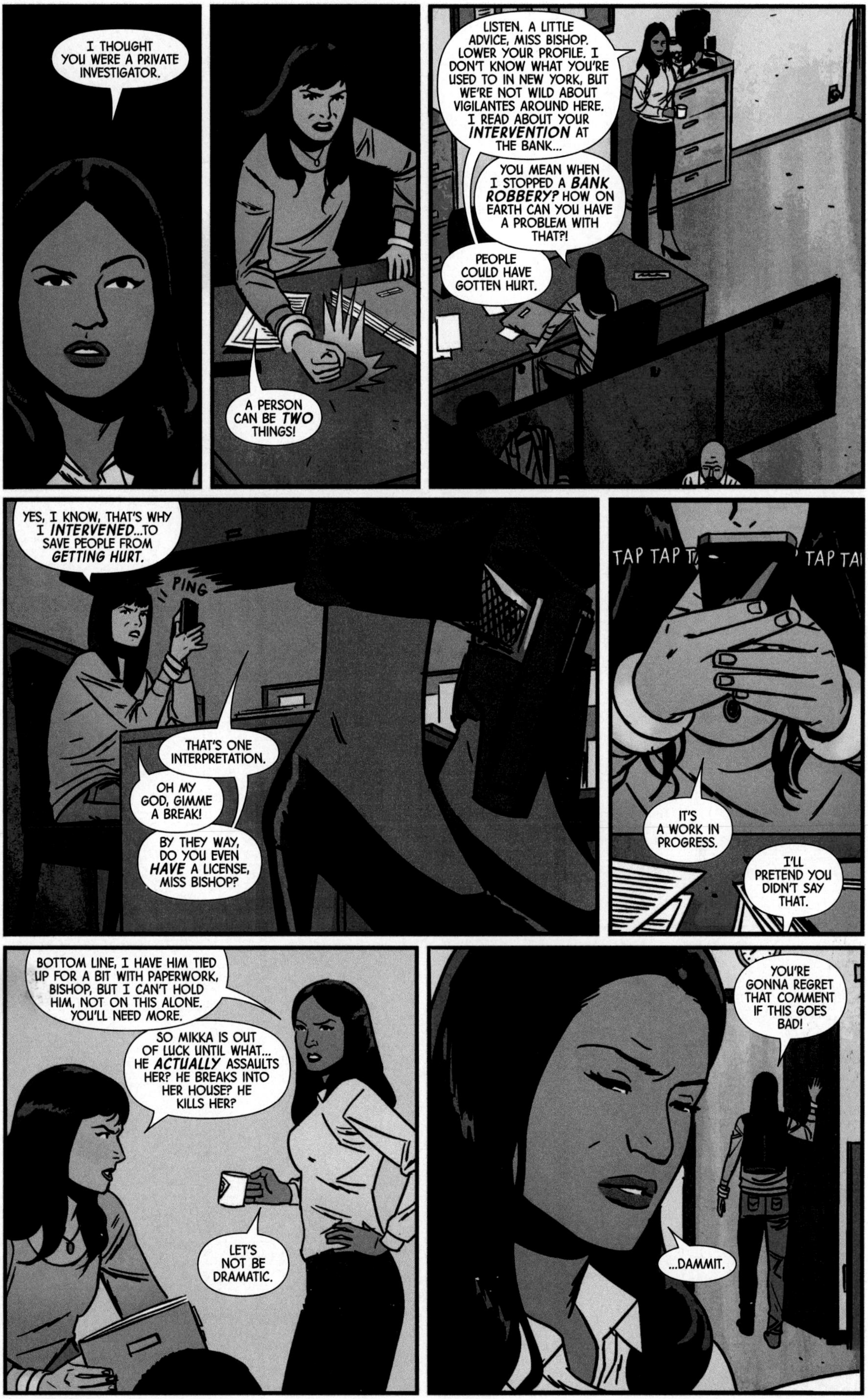
I THOUGHT YOU WERE A PRIVATE INVESTIGATOR.
A PERSON CAN BE TWO THINGS!
LISTEN. A LITTLE ADVICE, MISS BISHOP. LOWER YOUR PROFILE. I DON'T KNOW WHAT YOU'RE USED TO IN NEW YORK, BUT WE'RE NOT WILD ABOUT VIGILANTES AROUND HERE. I READ ABOUT YOUR INTERVENTION AT THE BANK...
YOU MEAN WHEN I STOPPED A BANK ROBBERY? HOW ON EARTH CAN YOU HAVE A PROBLEM WITH THAT?!
PEOPLE COULD HAVE GOTTEN HURT.
YES, I KNOW, THAT'S WHY I INTERVENED...TO SAVE PEOPLE FROM GETTING HURT.
PING
THAT'S ONE INTERPRETATION.
OH MY GOD, GIMME A BREAK!
BY THEY WAY, DO YOU EVEN HAVE A LICENSE, MISS BISHOP?
TAP TAP TAP TAP TAP
IT'S A WORK IN PROGRESS.
I'LL PRETEND YOU DIDN'T SAY THAT.
BOTTOM LINE, I HAVE HIM TIED UP FOR A BIT WITH PAPERWORK, BISHOP, BUT I CAN'T HOLD HIM, NOT ON THIS ALONE. YOU'LL NEED MORE.
SO MIKKA IS OUT OF LUCK UNTIL WHAT... HE ACTUALLY ASSAULTS HER? HE BREAKS INTO HER HOUSE? HE KILLS HER?
LET'S NOT BE DRAMATIC.
YOU'RE GONNA REGRET THAT COMMENT IF THIS GOES BAD!
...DAMMIT.

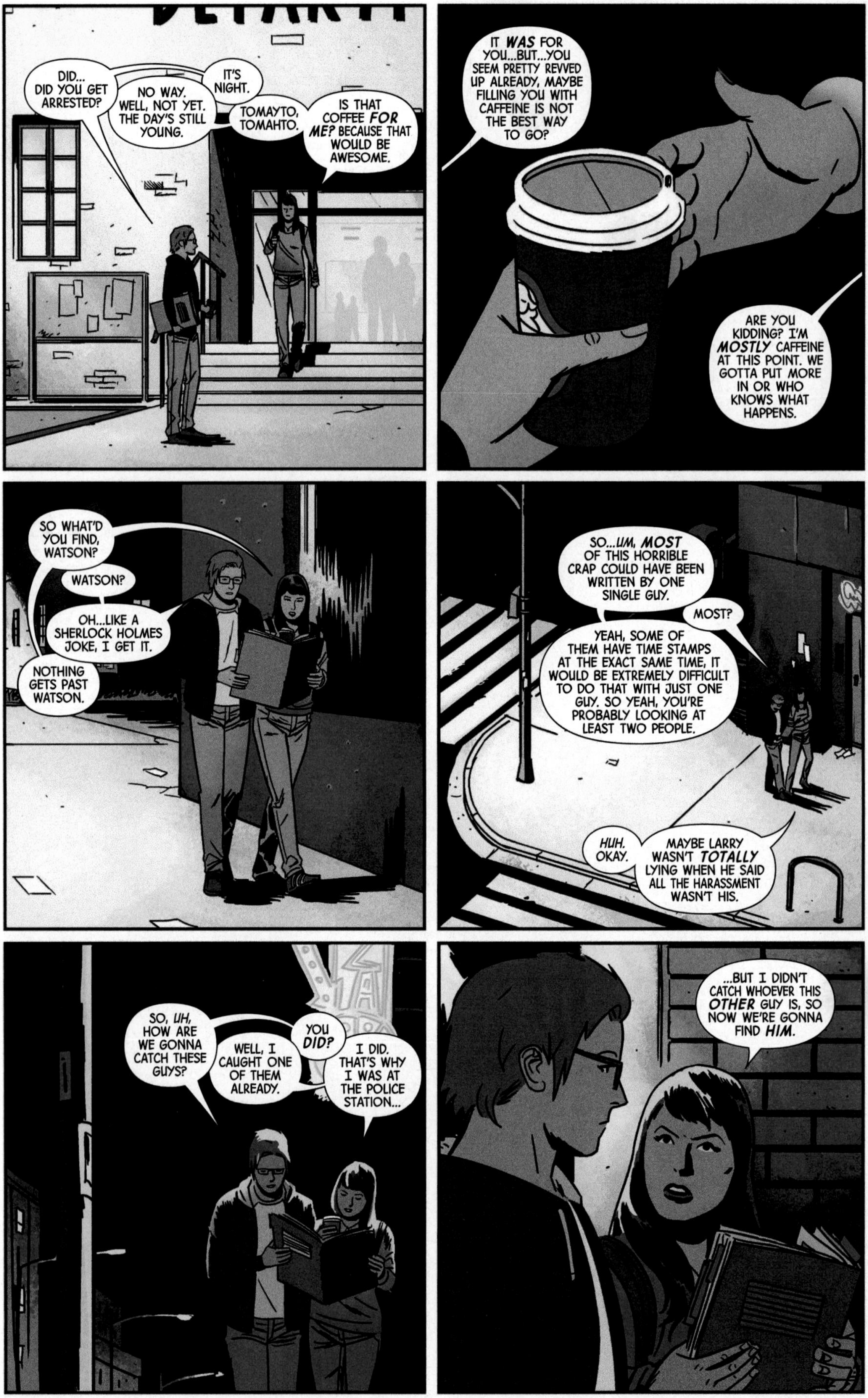

DID... DID YOU GET ARRESTED?
NO WAY. WELL, NOT YET. THE DAY'S STILL YOUNG.
IT'S NIGHT.
TOMAYTO, TOMAHTO.
IS THAT COFFEE FOR ME? BECAUSE THAT WOULD BE AWESOME.
IT WAS FOR YOU...BUT...YOU SEEM PRETTY REVVED UP ALREADY, MAYBE FILLING YOU WITH CAFFEINE IS NOT THE BEST WAY TO GO?
ARE YOU KIDDING? I'M MOSTLY CAFFEINE AT THIS POINT. WE GOTTA PUT MORE IN OR WHO KNOWS WHAT HAPPENS.
SO WHAT'D YOU FIND, WATSON?
WATSON?
OH...LIKE A SHERLOCK HOLMES JOKE, I GET IT.
NOTHING GETS PAST WATSON.
SO...UM, MOST OF THIS HORRIBLE CRAP COULD HAVE BEEN WRITTEN BY ONE SINGLE GUY.
MOST?
YEAH, SOME OF THEM HAVE TIME STAMPS AT THE EXACT SAME TIME, IT WOULD BE EXTREMELY DIFFICULT TO DO THAT WITH JUST ONE GUY. SO YEAH, YOU'RE PROBABLY LOOKING AT LEAST TWO PEOPLE.
MAYBE LARRY WASN'T TOTALLY LYING WHEN HE SAID ALL THE HARASSMENT WASN'T HIS.
HUH. OKAY.
SO, UH, HOW ARE WE GONNA CATCH THESE GUYS?
WELL, I CAUGHT ONE OF THEM ALREADY.
YOU DID?
I DID. THAT'S WHY I WAS AT THE POLICE STATION...
...BUT I DIDN'T CATCH WHOEVER THIS OTHER GUY IS, SO NOW WE'RE GONNA FIND HIM.

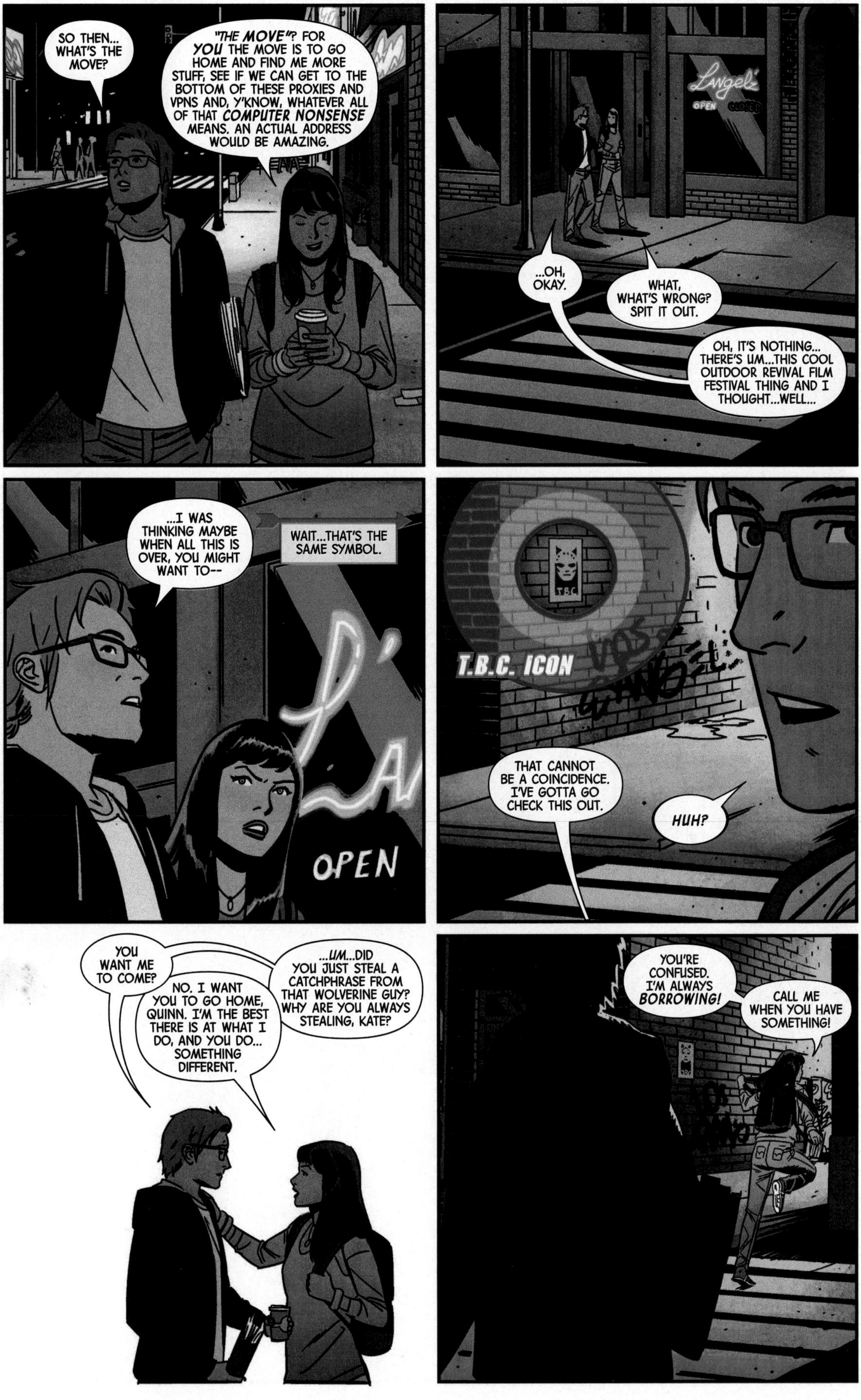
SO THEN... WHAT'S THE MOVE?
"THE MOVE"? FOR YOU THE MOVE IS TO GO HOME AND FIND ME MORE STUFF, SEE IF WE CAN GET TO THE BOTTOM OF THESE PROXIES AND VPNS AND, Y'KNOW, WHATEVER ALL OF THAT COMPUTER NONSENSE MEANS. AN ACTUAL ADDRESS WOULD BE AMAZING.
OPEN
...OH, OKAY.
WHAT, WHAT'S WRONG? SPIT IT OUT.
OH, IT'S NOTHING... THERE'S UM...THIS COOL OUTDOOR REVIVAL FILM FESTIVAL THING AND I THOUGHT...WELL...
...I WAS THINKING MAYBE WHEN ALL THIS IS OVER, YOU MIGHT WANT TO--
WAIT...THAT'S THE SAME SYMBOL.
OPEN
TBC
T.B.C. ICON
THAT CANNOT BE A COINCIDENCE. I'VE GOTTA GO CHECK THIS OUT.
HUH?
YOU WANT ME TO COME?
NO. I WANT YOU TO GO HOME, QUINN. I'M THE BEST THERE IS AT WHAT I DO, AND YOU DO... SOMETHING DIFFERENT.
...UM...DID YOU JUST STEAL A CATCHPHRASE FROM THAT WOLVERINE GUY? WHY ARE YOU ALWAYS STEALING, KATE?
YOU'RE CONFUSED. I'M ALWAYS BORROWING!
CALL ME WHEN YOU HAVE SOMETHING!

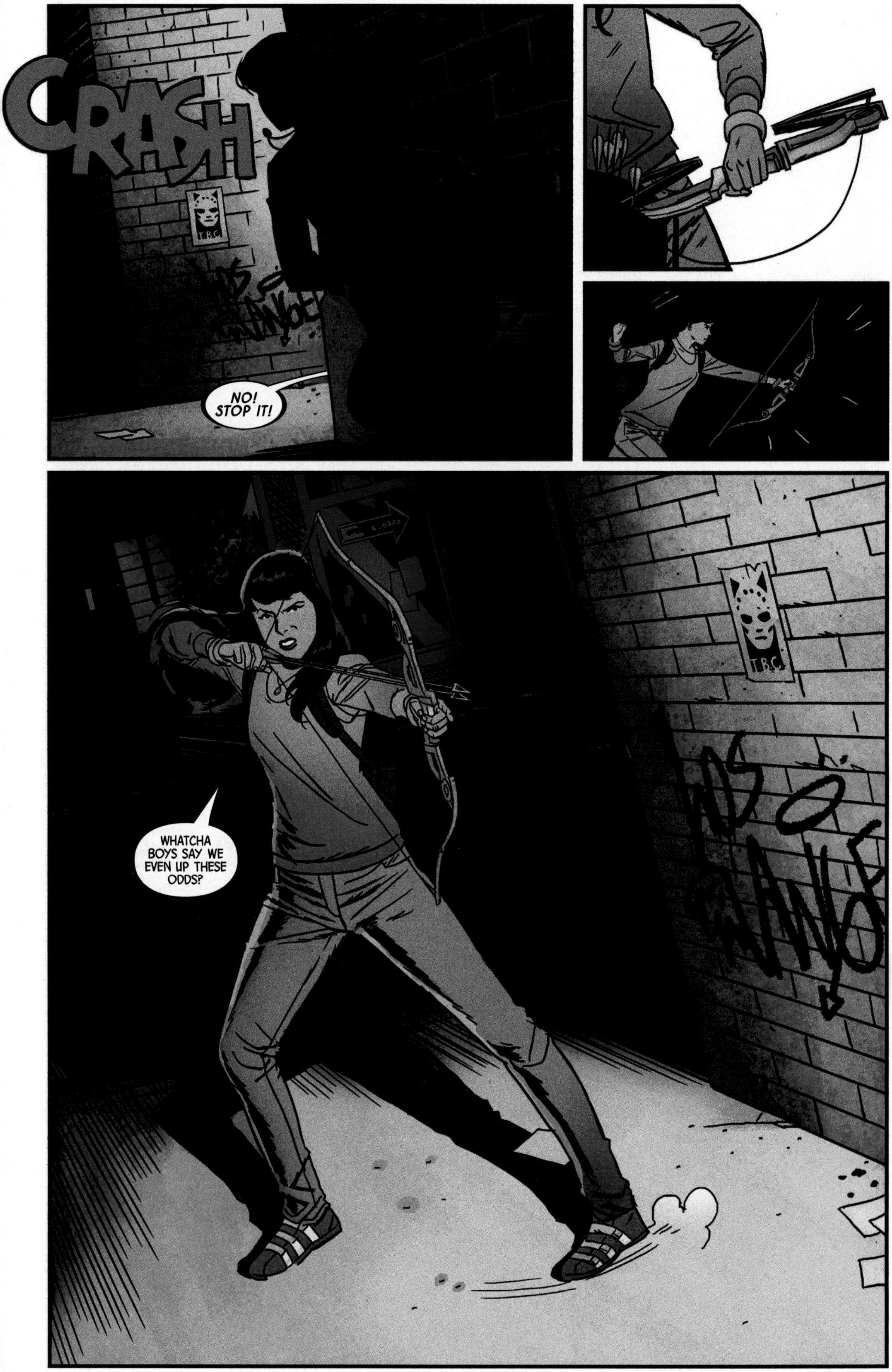
CRASH
NO! STOP IT!
WHATCHA BOYS SAY WE EVEN UP THESE ODDS?

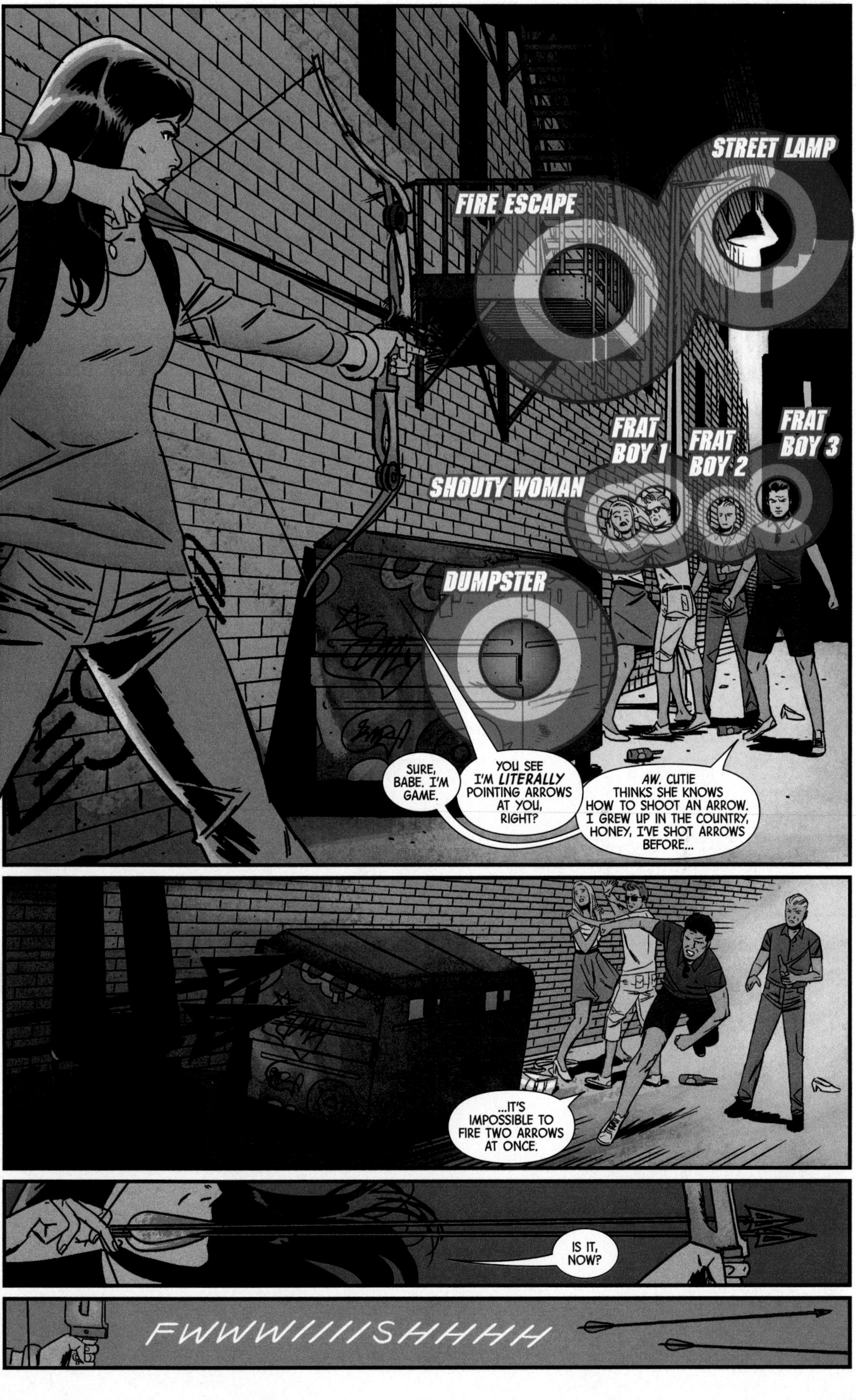
STREET LAMP
FIRE ESCAPE
FRAT BOY 1
FRAT BOY 2
FRAT BOY 3
SHOUTY WOMAN
DUMPSTER
SURE, BABE. I'M GAME.
YOU SEE I'M LITERALLY POINTING ARROWS AT YOU, RIGHT?
AW. CUTIE THINKS SHE KNOWS HOW TO SHOOT AN ARROW. I GREW UP IN THE COUNTRY, HONEY, I'VE SHOT ARROWS BEFORE...
...IT'S IMPOSSIBLE TO FIRE TWO ARROWS AT ONCE.
IS IT, NOW?
FWWWIIIISHHHH

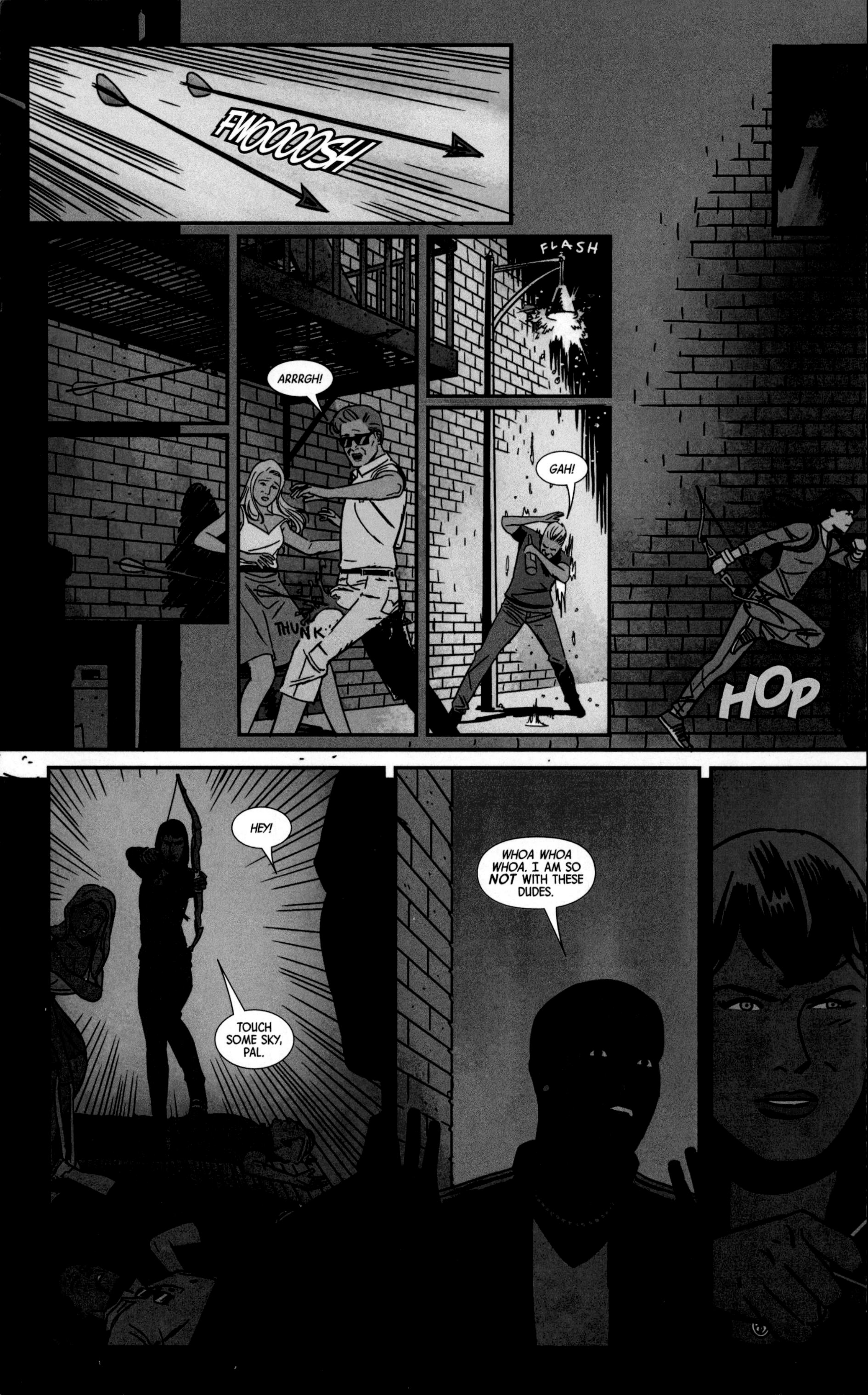
FWOOOOSH
ARRRGH!
THUNK
FLASH
GAH!
HOP
HEY!
TOUCH SOME SKY, PAL.
WHOA WHOA WHOA. I AM SO NOT WITH THESE DUDES.

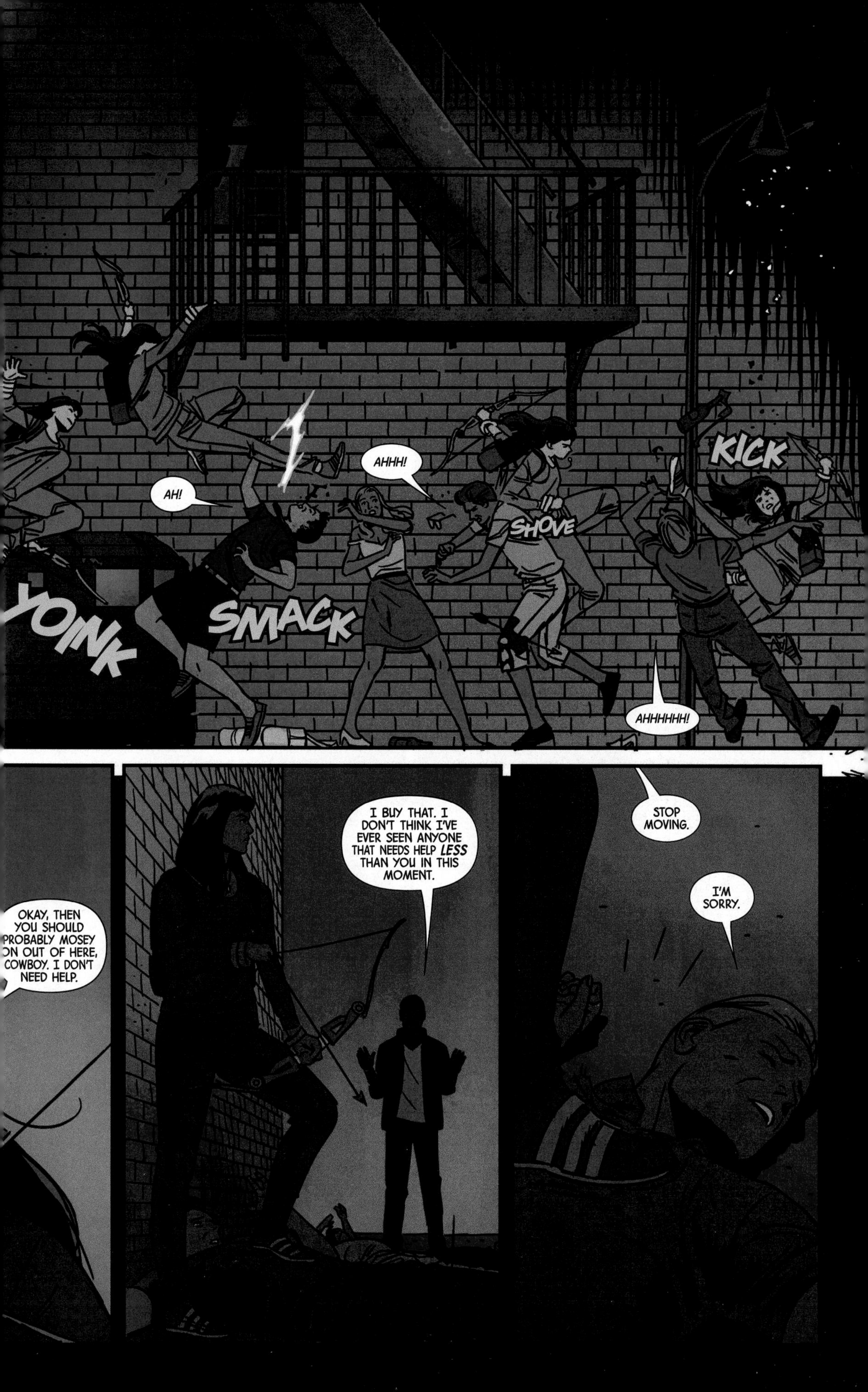
AH!
SMACK
YOINK
AHHH!
SHOVE
KICK
AHHHHHH!
OKAY, THEN YOU SHOULD PROBABLY MOSEY ON OUT OF HERE, COWBOY. I DON'T NEED HELP.
I BUY THAT. I DON'T THINK I'VE EVER SEEN ANYONE THAT NEEDS HELP *LESS* THAN YOU IN THIS MOMENT.
STOP MOVING.
I'M SORRY.

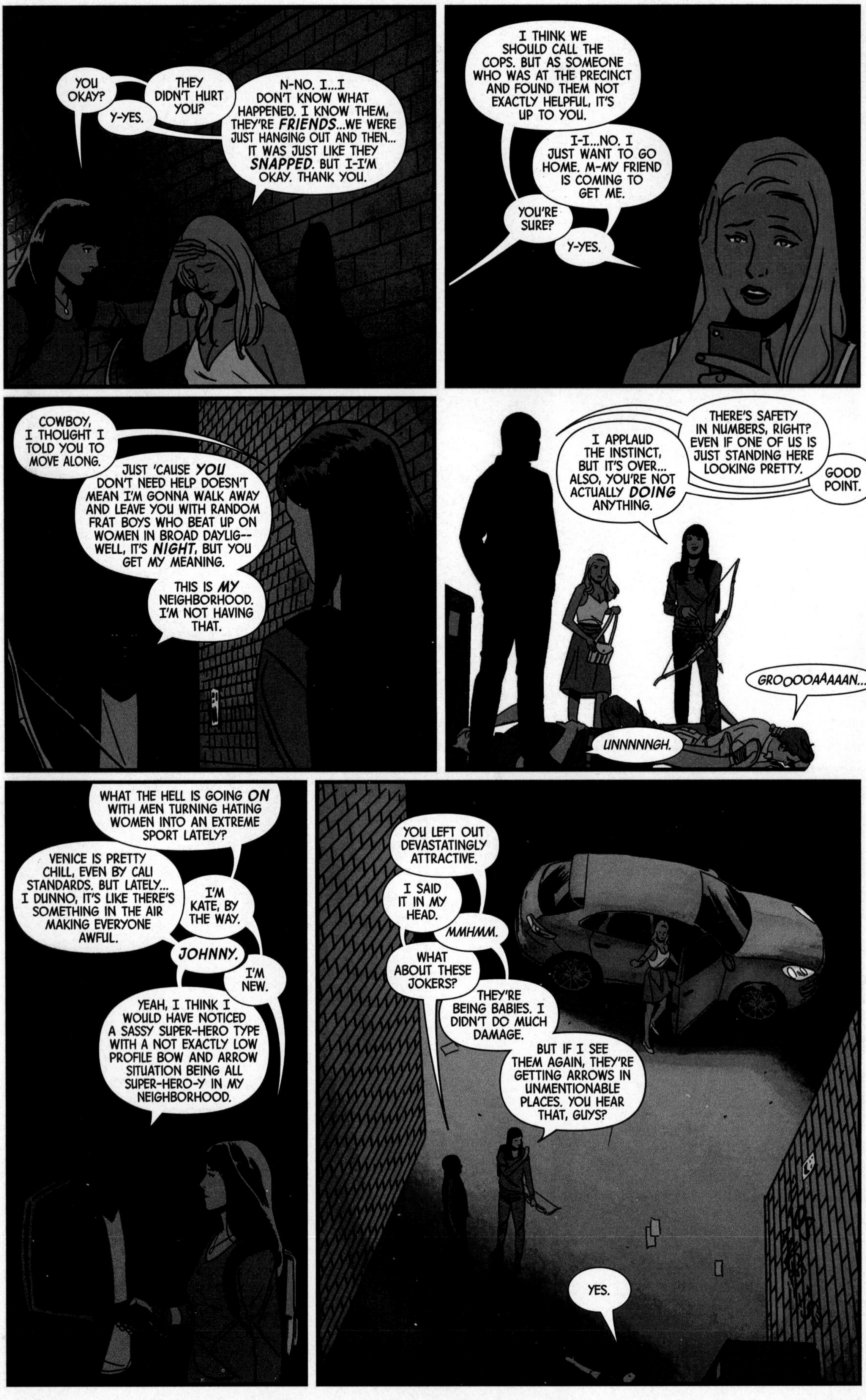
YOU OKAY?
THEY DIDN'T HURT YOU?
Y-YES.
N-NO. I...I DON'T KNOW WHAT HAPPENED. I KNOW THEM, THEY'RE FRIENDS...WE WERE JUST HANGING OUT AND THEN... IT WAS JUST LIKE THEY SNAPPED. BUT I-I'M OKAY. THANK YOU.
I THINK WE SHOULD CALL THE COPS. BUT AS SOMEONE WHO WAS AT THE PRECINCT AND FOUND THEM NOT EXACTLY HELPFUL, IT'S UP TO YOU.
I-I...NO. I JUST WANT TO GO HOME. M-MY FRIEND IS COMING TO GET ME.
YOU'RE SURE?
Y-YES.
COWBOY, I THOUGHT I TOLD YOU TO MOVE ALONG.
JUST 'CAUSE YOU DON'T NEED HELP DOESN'T MEAN I'M GONNA WALK AWAY AND LEAVE YOU WITH RANDOM FRAT BOYS WHO BEAT UP ON WOMEN IN BROAD DAYLIG-- WELL, IT'S NIGHT, BUT YOU GET MY MEANING.
THIS IS MY NEIGHBORHOOD. I'M NOT HAVING THAT.
I APPLAUD THE INSTINCT, BUT IT'S OVER... ALSO, YOU'RE NOT ACTUALLY DOING ANYTHING.
THERE'S SAFETY IN NUMBERS, RIGHT? EVEN IF ONE OF US IS JUST STANDING HERE LOOKING PRETTY.
GOOD POINT.
GROOOOAAAAAN...
UNNNNNGH.
WHAT THE HELL IS GOING ON WITH MEN TURNING HATING WOMEN INTO AN EXTREME SPORT LATELY?
VENICE IS PRETTY CHILL, EVEN BY CALI STANDARDS. BUT LATELY... I DUNNO, IT'S LIKE THERE'S SOMETHING IN THE AIR MAKING EVERYONE AWFUL.
I'M KATE, BY THE WAY.
JOHNNY.
I'M NEW.
YEAH, I THINK I WOULD HAVE NOTICED A SASSY SUPER-HERO TYPE WITH A NOT EXACTLY LOW PROFILE BOW AND ARROW SITUATION BEING ALL SUPER-HERO-Y IN MY NEIGHBORHOOD.
YOU LEFT OUT DEVASTATINGLY ATTRACTIVE.
I SAID IT IN MY HEAD.
MMHMM.
WHAT ABOUT THESE JOKERS?
THEY'RE BEING BABIES. I DIDN'T DO MUCH DAMAGE.
BUT IF I SEE THEM AGAIN, THEY'RE GETTING ARROWS IN UNMENTIONABLE PLACES. YOU HEAR THAT, GUYS?
YES.

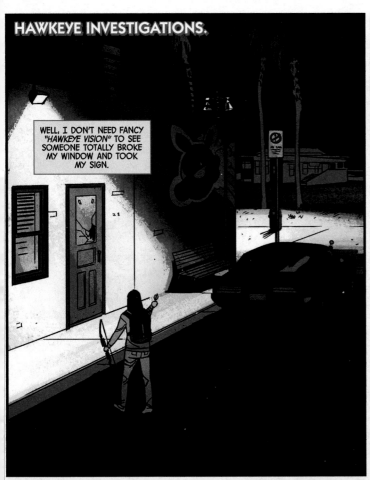

HAWKEYE INVESTIGATIONS.

WELL, I DON'T NEED FANCY *"HAWKEYE VISION"* TO SEE SOMEONE TOTALLY BROKE MY WINDOW AND TOOK MY SIGN.

CAN'T BELIEVE I'M GOING TO HAVE TO TRY TO DRAW THAT DAMN EYE ALL OVER AGAIN. TOTALLY GONNA PUT AN ARROW IN WHOEVER DID THAT.

AH-HA!

AH-HA? REALLY?

RAMONE?!

WHAT THE HELL? WHY DID YOU BREAK INTO MY PLACE?

I'M ASKING THE QUESTIONS. WHY ARE YOU CALLING *MY* GIRLFRIEND?

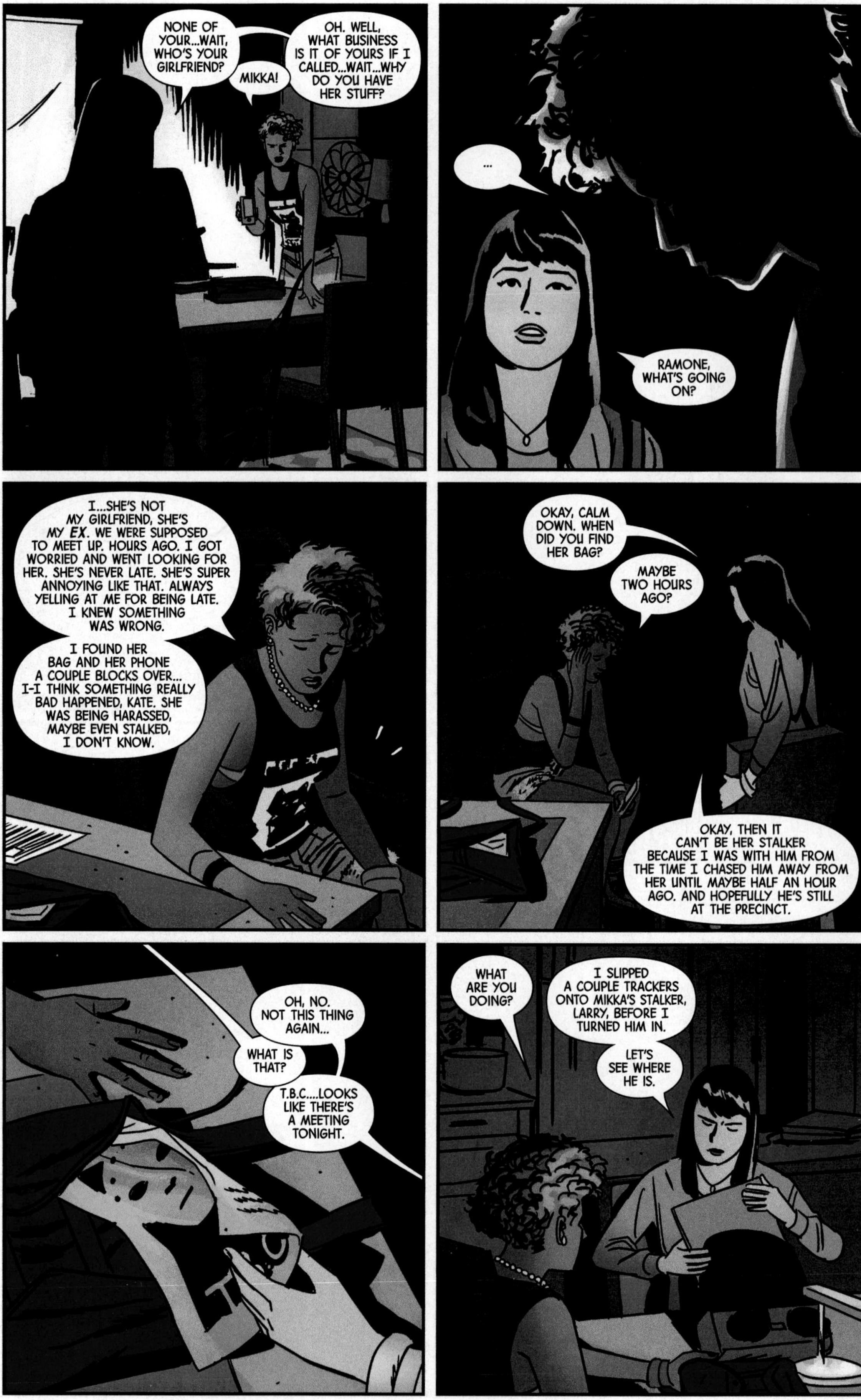

NONE OF YOUR...WAIT, WHO'S YOUR GIRLFRIEND?
OH. WELL, WHAT BUSINESS IS IT OF YOURS IF I CALLED...WAIT...WHY DO YOU HAVE HER STUFF?
MIKKA!
...
RAMONE, WHAT'S GOING ON?
I...SHE'S NOT MY GIRLFRIEND, SHE'S MY EX. WE WERE SUPPOSED TO MEET UP. HOURS AGO. I GOT WORRIED AND WENT LOOKING FOR HER. SHE'S NEVER LATE. SHE'S SUPER ANNOYING LIKE THAT. ALWAYS YELLING AT ME FOR BEING LATE. I KNEW SOMETHING WAS WRONG.
I FOUND HER BAG AND HER PHONE A COUPLE BLOCKS OVER... I-I THINK SOMETHING REALLY BAD HAPPENED, KATE. SHE WAS BEING HARASSED, MAYBE EVEN STALKED, I DON'T KNOW.
OKAY, CALM DOWN. WHEN DID YOU FIND HER BAG?
MAYBE TWO HOURS AGO?
OKAY, THEN IT CAN'T BE HER STALKER BECAUSE I WAS WITH HIM FROM THE TIME I CHASED HIM AWAY FROM HER UNTIL MAYBE HALF AN HOUR AGO. AND HOPEFULLY HE'S STILL AT THE PRECINCT.
OH, NO. NOT THIS THING AGAIN...
WHAT IS THAT?
T.B.C....LOOKS LIKE THERE'S A MEETING TONIGHT.
WHAT ARE YOU DOING?
I SLIPPED A COUPLE TRACKERS ONTO MIKKA'S STALKER, LARRY, BEFORE I TURNED HIM IN.
LET'S SEE WHERE HE IS.

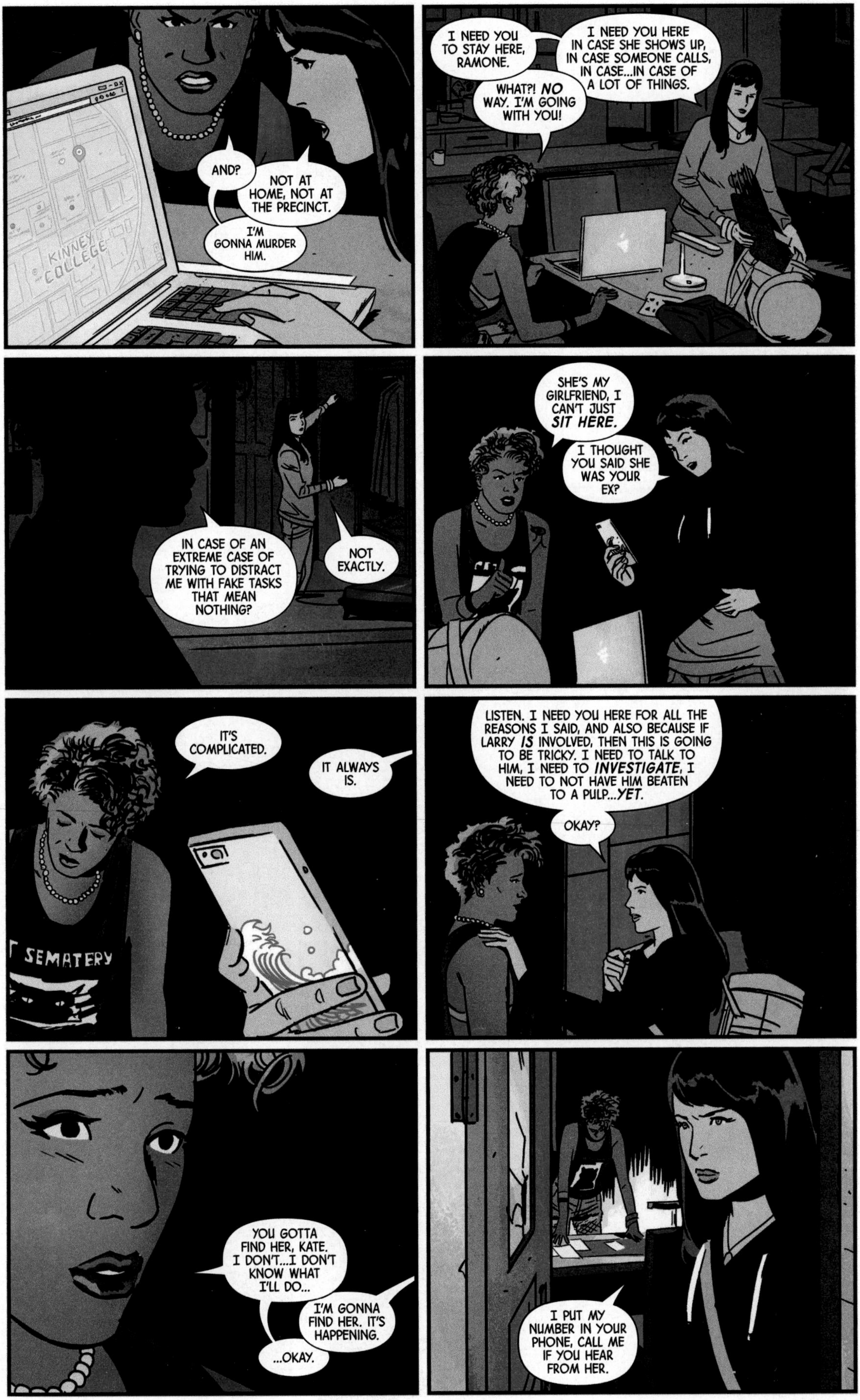
KINNEY COLLEGE
AND?
NOT AT HOME, NOT AT THE PRECINCT.
I'M GONNA MURDER HIM.
I NEED YOU TO STAY HERE, RAMONE.
I NEED YOU HERE IN CASE SHE SHOWS UP, IN CASE SOMEONE CALLS, IN CASE...IN CASE OF A LOT OF THINGS.
WHAT?! NO WAY. I'M GOING WITH YOU!
IN CASE OF AN EXTREME CASE OF TRYING TO DISTRACT ME WITH FAKE TASKS THAT MEAN NOTHING?
NOT EXACTLY.
SHE'S MY GIRLFRIEND, I CAN'T JUST SIT HERE.
I THOUGHT YOU SAID SHE WAS YOUR EX?
IT'S COMPLICATED.
IT ALWAYS IS.
SEMATERY
LISTEN. I NEED YOU HERE FOR ALL THE REASONS I SAID, AND ALSO BECAUSE IF LARRY IS INVOLVED, THEN THIS IS GOING TO BE TRICKY. I NEED TO TALK TO HIM, I NEED TO INVESTIGATE, I NEED TO NOT HAVE HIM BEATEN TO A PULP...YET.
OKAY?
YOU GOTTA FIND HER, KATE. I DON'T...I DON'T KNOW WHAT I'LL DO...
I'M GONNA FIND HER. IT'S HAPPENING.
...OKAY.
I PUT MY NUMBER IN YOUR PHONE, CALL ME IF YOU HEAR FROM HER.

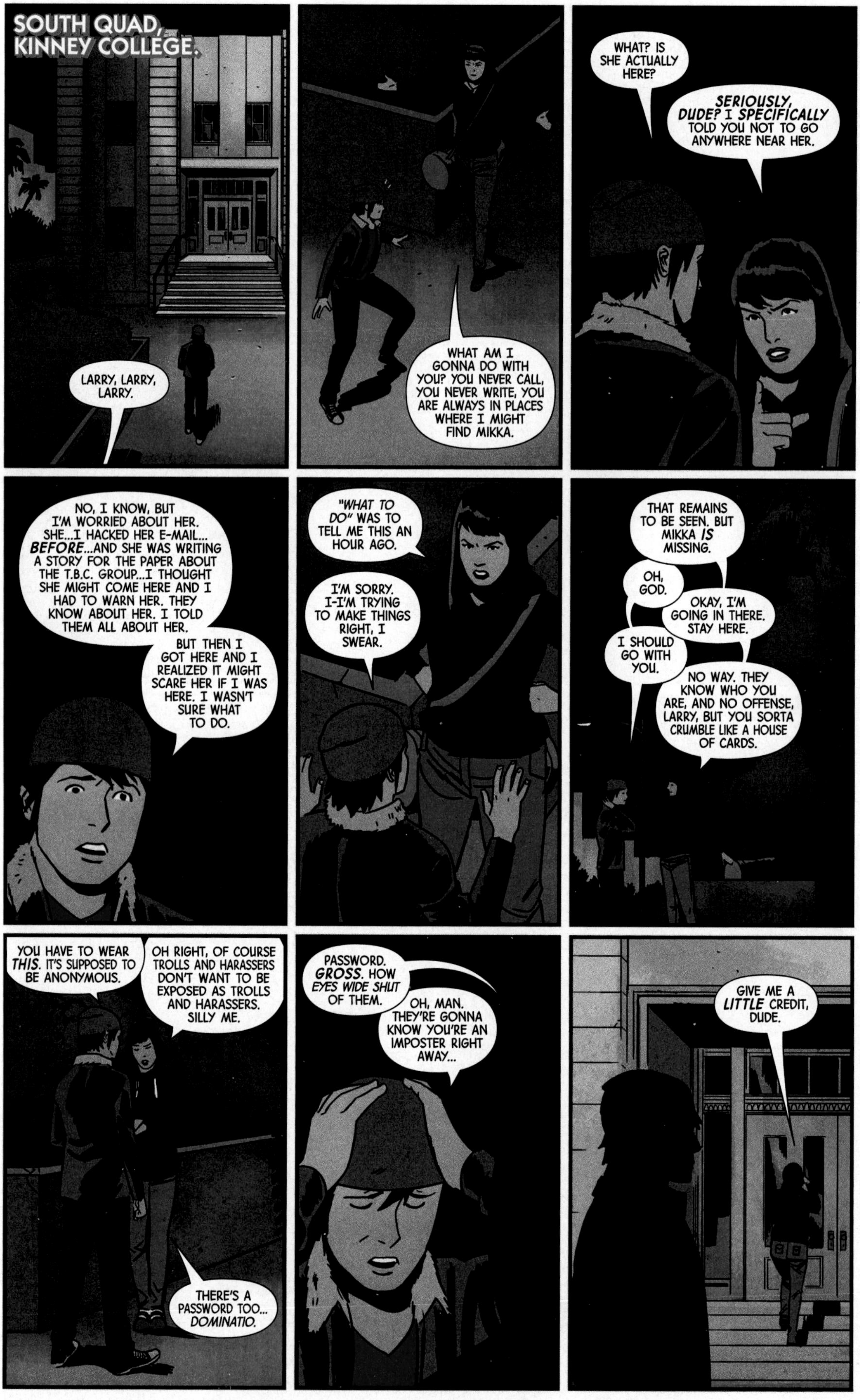
SOUTH QUAD, KINNEY COLLEGE.
LARRY, LARRY, LARRY.
WHAT AM I GONNA DO WITH YOU? YOU NEVER CALL, YOU NEVER WRITE, YOU ARE ALWAYS IN PLACES WHERE I MIGHT FIND MIKKA.
WHAT? IS SHE ACTUALLY HERE?
SERIOUSLY, DUDE? I SPECIFICALLY TOLD YOU NOT TO GO ANYWHERE NEAR HER.
NO, I KNOW, BUT I'M WORRIED ABOUT HER. SHE...I HACKED HER E-MAIL... BEFORE...AND SHE WAS WRITING A STORY FOR THE PAPER ABOUT THE T.B.C. GROUP...I THOUGHT SHE MIGHT COME HERE AND I HAD TO WARN HER. THEY KNOW ABOUT HER. I TOLD THEM ALL ABOUT HER.
BUT THEN I GOT HERE AND I REALIZED IT MIGHT SCARE HER IF I WAS HERE. I WASN'T SURE WHAT TO DO.
"WHAT TO DO" WAS TO TELL ME THIS AN HOUR AGO.
I'M SORRY. I-I'M TRYING TO MAKE THINGS RIGHT, I SWEAR.
THAT REMAINS TO BE SEEN. BUT MIKKA IS MISSING.
OH, GOD.
OKAY, I'M GOING IN THERE. STAY HERE.
I SHOULD GO WITH YOU.
NO WAY. THEY KNOW WHO YOU ARE, AND NO OFFENSE, LARRY, BUT YOU SORTA CRUMBLE LIKE A HOUSE OF CARDS.
YOU HAVE TO WEAR THIS. IT'S SUPPOSED TO BE ANONYMOUS.
OH RIGHT, OF COURSE TROLLS AND HARASSERS DON'T WANT TO BE EXPOSED AS TROLLS AND HARASSERS. SILLY ME.
THERE'S A PASSWORD TOO... DOMINATIO.
PASSWORD. GROSS. HOW EYES WIDE SHUT OF THEM.
OH, MAN. THEY'RE GONNA KNOW YOU'RE AN IMPOSTER RIGHT AWAY...
GIVE ME A LITTLE CREDIT, DUDE.

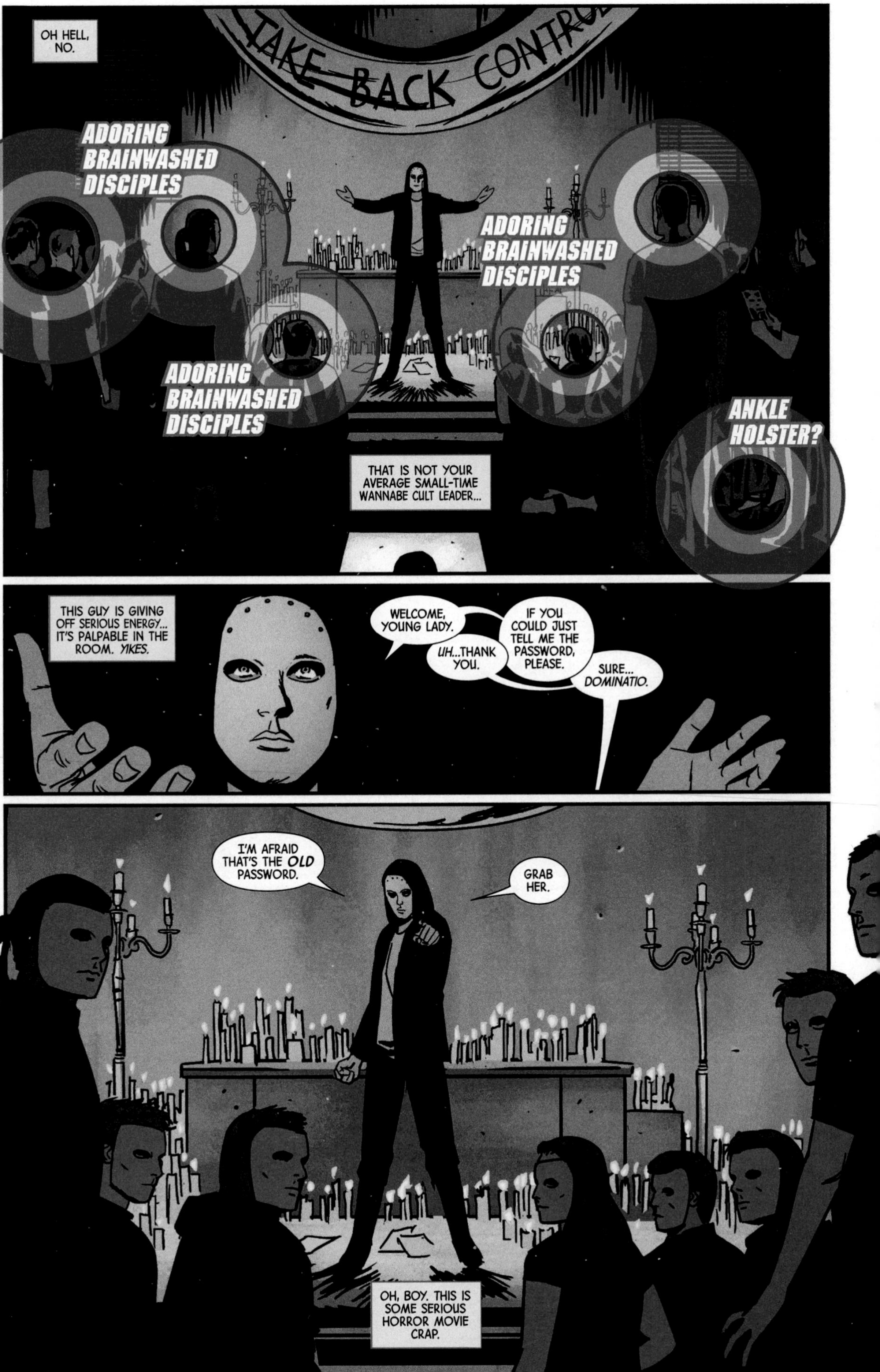
TAKE BACK CONTROL
OH HELL, NO.
ADORING BRAINWASHED DISCIPLES
ADORING BRAINWASHED DISCIPLES
ADORING BRAINWASHED DISCIPLES
ANKLE HOLSTER?
THAT IS NOT YOUR AVERAGE SMALL-TIME WANNABE CULT LEADER...
THIS GUY IS GIVING OFF SERIOUS ENERGY... IT'S PALPABLE IN THE ROOM. *YIKES.*
WELCOME, YOUNG LADY.
UH...THANK YOU.
IF YOU COULD JUST TELL ME THE PASSWORD, PLEASE.
SURE... *DOMINATIO.*
I'M AFRAID THAT'S THE *OLD* PASSWORD.
GRAB HER.
OH, BOY. THIS IS SOME SERIOUS HORROR MOVIE CRAP.

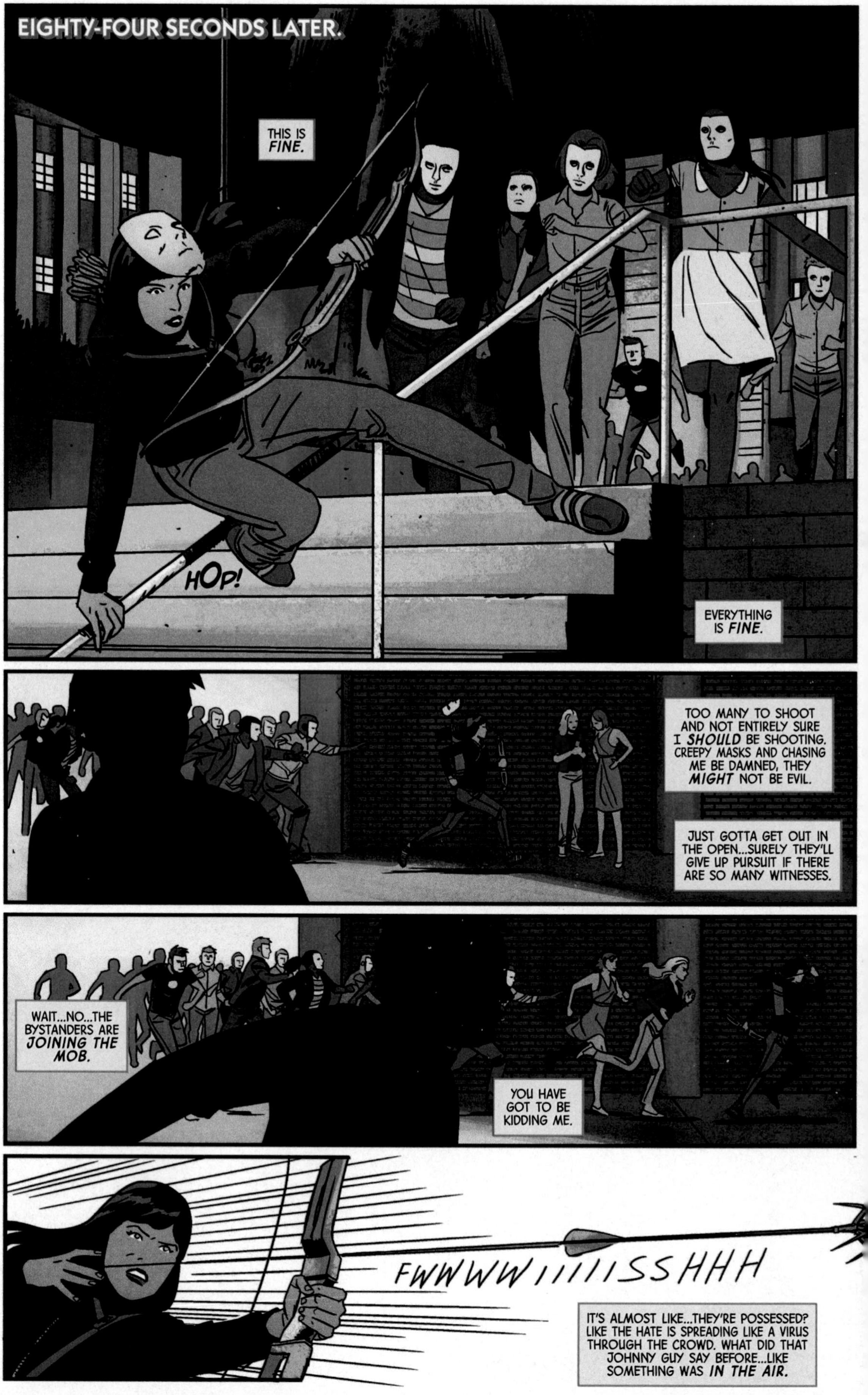
EIGHTY-FOUR SECONDS LATER.
THIS IS FINE.
HOP!
EVERYTHING IS FINE.
TOO MANY TO SHOOT AND NOT ENTIRELY SURE I SHOULD BE SHOOTING. CREEPY MASKS AND CHASING ME BE DAMNED, THEY MIGHT NOT BE EVIL.
JUST GOTTA GET OUT IN THE OPEN...SURELY THEY'LL GIVE UP PURSUIT IF THERE ARE SO MANY WITNESSES.
WAIT...NO...THE BYSTANDERS ARE JOINING THE MOB.
YOU HAVE GOT TO BE KIDDING ME.
FWWWWIIIIISSHHH
IT'S ALMOST LIKE...THEY'RE POSSESSED? LIKE THE HATE IS SPREADING LIKE A VIRUS THROUGH THE CROWD. WHAT DID THAT JOHNNY GUY SAY BEFORE...LIKE SOMETHING WAS IN THE AIR.

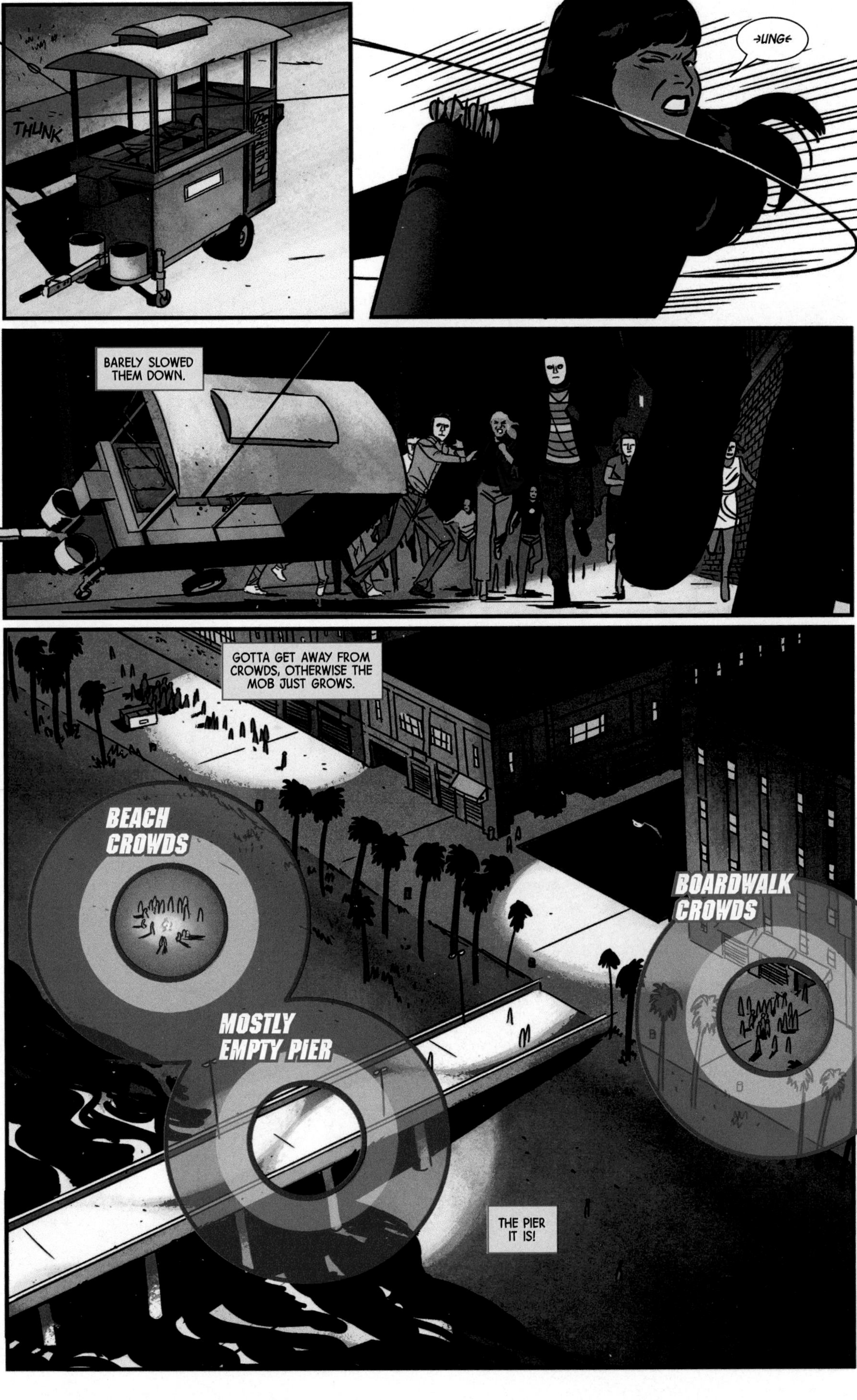
THUNK
LUNG
BARELY SLOWED THEM DOWN.
GOTTA GET AWAY FROM CROWDS, OTHERWISE THE MOB JUST GROWS.
BEACH CROWDS
MOSTLY EMPTY PIER
BOARDWALK CROWDS
THE PIER IT IS!

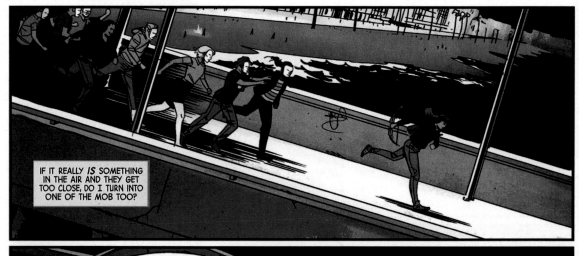

IF IT REALLY *IS* SOMETHING IN THE AIR AND THEY GET TOO CLOSE, DO I TURN INTO ONE OF THE MOB TOO?

I CAN'T RISK HURTING THEM. AT LEAST *SOME* OF THEM ARE COMPLETELY INNOCENT.

BUT I DON'T THINK I CAN RISK LETTING THEM TOO CLOSE OR MAYBE IT'S ALL OVER FOR ME AND PESKY THINGS LIKE FREE THOUGHT...

...AND I'M RUNNING OUT OF RUNWAY.

WELL, WELCOME TO LOS ANGELES, KATE...NOT SURE YOU'RE SURVIVING THE EXPERIENCE!

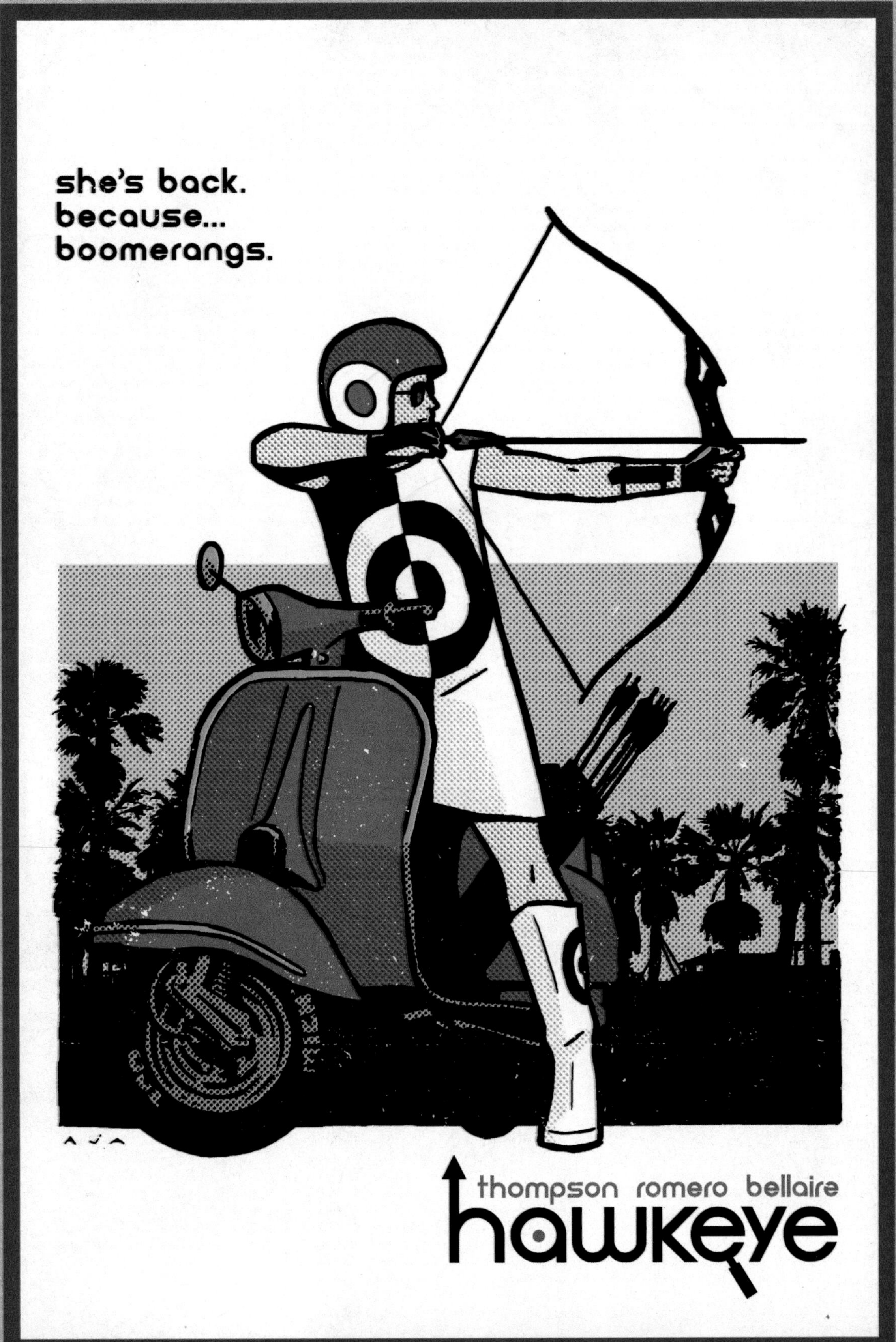

#1 variant by **David Aja**
dress design by **Angela Williams**

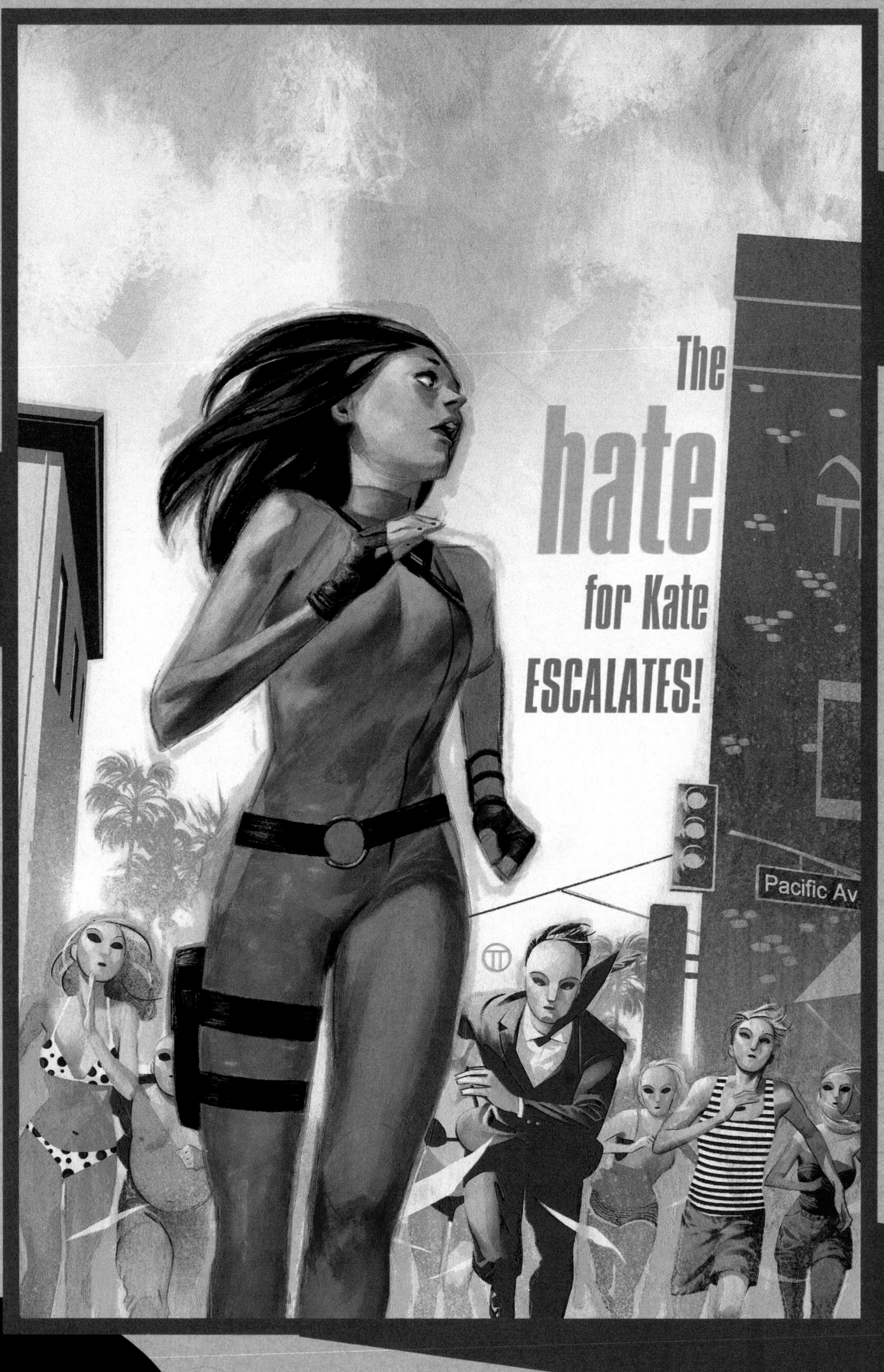
The hate for Kate ESCALATES!
Pacific Av

3

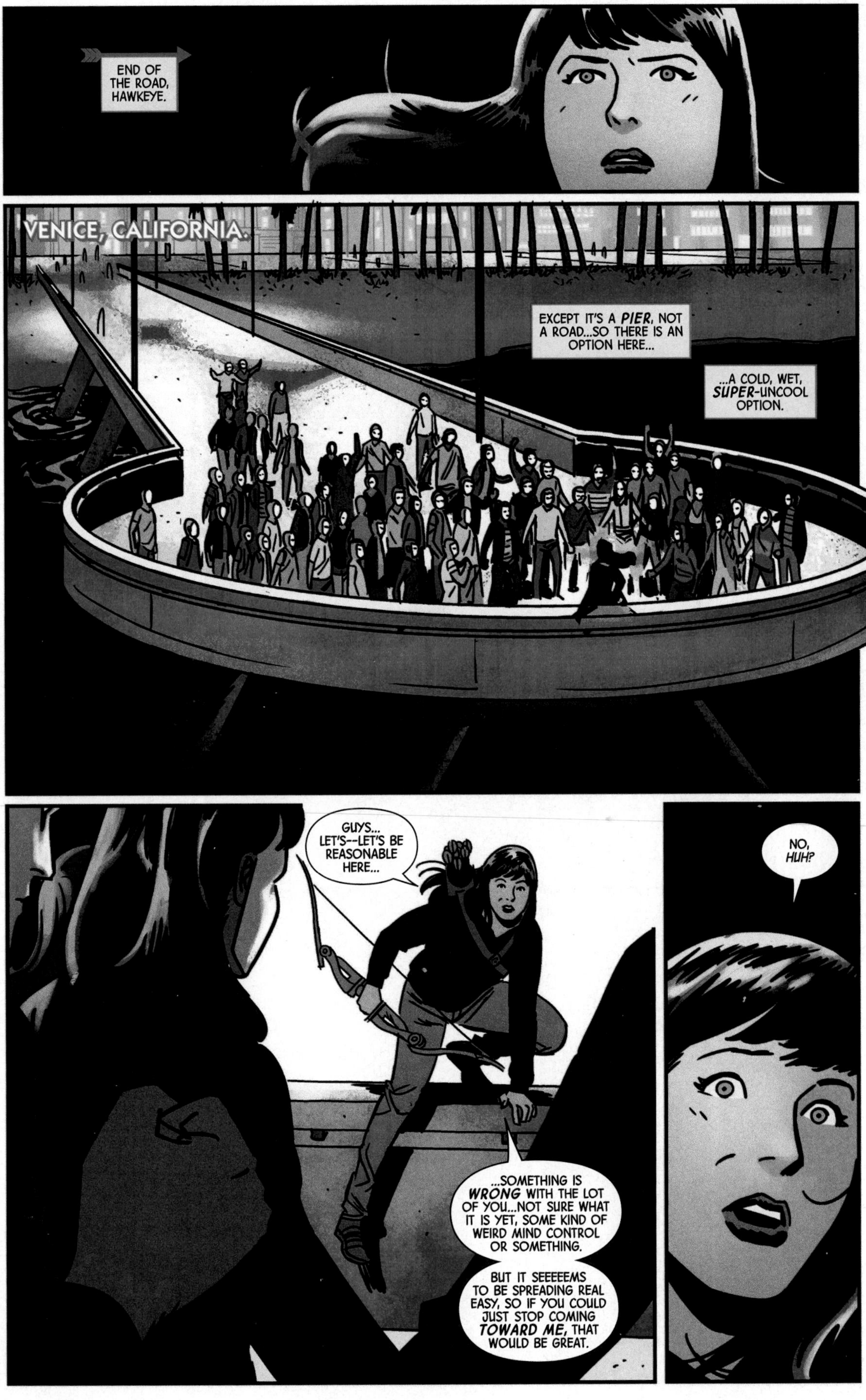
END OF THE ROAD, HAWKEYE.
VENICE, CALIFORNIA.
EXCEPT IT'S A PIER, NOT A ROAD...SO THERE IS AN OPTION HERE...
...A COLD, WET, SUPER-UNCOOL OPTION.
GUYS... LET'S--LET'S BE REASONABLE HERE...
...SOMETHING IS WRONG WITH THE LOT OF YOU...NOT SURE WHAT IT IS YET, SOME KIND OF WEIRD MIND CONTROL OR SOMETHING.
BUT IT SEEEEEMS TO BE SPREADING REAL EASY, SO IF YOU COULD JUST STOP COMING TOWARD ME, THAT WOULD BE GREAT.
NO, HUH?

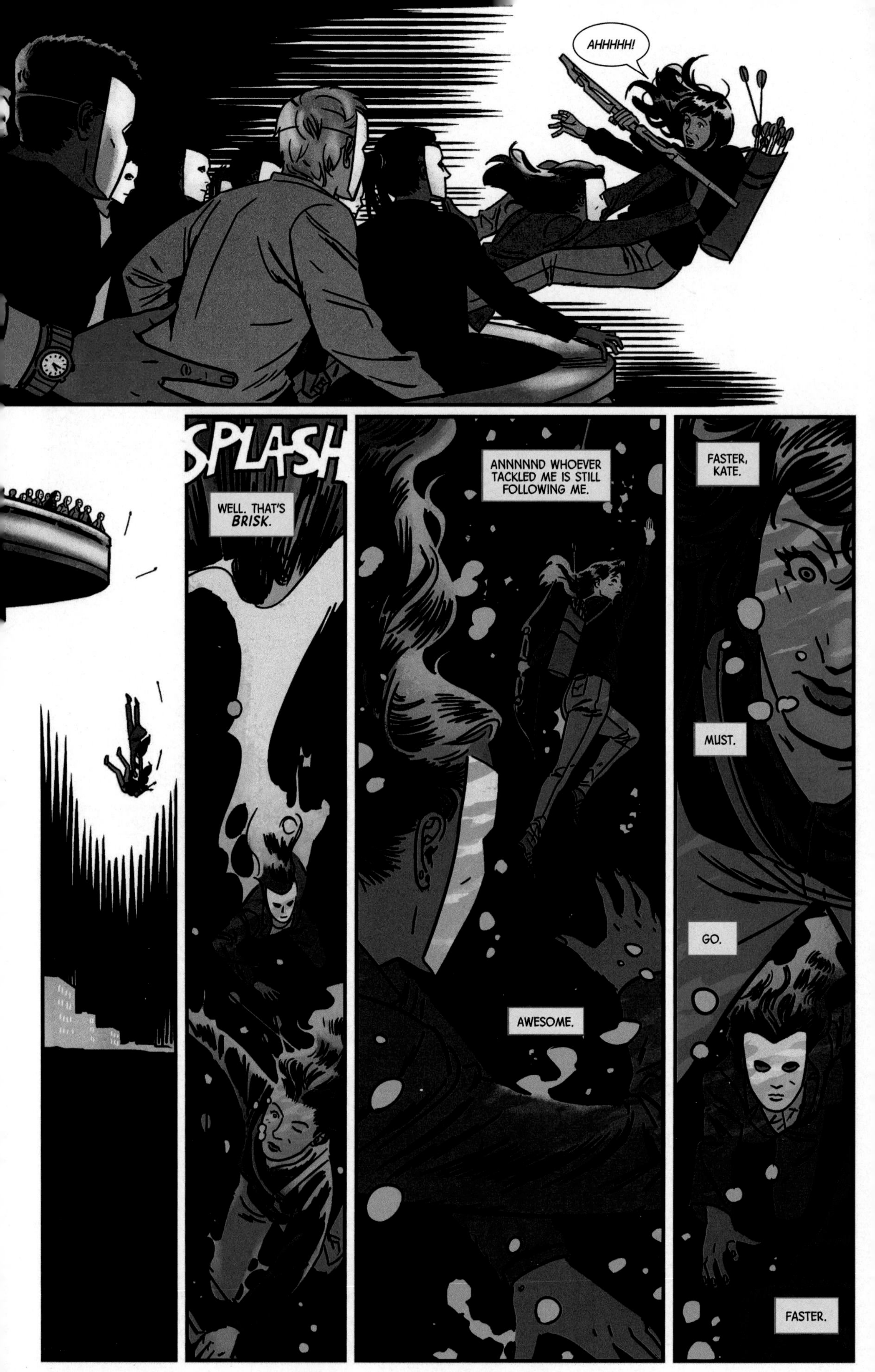
AHHHHH!
SPLASH
WELL. THAT'S *BRISK*.
ANNNNND WHOEVER TACKLED ME IS STILL FOLLOWING ME.
AWESOME.
FASTER, KATE.
MUST.
GO.
FASTER.

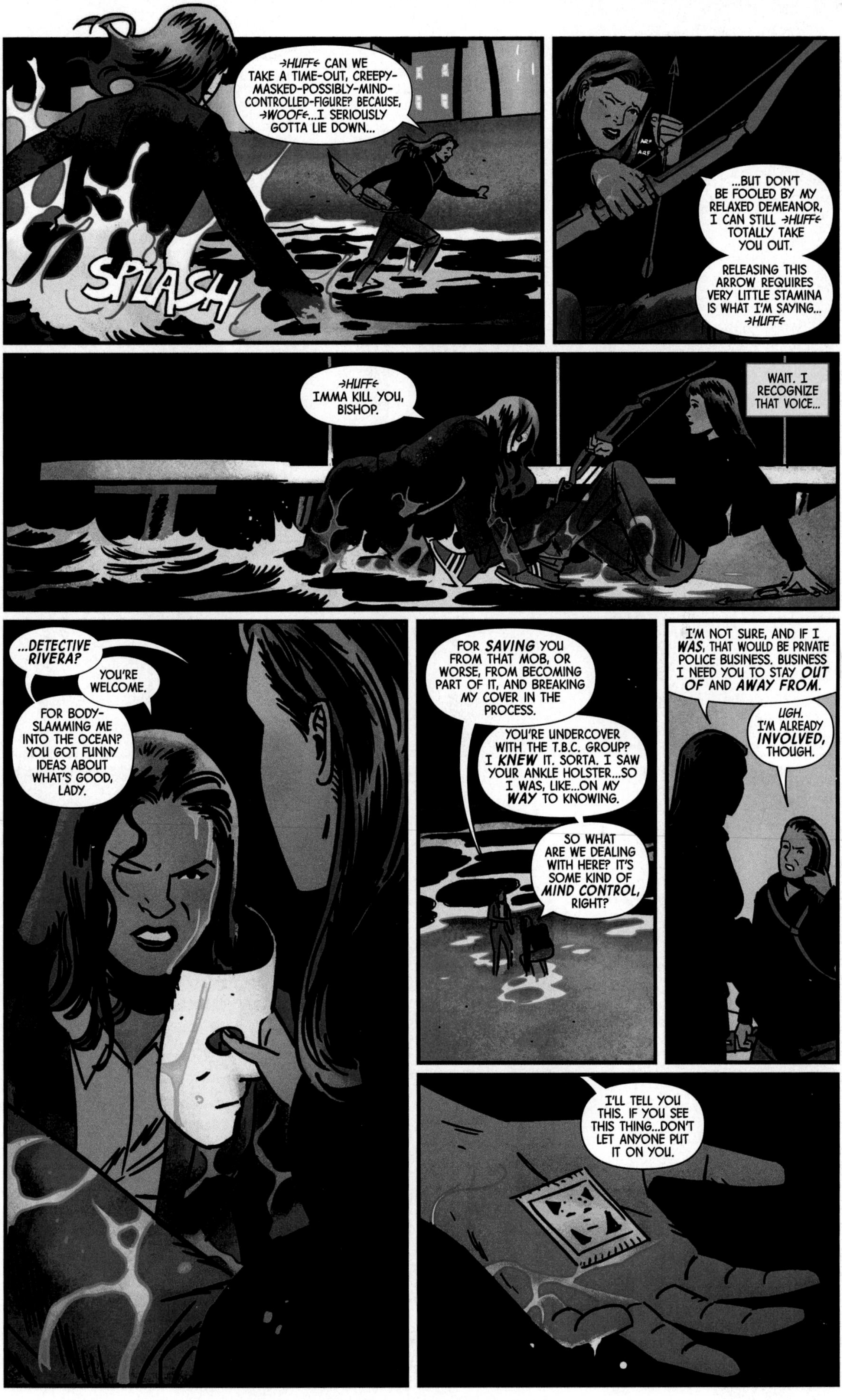

→HUFF← CAN WE TAKE A TIME-OUT, CREEPY-MASKED-POSSIBLY-MIND-CONTROLLED-FIGURE? BECAUSE, →WOOF←...I SERIOUSLY GOTTA LIE DOWN...
SPLASH
...BUT DON'T BE FOOLED BY MY RELAXED DEMEANOR, I CAN STILL →HUFF← TOTALLY TAKE YOU OUT.
RELEASING THIS ARROW REQUIRES VERY LITTLE STAMINA IS WHAT I'M SAYING... →HUFF←
→HUFF← IMMA KILL YOU, BISHOP.
WAIT. I RECOGNIZE THAT VOICE...
...DETECTIVE RIVERA?
YOU'RE WELCOME.
FOR BODY-SLAMMING ME INTO THE OCEAN? YOU GOT FUNNY IDEAS ABOUT WHAT'S GOOD, LADY.
FOR SAVING YOU FROM THAT MOB, OR WORSE, FROM BECOMING PART OF IT, AND BREAKING MY COVER IN THE PROCESS.
YOU'RE UNDERCOVER WITH THE T.B.C. GROUP? I KNEW IT. SORTA. I SAW YOUR ANKLE HOLSTER...SO I WAS, LIKE...ON MY WAY TO KNOWING.
SO WHAT ARE WE DEALING WITH HERE? IT'S SOME KIND OF MIND CONTROL, RIGHT?
I'M NOT SURE, AND IF I WAS, THAT WOULD BE PRIVATE POLICE BUSINESS. BUSINESS I NEED YOU TO STAY OUT OF AND AWAY FROM.
UGH. I'M ALREADY INVOLVED, THOUGH.
I'LL TELL YOU THIS. IF YOU SEE THIS THING...DON'T LET ANYONE PUT IT ON YOU.

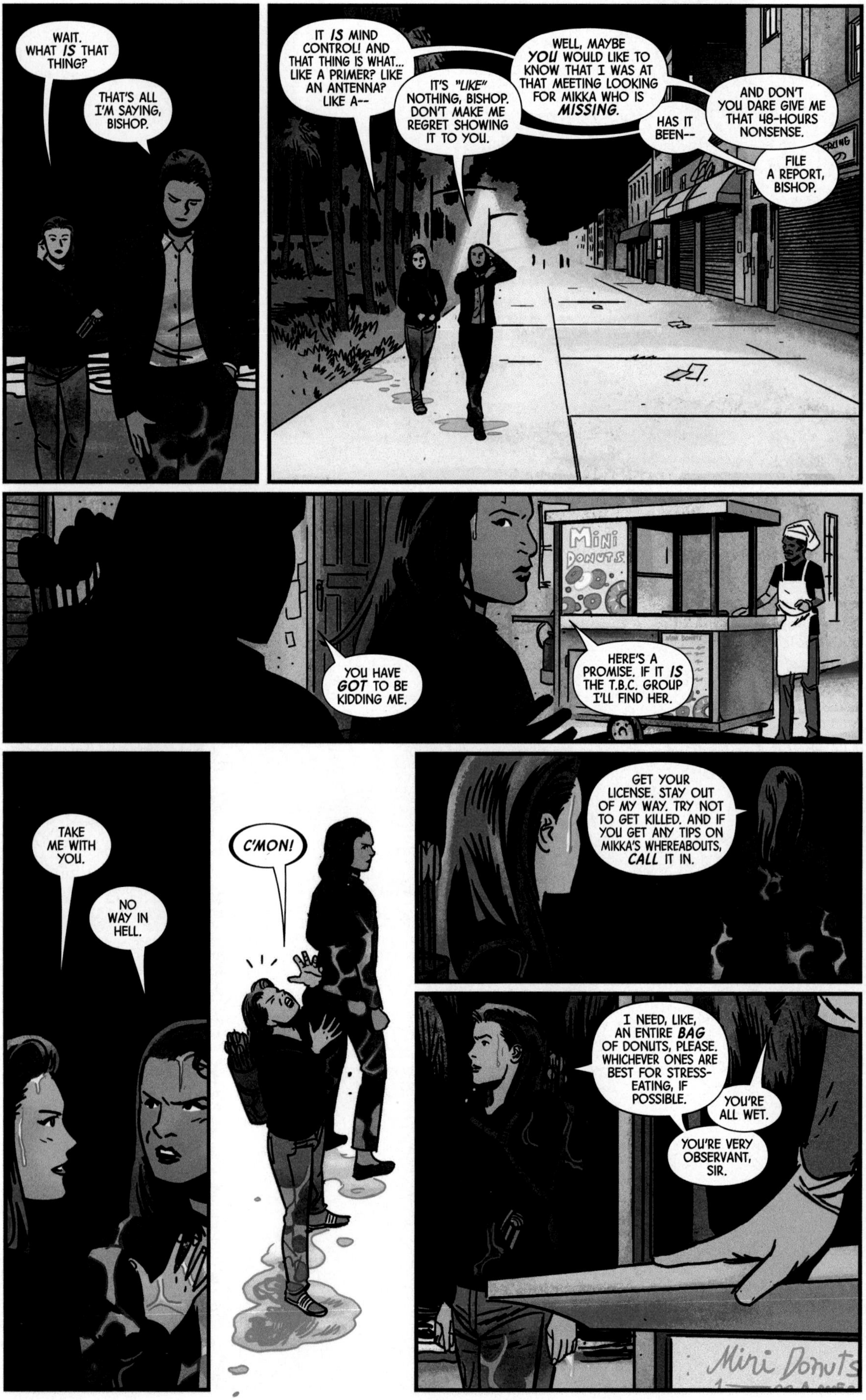
WAIT. WHAT *IS* THAT THING?
THAT'S ALL I'M SAYING, BISHOP.
IT *IS* MIND CONTROL! AND THAT THING IS WHAT... LIKE A PRIMER? LIKE AN ANTENNA? LIKE A--
IT'S *"LIKE"* NOTHING, BISHOP. DON'T MAKE ME REGRET SHOWING IT TO YOU.
WELL, MAYBE *YOU* WOULD LIKE TO KNOW THAT I WAS AT THAT MEETING LOOKING FOR MIKKA WHO IS *MISSING*.
HAS IT BEEN--
AND DON'T YOU DARE GIVE ME THAT 48-HOURS NONSENSE.
FILE A REPORT, BISHOP.
MINI DONUTS
YOU HAVE *GOT* TO BE KIDDING ME.
HERE'S A PROMISE. IF IT *IS* THE T.B.C. GROUP I'LL FIND HER.
TAKE ME WITH YOU.
NO WAY IN HELL.
C'MON!
GET YOUR LICENSE. STAY OUT OF MY WAY. TRY NOT TO GET KILLED. AND IF YOU GET ANY TIPS ON MIKKA'S WHEREABOUTS, *CALL* IT IN.
I NEED, LIKE, AN ENTIRE *BAG* OF DONUTS, PLEASE. WHICHEVER ONES ARE BEST FOR STRESS-EATING, IF POSSIBLE.
YOU'RE ALL WET.
YOU'RE VERY OBSERVANT, SIR.
Mini Donuts

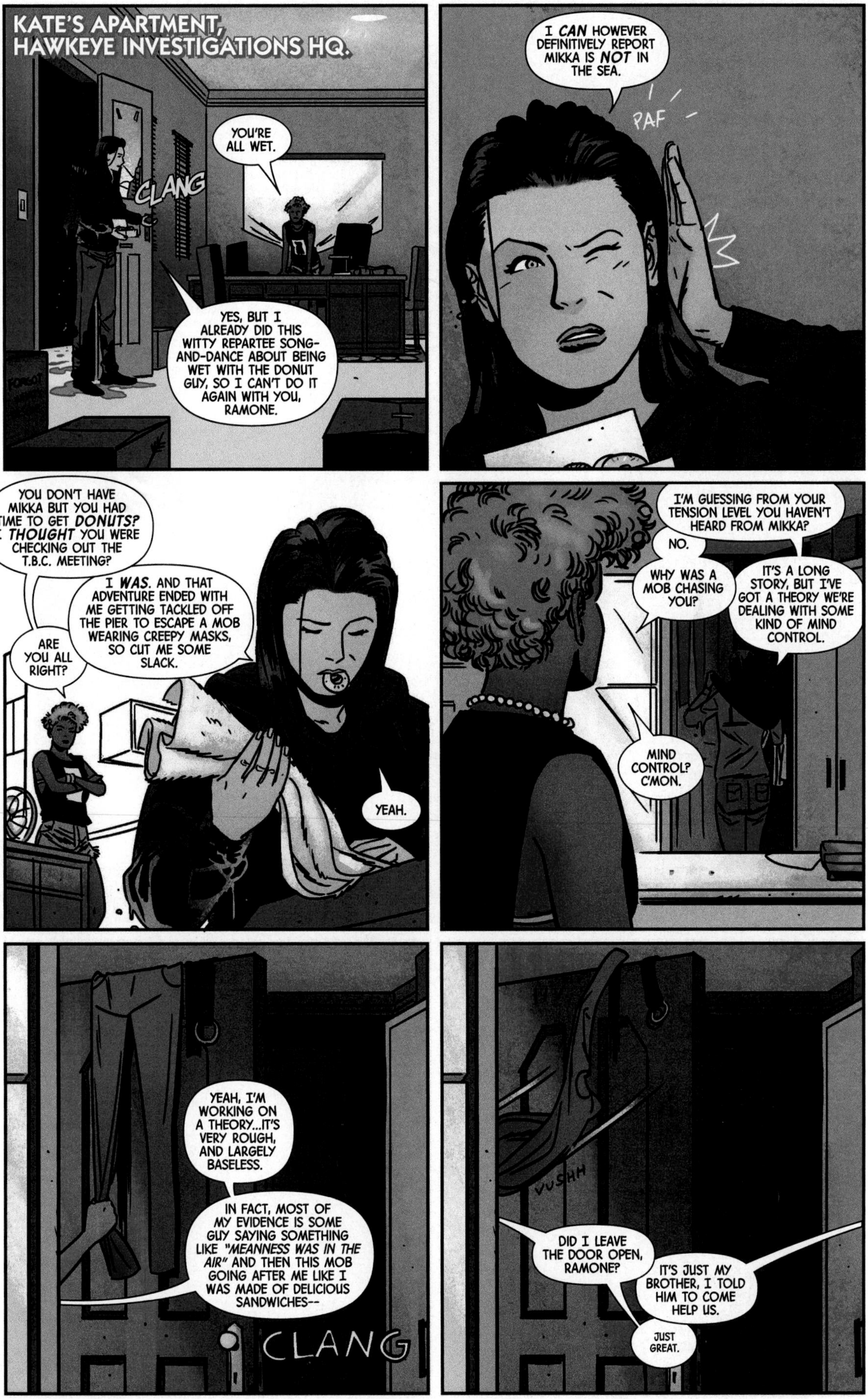
KATE'S APARTMENT, HAWKEYE INVESTIGATIONS HQ.
YOU'RE ALL WET.
CLANG
YES, BUT I ALREADY DID THIS WITTY REPARTEE SONG-AND-DANCE ABOUT BEING WET WITH THE DONUT GUY, SO I CAN'T DO IT AGAIN WITH YOU, RAMONE.
I CAN HOWEVER DEFINITIVELY REPORT MIKKA IS NOT IN THE SEA.
PAF
YOU DON'T HAVE MIKKA BUT YOU HAD TIME TO GET DONUTS? I THOUGHT YOU WERE CHECKING OUT THE T.B.C. MEETING?
I WAS. AND THAT ADVENTURE ENDED WITH ME GETTING TACKLED OFF THE PIER TO ESCAPE A MOB WEARING CREEPY MASKS, SO CUT ME SOME SLACK.
ARE YOU ALL RIGHT?
YEAH.
I'M GUESSING FROM YOUR TENSION LEVEL YOU HAVEN'T HEARD FROM MIKKA?
NO.
WHY WAS A MOB CHASING YOU?
IT'S A LONG STORY, BUT I'VE GOT A THEORY WE'RE DEALING WITH SOME KIND OF MIND CONTROL.
MIND CONTROL? C'MON.
YEAH, I'M WORKING ON A THEORY...IT'S VERY ROUGH, AND LARGELY BASELESS.
IN FACT, MOST OF MY EVIDENCE IS SOME GUY SAYING SOMETHING LIKE "MEANNESS WAS IN THE AIR" AND THEN THIS MOB GOING AFTER ME LIKE I WAS MADE OF DELICIOUS SANDWICHES--
CLANG
VUSHH
DID I LEAVE THE DOOR OPEN, RAMONE?
IT'S JUST MY BROTHER, I TOLD HIM TO COME HELP US.
JUST GREAT.

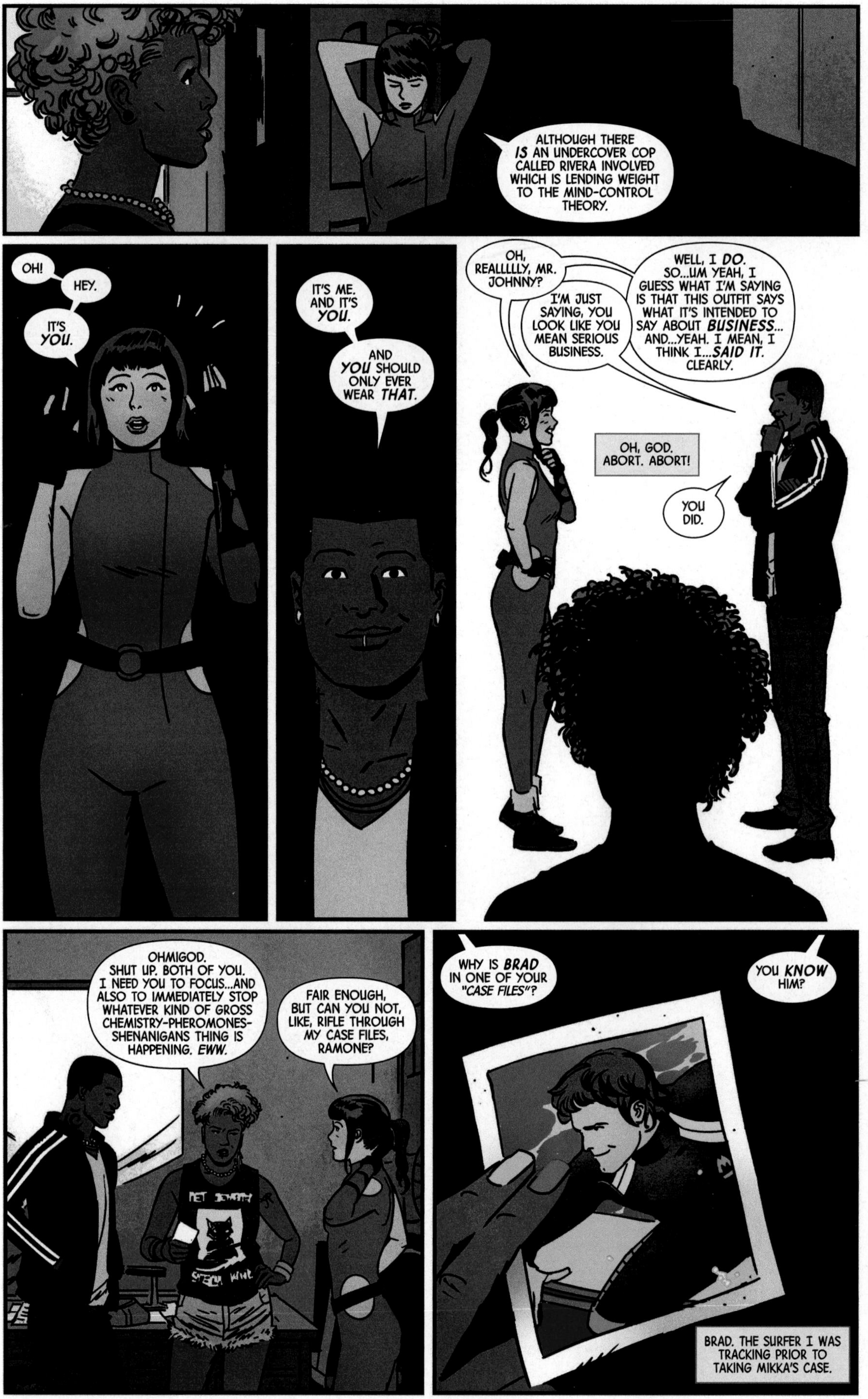
ALTHOUGH THERE IS AN UNDERCOVER COP CALLED RIVERA INVOLVED WHICH IS LENDING WEIGHT TO THE MIND-CONTROL THEORY.
OH!
HEY.
IT'S YOU.
IT'S ME. AND IT'S YOU.
AND YOU SHOULD ONLY EVER WEAR THAT.
OH, REALLLLLY, MR. JOHNNY?
I'M JUST SAYING, YOU LOOK LIKE YOU MEAN SERIOUS BUSINESS.
WELL, I DO. SO...UM YEAH, I GUESS WHAT I'M SAYING IS THAT THIS OUTFIT SAYS WHAT IT'S INTENDED TO SAY ABOUT BUSINESS... AND...YEAH. I MEAN, I THINK I...SAID IT. CLEARLY.
OH, GOD. ABORT. ABORT!
YOU DID.
OHMIGOD. SHUT UP. BOTH OF YOU. I NEED YOU TO FOCUS...AND ALSO TO IMMEDIATELY STOP WHATEVER KIND OF GROSS CHEMISTRY-PHEROMONES-SHENANIGANS THING IS HAPPENING. EWW.
FAIR ENOUGH, BUT CAN YOU NOT, LIKE, RIFLE THROUGH MY CASE FILES, RAMONE?
WHY IS BRAD IN ONE OF YOUR "CASE FILES"?
YOU KNOW HIM?
BRAD. THE SURFER I WAS TRACKING PRIOR TO TAKING MIKKA'S CASE.

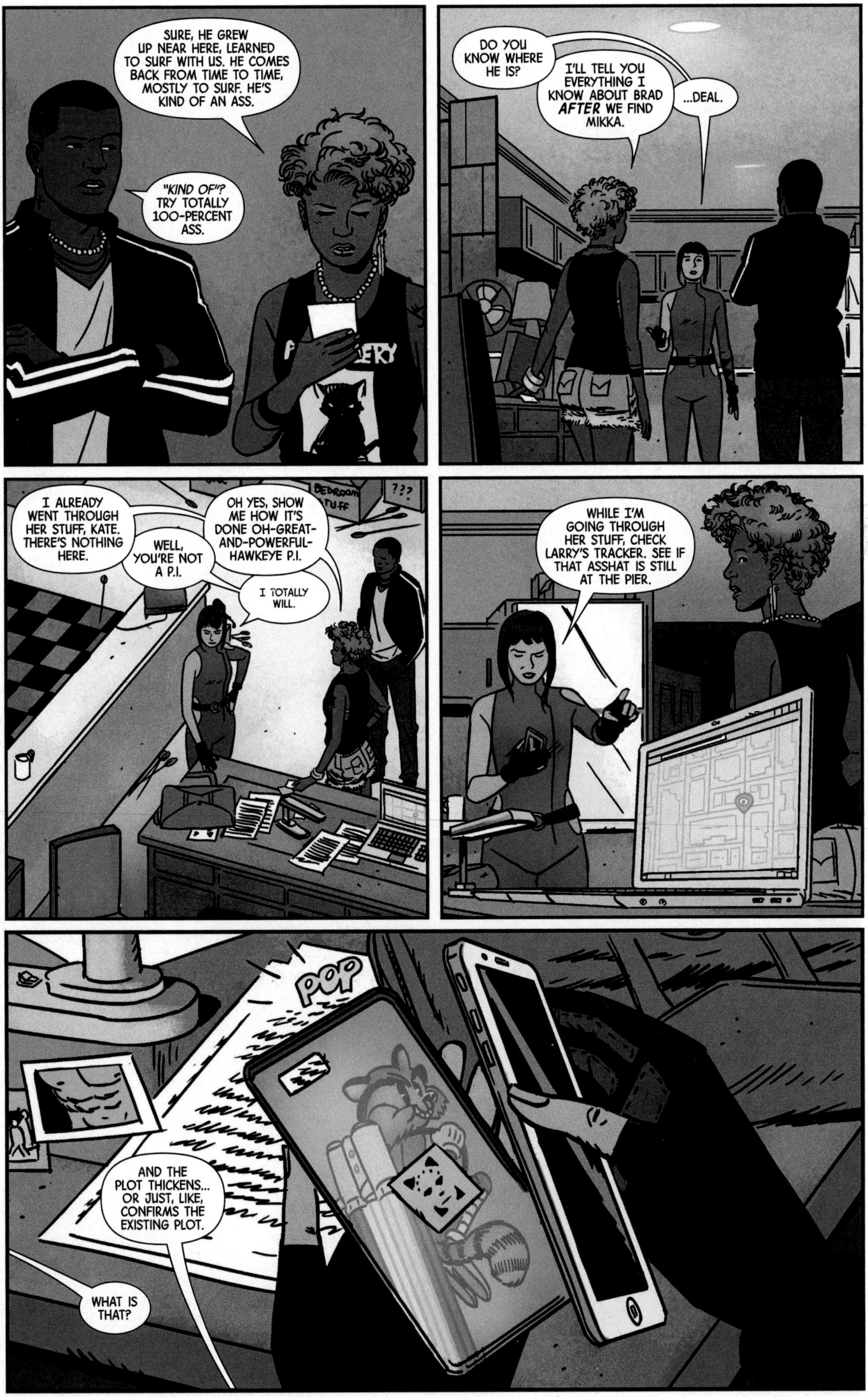
SURE, HE GREW UP NEAR HERE, LEARNED TO SURF WITH US. HE COMES BACK FROM TIME TO TIME, MOSTLY TO SURF. HE'S KIND OF AN ASS.
"KIND OF"? TRY TOTALLY 100-PERCENT ASS.
DO YOU KNOW WHERE HE IS?
I'LL TELL YOU EVERYTHING I KNOW ABOUT BRAD AFTER WE FIND MIKKA.
...DEAL.
BEDROOM STUFF
???
I ALREADY WENT THROUGH HER STUFF, KATE. THERE'S NOTHING HERE.
WELL, YOU'RE NOT A P.I.
OH YES, SHOW ME HOW IT'S DONE OH-GREAT-AND-POWERFUL-HAWKEYE P.I.
I TOTALLY WILL.
WHILE I'M GOING THROUGH HER STUFF, CHECK LARRY'S TRACKER. SEE IF THAT ASSHAT IS STILL AT THE PIER.
POP
AND THE PLOT THICKENS... OR JUST, LIKE, CONFIRMS THE EXISTING PLOT.
WHAT IS THAT?

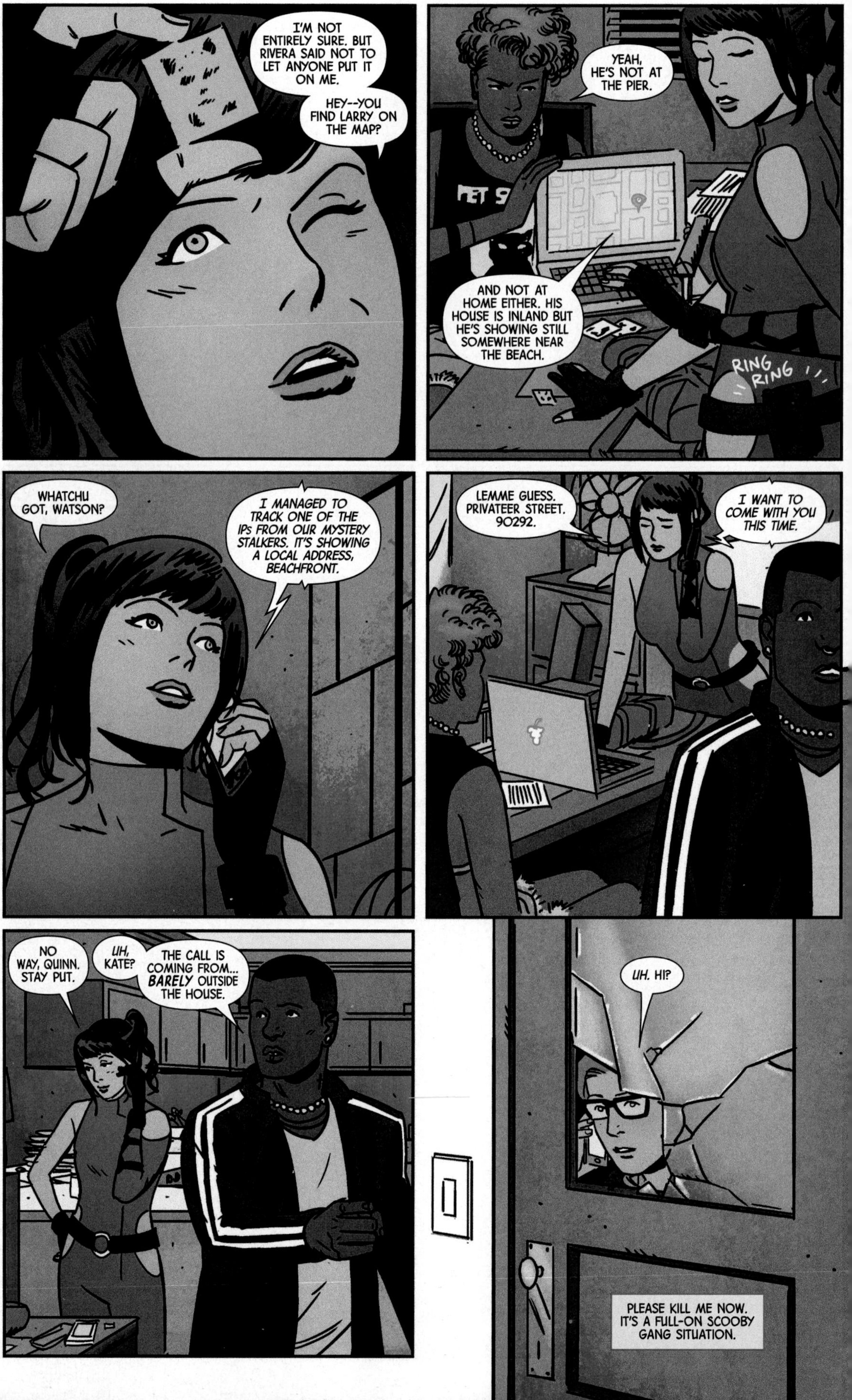
I'M NOT ENTIRELY SURE. BUT RIVERA SAID NOT TO LET ANYONE PUT IT ON ME.
HEY--YOU FIND LARRY ON THE MAP?
YEAH, HE'S NOT AT THE PIER.
AND NOT AT HOME EITHER. HIS HOUSE IS INLAND BUT HE'S SHOWING STILL SOMEWHERE NEAR THE BEACH.
RING RING
WHATCHU GOT, WATSON?
I MANAGED TO TRACK ONE OF THE IPs FROM OUR MYSTERY STALKERS. IT'S SHOWING A LOCAL ADDRESS, BEACHFRONT.
LEMME GUESS. PRIVATEER STREET. 90292.
I WANT TO COME WITH YOU THIS TIME.
NO WAY, QUINN. STAY PUT.
UH, KATE?
THE CALL IS COMING FROM... BARELY OUTSIDE THE HOUSE.
UH. HI?
PLEASE KILL ME NOW. IT'S A FULL-ON SCOOBY GANG SITUATION.

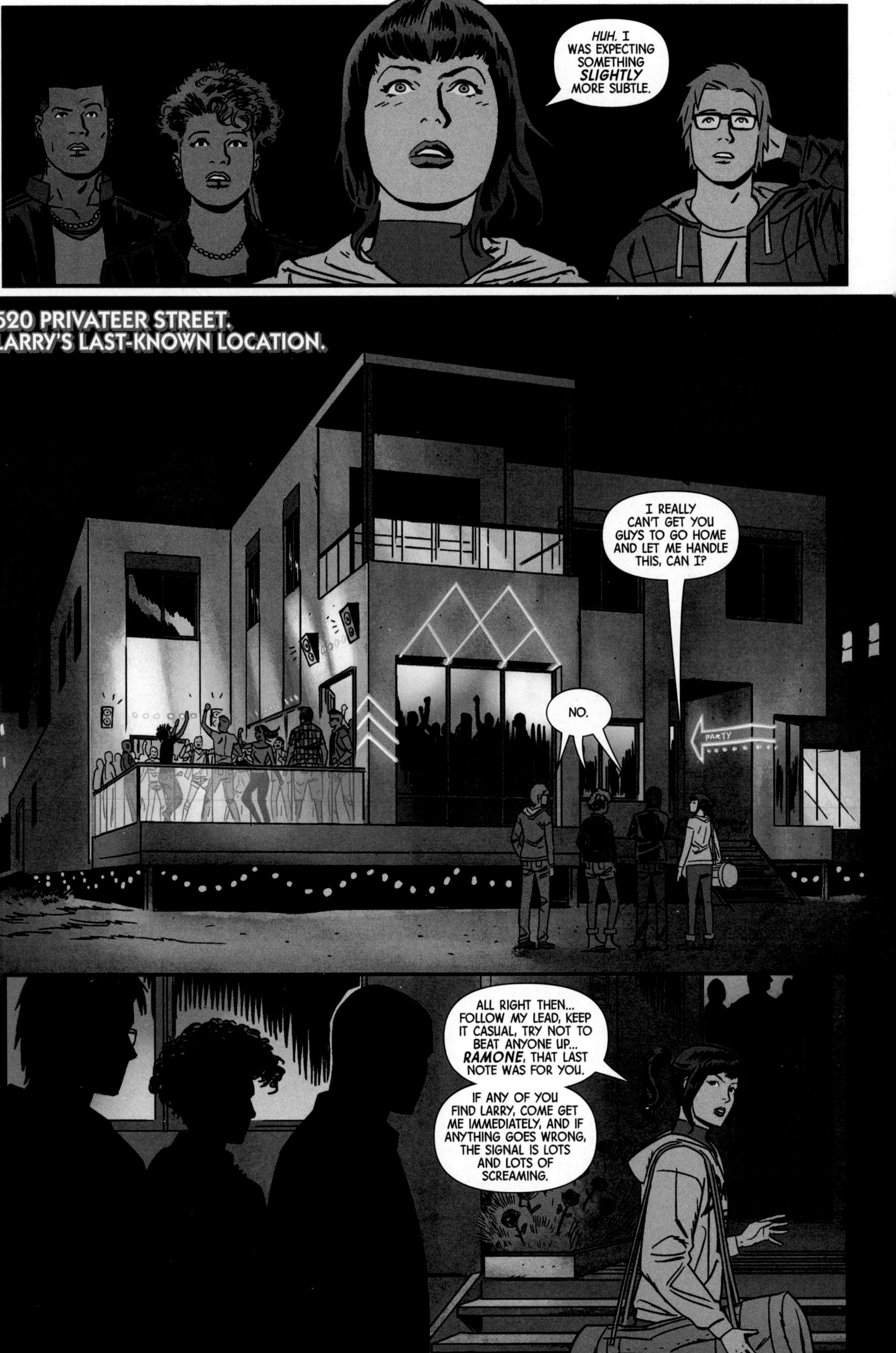
HUH. I WAS EXPECTING SOMETHING SLIGHTLY MORE SUBTLE.
520 PRIVATEER STREET. LARRY'S LAST-KNOWN LOCATION.
I REALLY CAN'T GET YOU GUYS TO GO HOME AND LET ME HANDLE THIS, CAN I?
NO.
PARTY
ALL RIGHT THEN... FOLLOW MY LEAD, KEEP IT CASUAL, TRY NOT TO BEAT ANYONE UP... RAMONE, THAT LAST NOTE WAS FOR YOU.
IF ANY OF YOU FIND LARRY, COME GET ME IMMEDIATELY, AND IF ANYTHING GOES WRONG, THE SIGNAL IS LOTS AND LOTS OF SCREAMING.

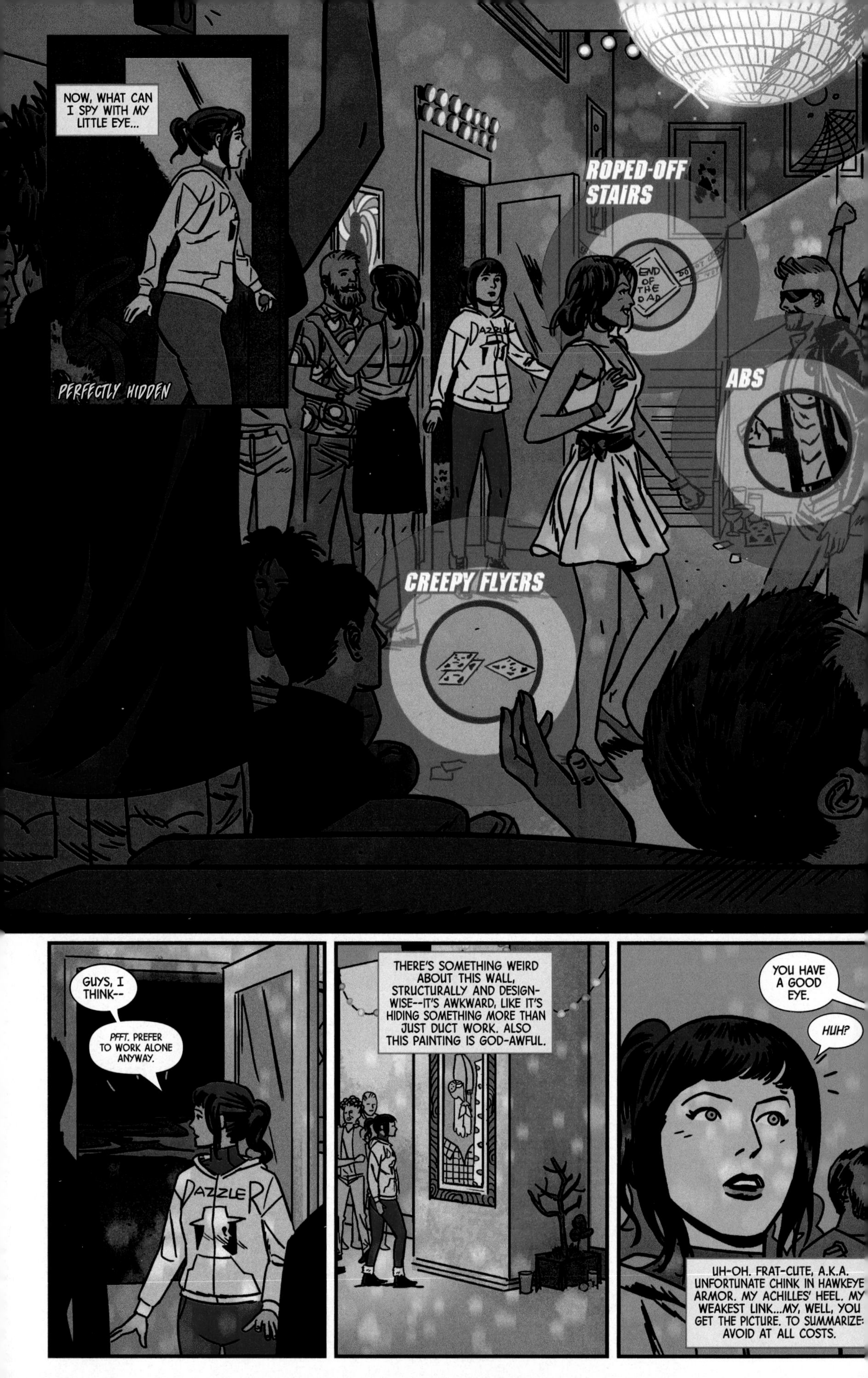
NOW, WHAT CAN I SPY WITH MY LITTLE EYE...
PERFECTLY HIDDEN
ROPED-OFF STAIRS
END OF THE ROAD
ABS
CREEPY FLYERS
GUYS, I THINK--
PFFT. PREFER TO WORK ALONE ANYWAY.
DAZZLER
THERE'S SOMETHING WEIRD ABOUT THIS WALL, STRUCTURALLY AND DESIGN-WISE--IT'S AWKWARD, LIKE IT'S HIDING SOMETHING MORE THAN JUST DUCT WORK. ALSO THIS PAINTING IS GOD-AWFUL.
YOU HAVE A GOOD EYE.
HUH?
UH-OH. FRAT-CUTE, A.K.A. UNFORTUNATE CHINK IN HAWKEYE ARMOR. MY ACHILLES' HEEL. MY WEAKEST LINK...MY, WELL, YOU GET THE PICTURE. TO SUMMARIZE: AVOID AT ALL COSTS.

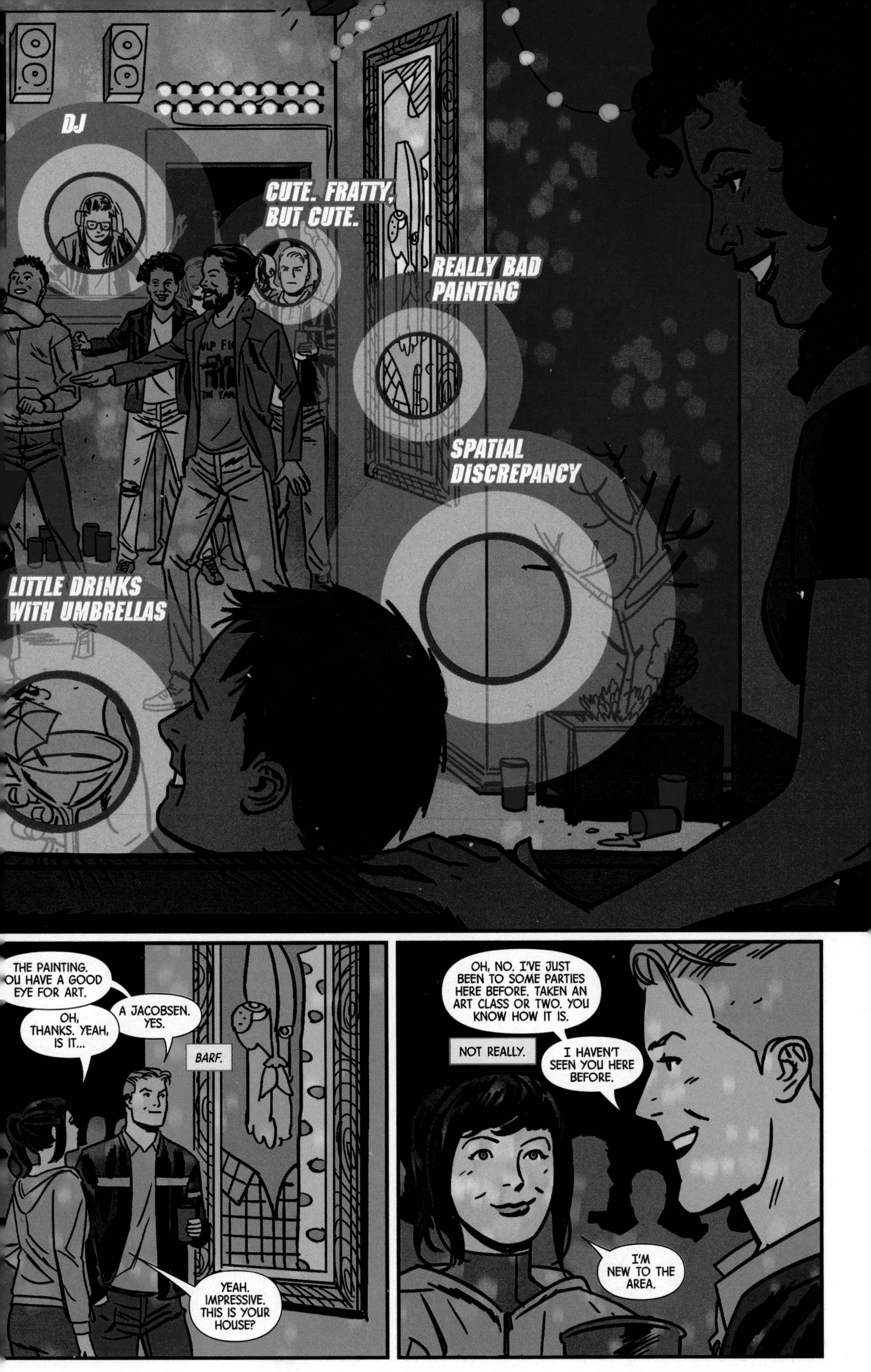
DJ
CUTE. FRATTY, BUT CUTE.
REALLY BAD PAINTING
SPATIAL DISCREPANCY
LITTLE DRINKS WITH UMBRELLAS
THE PAINTING. OU HAVE A GOOD EYE FOR ART.
OH, THANKS. YEAH, IS IT...
A JACOBSEN. YES.
BARF.
YEAH. IMPRESSIVE. THIS IS YOUR HOUSE?
OH, NO. I'VE JUST BEEN TO SOME PARTIES HERE BEFORE. TAKEN AN ART CLASS OR TWO. YOU KNOW HOW IT IS.
NOT REALLY.
I HAVEN'T SEEN YOU HERE BEFORE.
I'M NEW TO THE AREA.

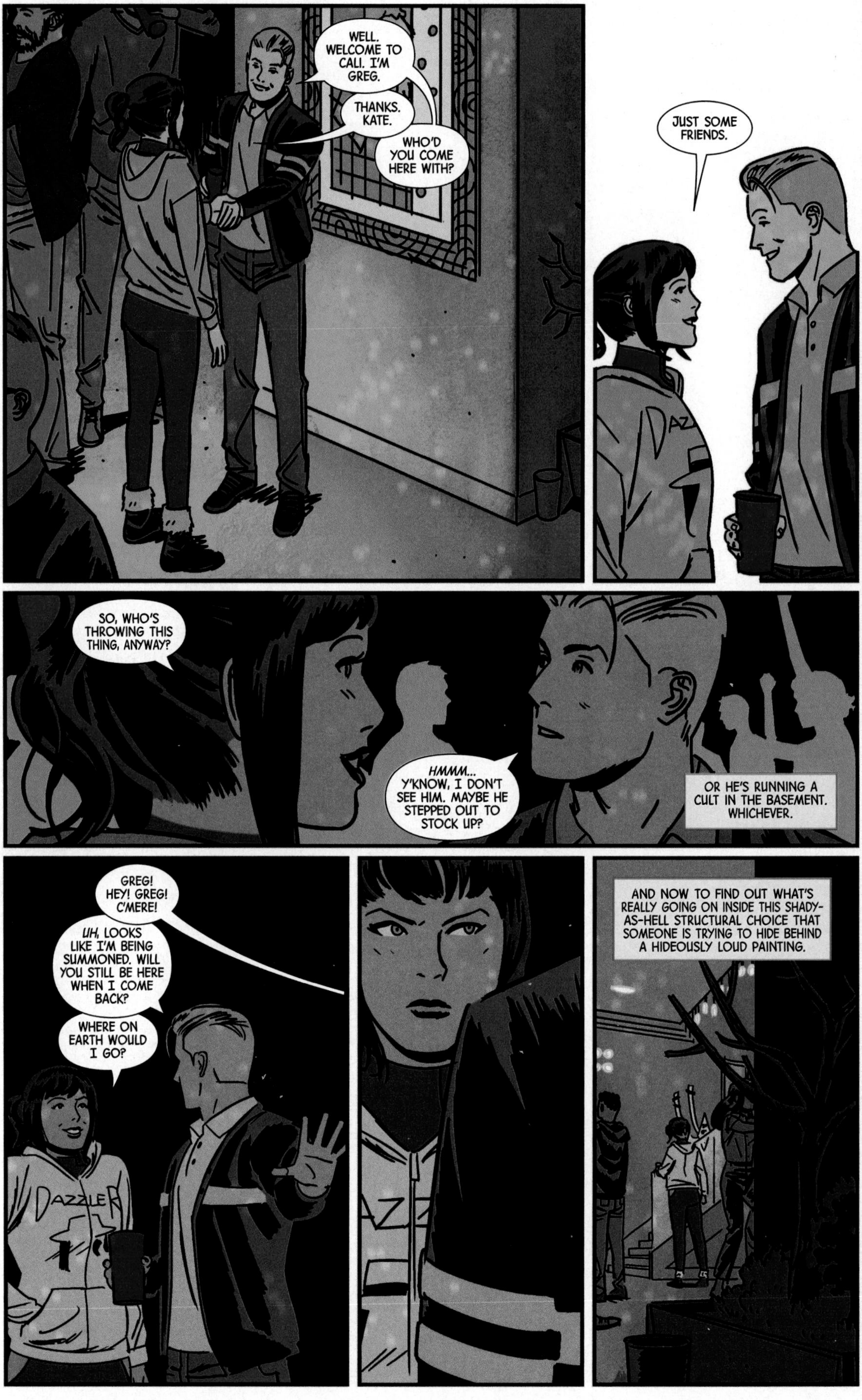
WELL. WELCOME TO CALI. I'M GREG.
THANKS. KATE.
WHO'D YOU COME HERE WITH?
JUST SOME FRIENDS.
SO, WHO'S THROWING THIS THING, ANYWAY?
HMMM... Y'KNOW, I DON'T SEE HIM. MAYBE HE STEPPED OUT TO STOCK UP?
OR HE'S RUNNING A CULT IN THE BASEMENT. WHICHEVER.
GREG! HEY! GREG! C'MERE!
UH, LOOKS LIKE I'M BEING SUMMONED. WILL YOU STILL BE HERE WHEN I COME BACK?
WHERE ON EARTH WOULD I GO?
AND NOW TO FIND OUT WHAT'S REALLY GOING ON INSIDE THIS SHADY-AS-HELL STRUCTURAL CHOICE THAT SOMEONE IS TRYING TO HIDE BEHIND A HIDEOUSLY LOUD PAINTING.

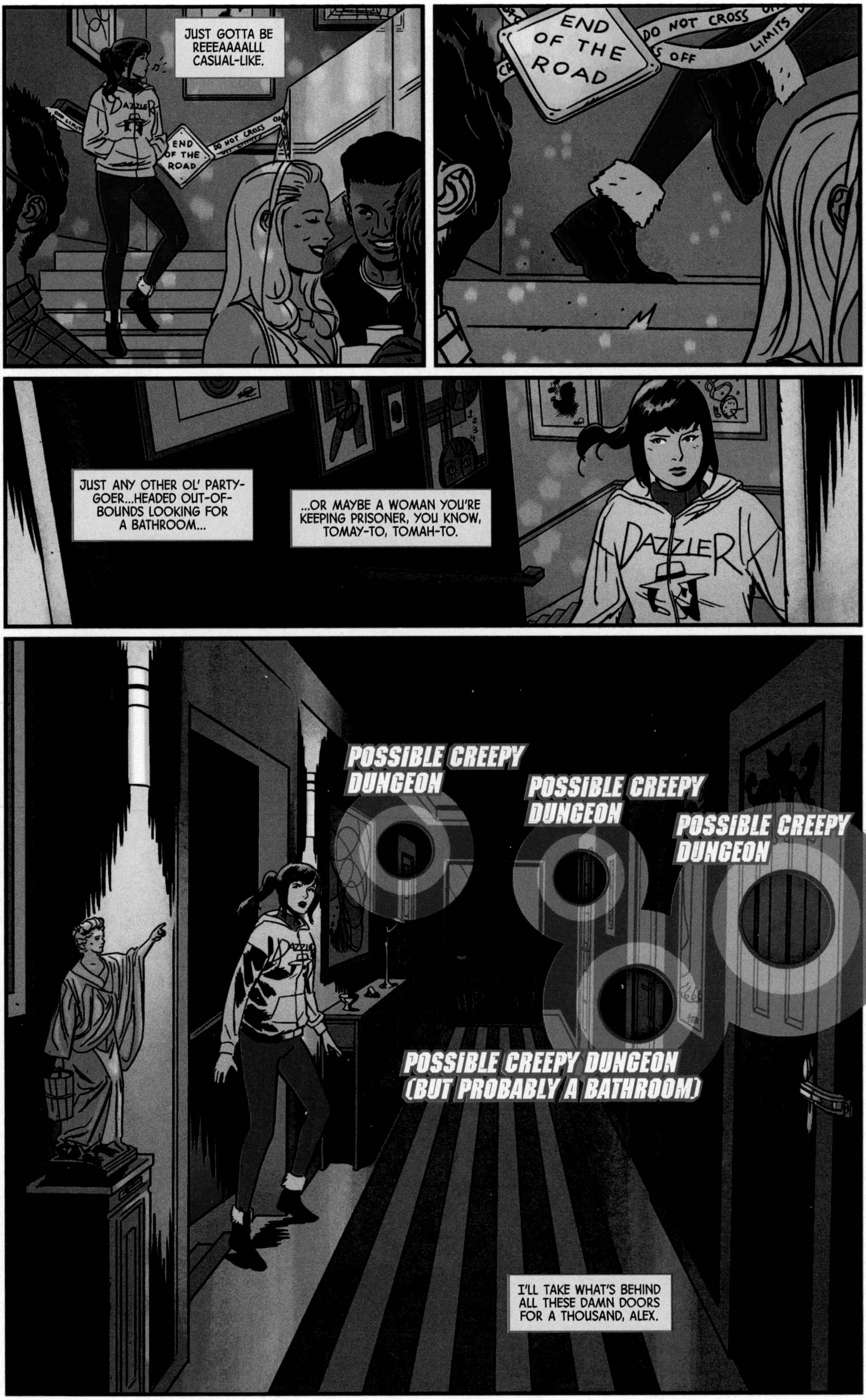
JUST GOTTA BE REEEAAAALLL CASUAL-LIKE.
END OF THE ROAD
DO NOT CROSS
JUST ANY OTHER OL' PARTY-GOER...HEADED OUT-OF-BOUNDS LOOKING FOR A BATHROOM...
...OR MAYBE A WOMAN YOU'RE KEEPING PRISONER, YOU KNOW, TOMAY-TO, TOMAH-TO.
DAZZLER
POSSIBLE CREEPY DUNGEON
POSSIBLE CREEPY DUNGEON
POSSIBLE CREEPY DUNGEON
POSSIBLE CREEPY DUNGEON (BUT PROBABLY A BATHROOM)
I'LL TAKE WHAT'S BEHIND ALL THESE DAMN DOORS FOR A THOUSAND, ALEX.

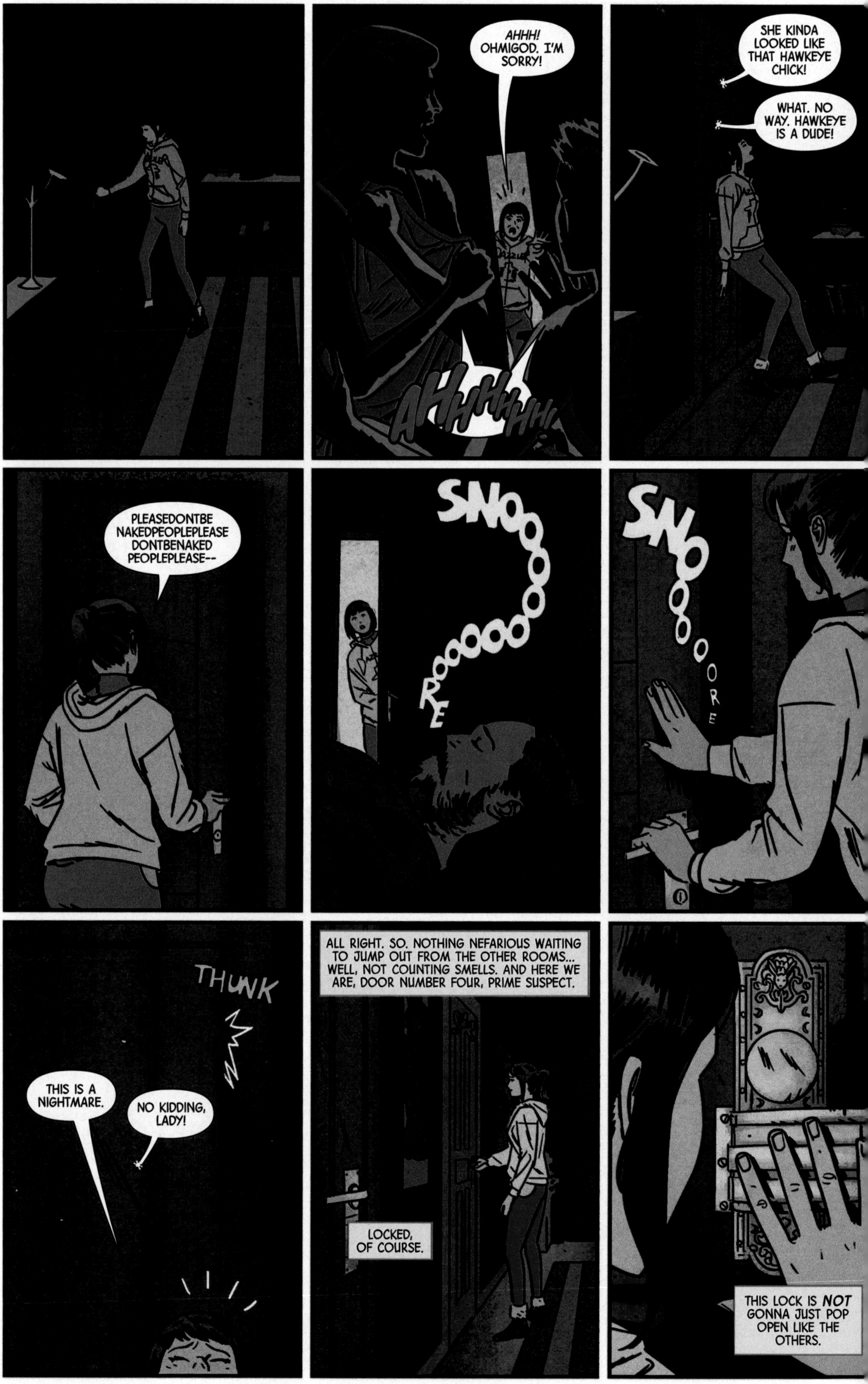
AHHH! OHMIGOD. I'M SORRY!
AHHHHHHHH!
SHE KINDA LOOKED LIKE THAT HAWKEYE CHICK!
WHAT. NO WAY. HAWKEYE IS A DUDE!
PLEASEDONTBE NAKEDPEOPLEPLEASE DONTBENAKED PEOPLEPLEASE--
SNOOOOOOOOOOOOOOORE
SNOOOOOOOORE
THUNK
THIS IS A NIGHTMARE.
NO KIDDING, LADY!
ALL RIGHT. SO. NOTHING NEFARIOUS WAITING TO JUMP OUT FROM THE OTHER ROOMS... WELL, NOT COUNTING SMELLS. AND HERE WE ARE, DOOR NUMBER FOUR, PRIME SUSPECT.
LOCKED, OF COURSE.
THIS LOCK IS NOT GONNA JUST POP OPEN LIKE THE OTHERS.

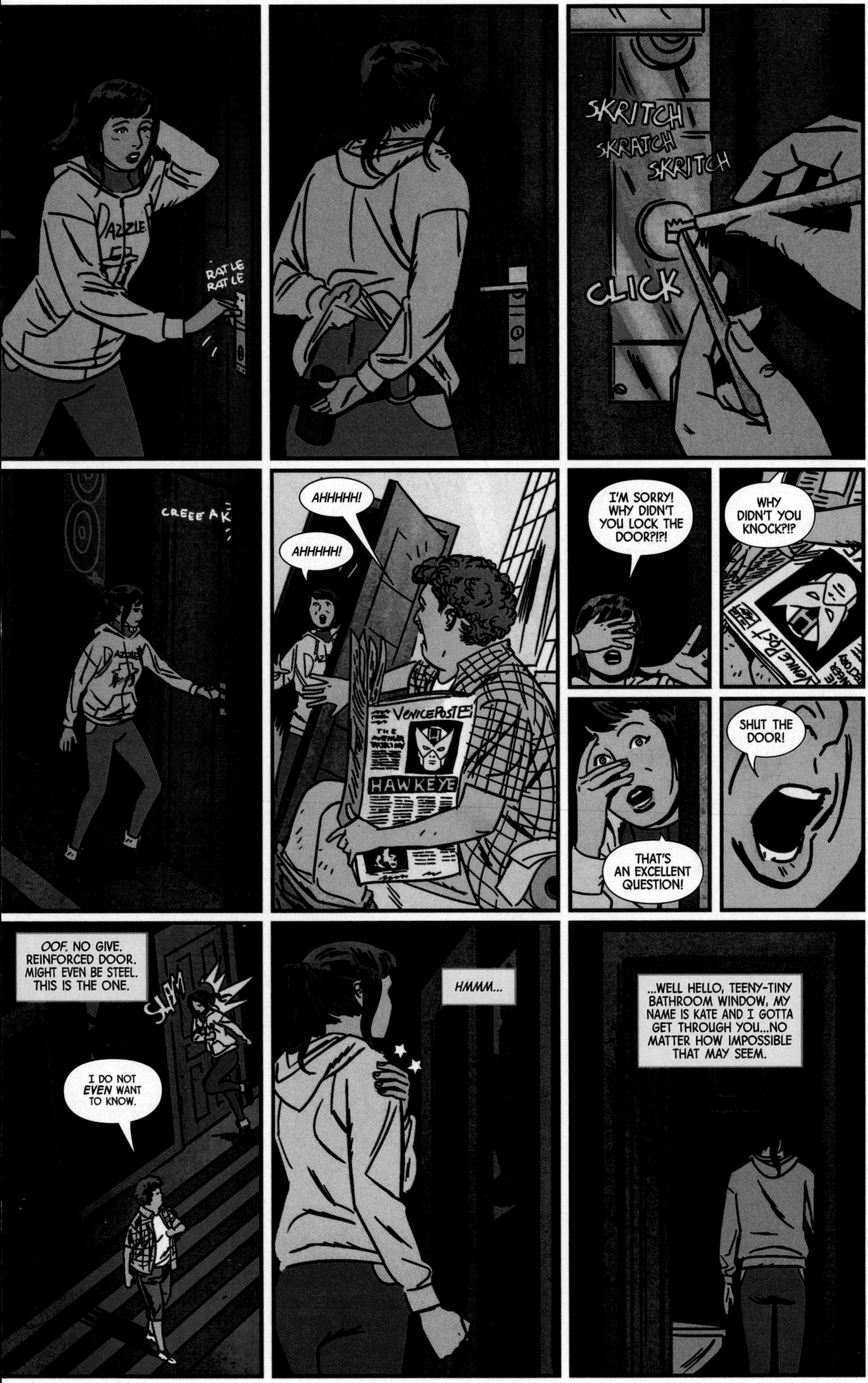

RATLE RATLE
SKRITCH
SKRATCH
SKRITCH
CLICK
CREEEAK
AHHHHH!
AHHHHH!
VENICE POST
HAWKEYE
I'M SORRY! WHY DIDN'T YOU LOCK THE DOOR?!?!
WHY DIDN'T YOU KNOCK?!?
THAT'S AN EXCELLENT QUESTION!
SHUT THE DOOR!
OOF. NO GIVE. REINFORCED DOOR. MIGHT EVEN BE STEEL. THIS IS THE ONE.
SLAM
I DO NOT EVEN WANT TO KNOW.
HMMM...
...WELL HELLO, TEENY-TINY BATHROOM WINDOW, MY NAME IS KATE AND I GOTTA GET THROUGH YOU...NO MATTER HOW IMPOSSIBLE THAT MAY SEEM.

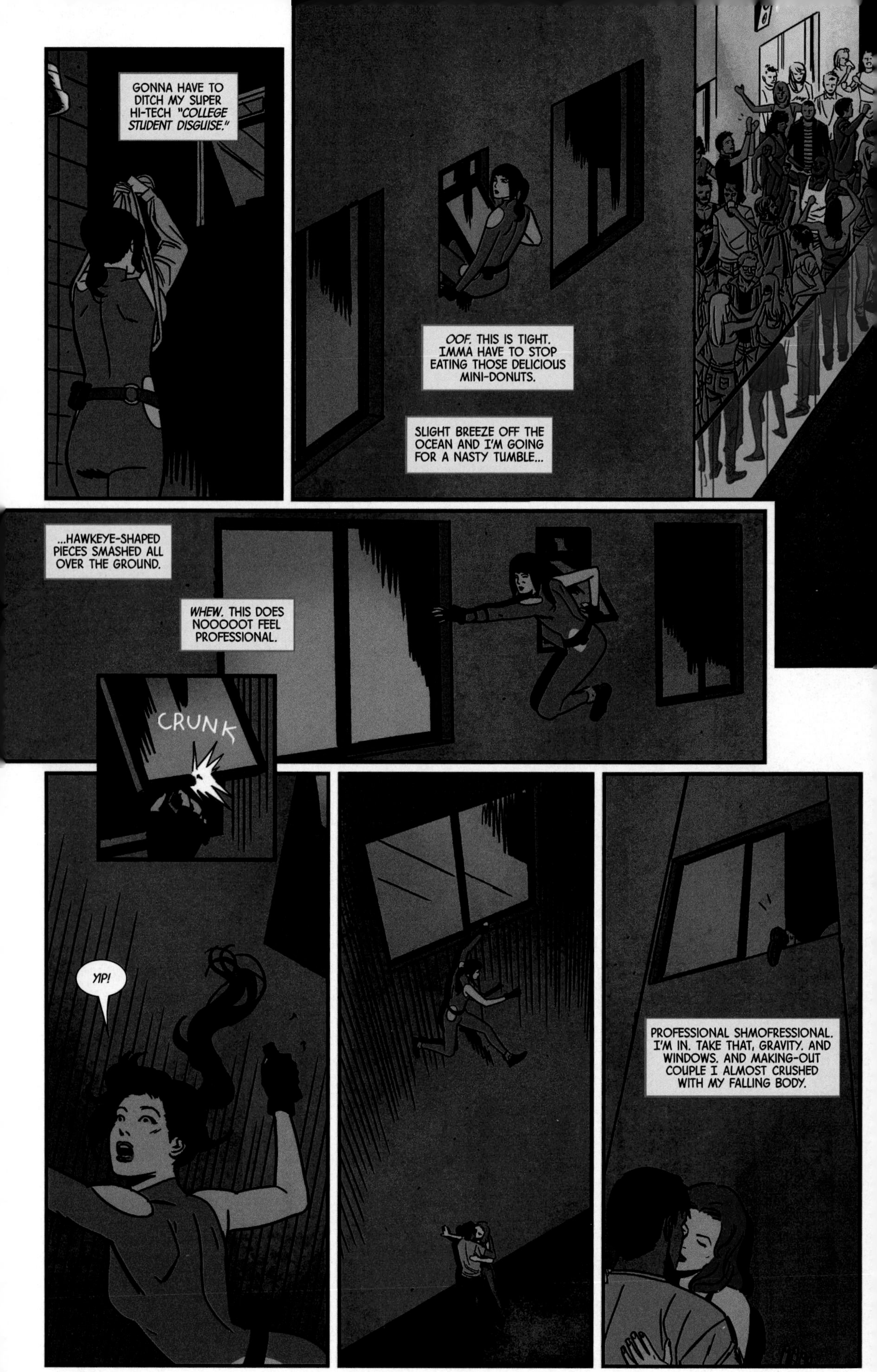
GONNA HAVE TO DITCH MY SUPER HI-TECH "COLLEGE STUDENT DISGUISE."
OOF. THIS IS TIGHT. IMMA HAVE TO STOP EATING THOSE DELICIOUS MINI-DONUTS.
SLIGHT BREEZE OFF THE OCEAN AND I'M GOING FOR A NASTY TUMBLE...
...HAWKEYE-SHAPED PIECES SMASHED ALL OVER THE GROUND.
WHEW. THIS DOES NOOOOOT FEEL PROFESSIONAL.
CRUNK
YIP!
PROFESSIONAL SHMOFRESSIONAL. I'M IN. TAKE THAT, GRAVITY. AND WINDOWS. AND MAKING-OUT COUPLE I ALMOST CRUSHED WITH MY FALLING BODY.

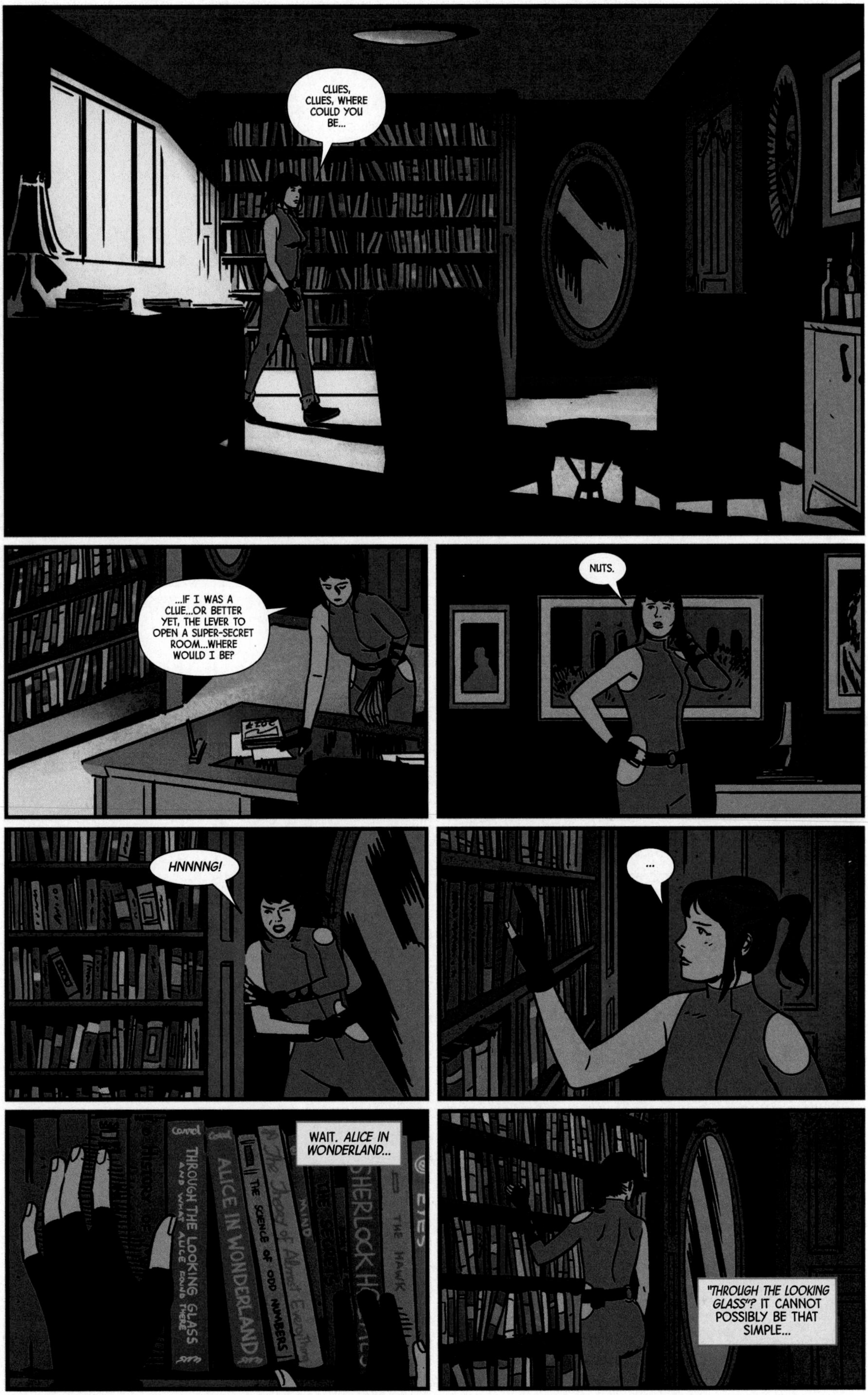
CLUES, CLUES, WHERE COULD YOU BE...
...IF I WAS A CLUE...OR BETTER YET, THE LEVER TO OPEN A SUPER-SECRET ROOM...WHERE WOULD I BE?
NUTS.
HNNNNG!
...
WAIT. ALICE IN WONDERLAND...
THROUGH THE LOOKING GLASS AND WHAT ALICE FOUND THERE
ALICE IN WONDERLAND
THE SCIENCE OF ODD NUMBERS
SHERLOCK H
THE HAWK
"THROUGH THE LOOKING GLASS"? IT CANNOT POSSIBLY BE THAT SIMPLE...

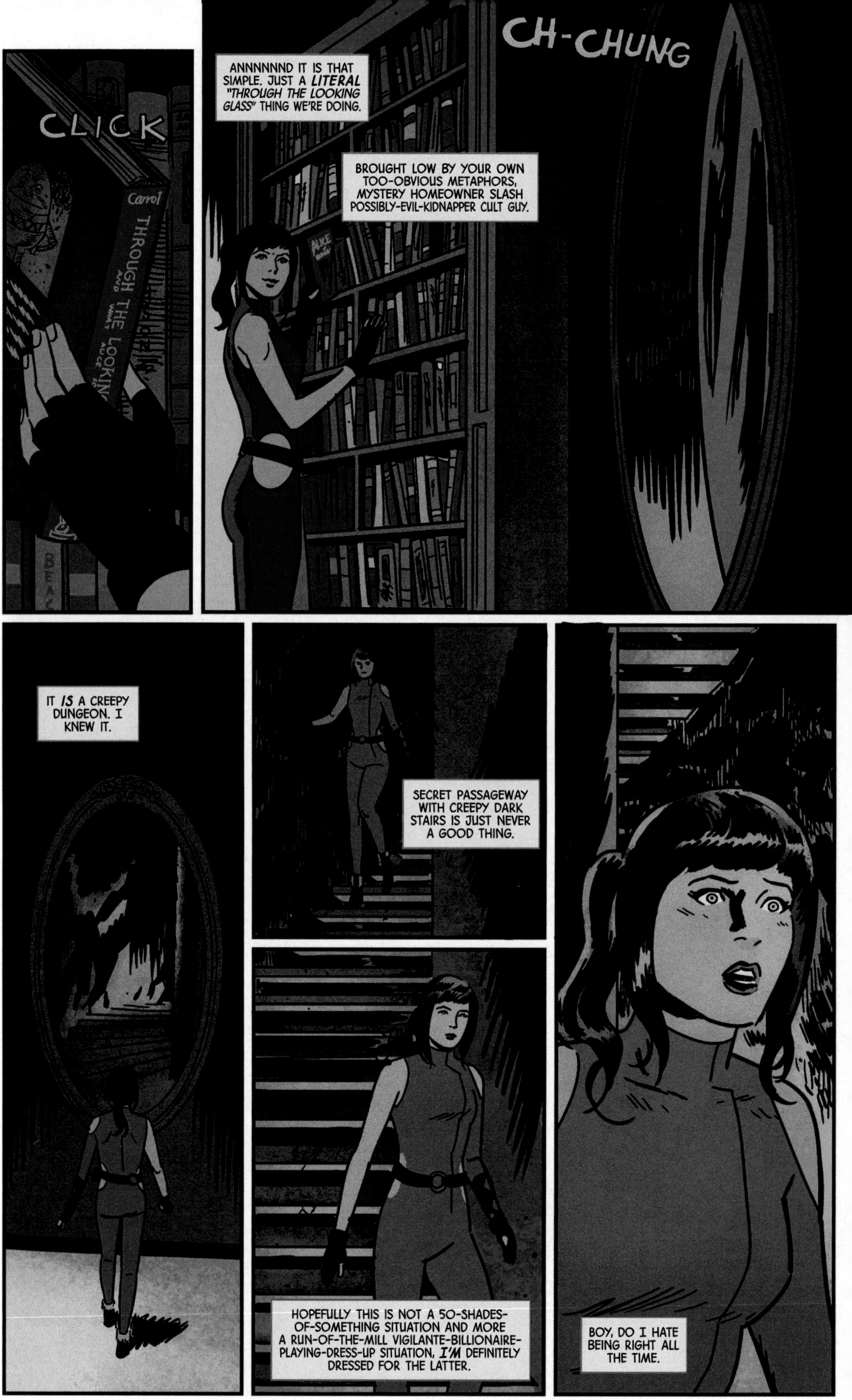
CLICK
Carrol
THROUGH THE LOOKING
ANNNNNND IT IS THAT SIMPLE. JUST A LITERAL "THROUGH THE LOOKING GLASS" THING WE'RE DOING.
BROUGHT LOW BY YOUR OWN TOO-OBVIOUS METAPHORS, MYSTERY HOMEOWNER SLASH POSSIBLY-EVIL-KIDNAPPER CULT GUY.
CH-CHUNG
IT IS A CREEPY DUNGEON. I KNEW IT.
SECRET PASSAGEWAY WITH CREEPY DARK STAIRS IS JUST NEVER A GOOD THING.
HOPEFULLY THIS IS NOT A 50-SHADES-OF-SOMETHING SITUATION AND MORE A RUN-OF-THE-MILL VIGILANTE-BILLIONAIRE-PLAYING-DRESS-UP SITUATION, I'M DEFINITELY DRESSED FOR THE LATTER.
BOY, DO I HATE BEING RIGHT ALL THE TIME.

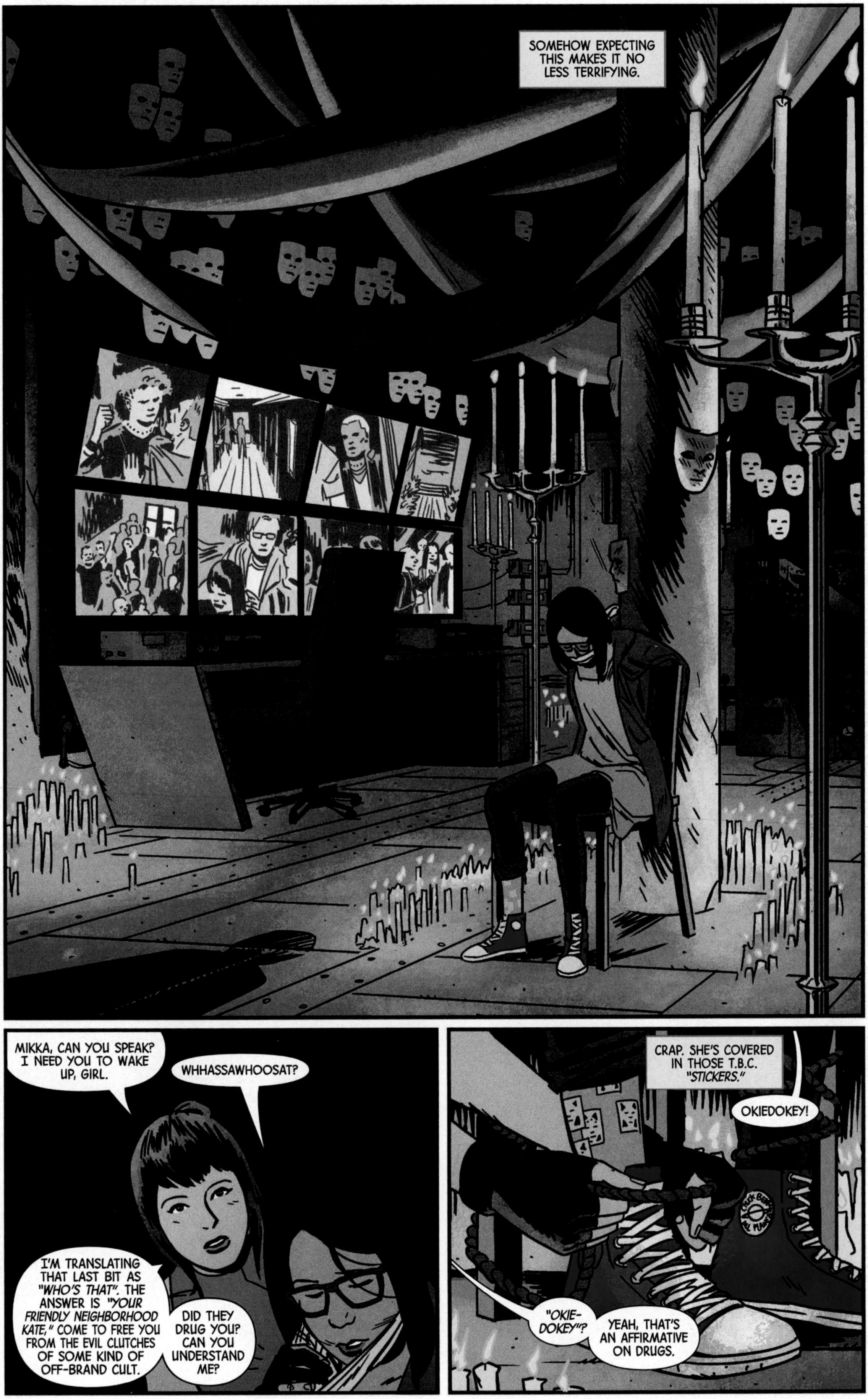
SOMEHOW EXPECTING THIS MAKES IT NO LESS TERRIFYING.
MIKKA, CAN YOU SPEAK? I NEED YOU TO WAKE UP, GIRL.
WHHASSAWHOOSAT?
I'M TRANSLATING THAT LAST BIT AS "WHO'S THAT". THE ANSWER IS "YOUR FRIENDLY NEIGHBORHOOD KATE," COME TO FREE YOU FROM THE EVIL CLUTCHES OF SOME KIND OF OFF-BRAND CULT.
DID THEY DRUG YOU? CAN YOU UNDERSTAND ME?
CRAP. SHE'S COVERED IN THOSE T.B.C. "STICKERS."
OKIEDOKEY!
"OKIE-DOKEY"?
YEAH, THAT'S AN AFFIRMATIVE ON DRUGS.

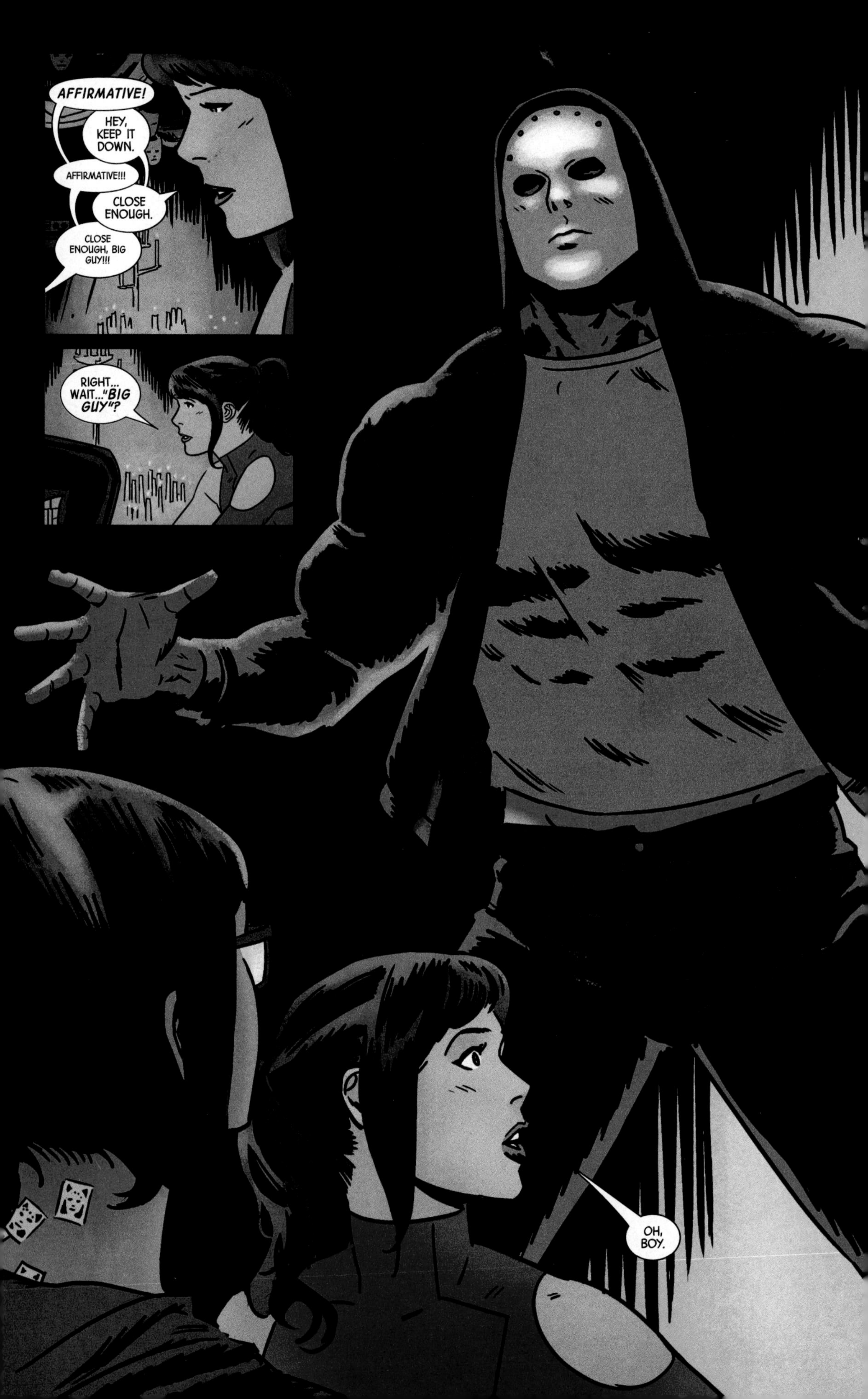
AFFIRMATIVE!
HEY, KEEP IT DOWN.
AFFIRMATIVE!!!
CLOSE ENOUGH.
CLOSE ENOUGH, BIG GUY!!!
RIGHT... WAIT..."BIG GUY"?
OH, BOY.

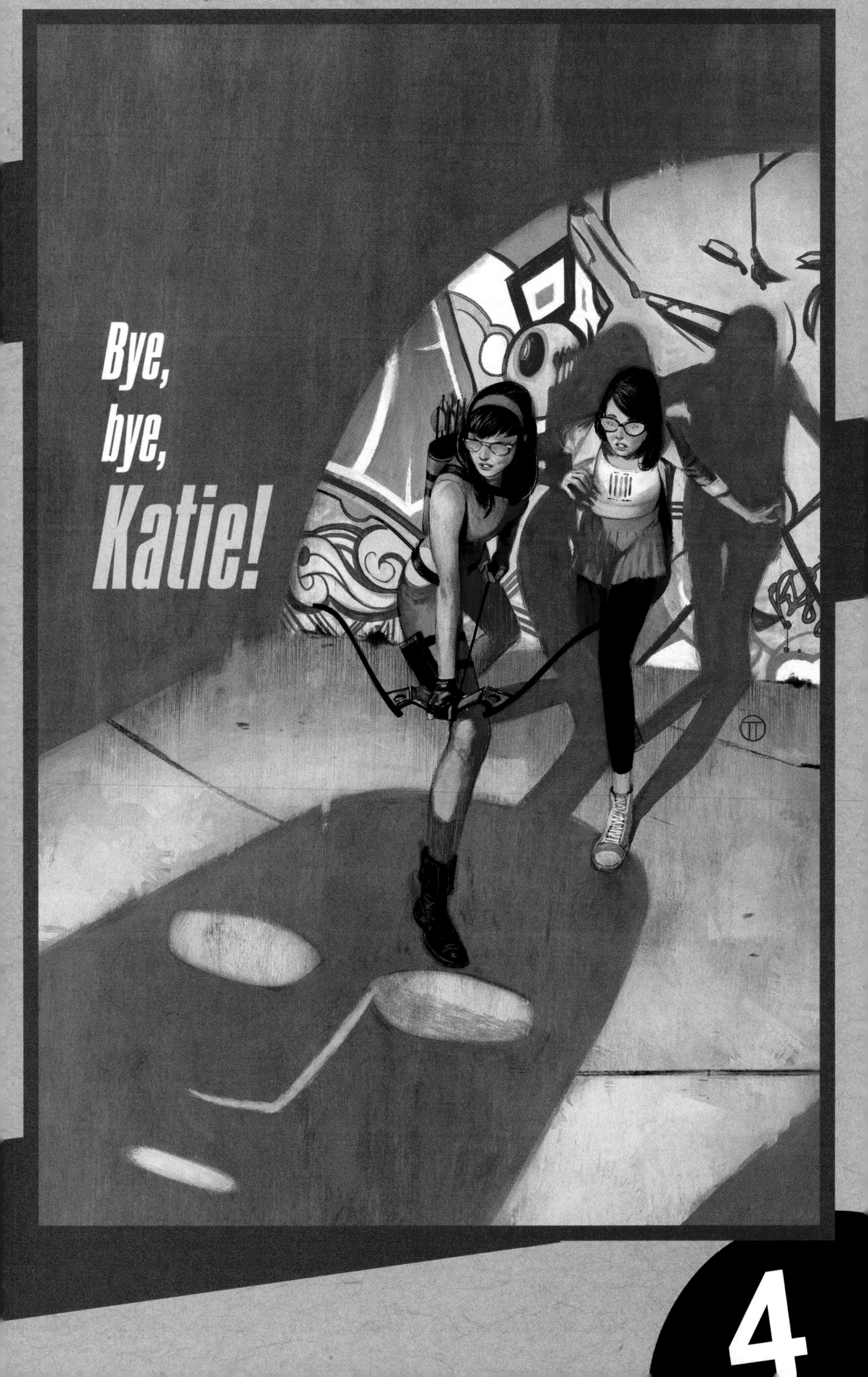
Bye, bye, Katie!
4

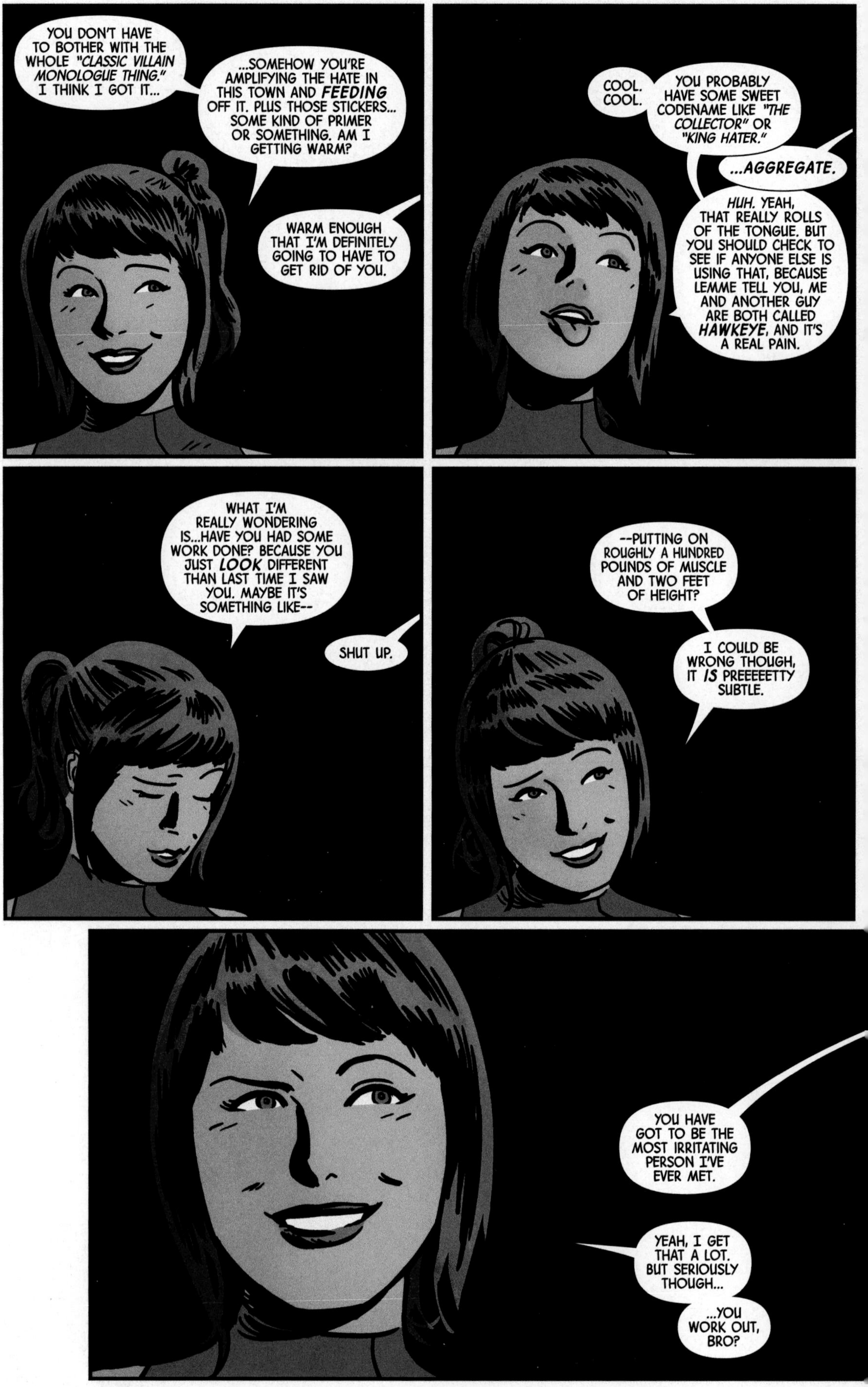

YOU DON'T HAVE TO BOTHER WITH THE WHOLE "CLASSIC VILLAIN MONOLOGUE THING." I THINK I GOT IT...
...SOMEHOW YOU'RE AMPLIFYING THE HATE IN THIS TOWN AND FEEDING OFF IT. PLUS THOSE STICKERS... SOME KIND OF PRIMER OR SOMETHING. AM I GETTING WARM?
WARM ENOUGH THAT I'M DEFINITELY GOING TO HAVE TO GET RID OF YOU.
COOL. COOL.
YOU PROBABLY HAVE SOME SWEET CODENAME LIKE "THE COLLECTOR" OR "KING HATER."
...AGGREGATE.
HUH. YEAH, THAT REALLY ROLLS OF THE TONGUE. BUT YOU SHOULD CHECK TO SEE IF ANYONE ELSE IS USING THAT, BECAUSE LEMME TELL YOU, ME AND ANOTHER GUY ARE BOTH CALLED HAWKEYE, AND IT'S A REAL PAIN.
WHAT I'M REALLY WONDERING IS...HAVE YOU HAD SOME WORK DONE? BECAUSE YOU JUST LOOK DIFFERENT THAN LAST TIME I SAW YOU. MAYBE IT'S SOMETHING LIKE--
SHUT UP.
--PUTTING ON ROUGHLY A HUNDRED POUNDS OF MUSCLE AND TWO FEET OF HEIGHT?
I COULD BE WRONG THOUGH, IT IS PREEEEETTY SUBTLE.
YOU HAVE GOT TO BE THE MOST IRRITATING PERSON I'VE EVER MET.
YEAH, I GET THAT A LOT. BUT SERIOUSLY THOUGH...
...YOU WORK OUT, BRO?

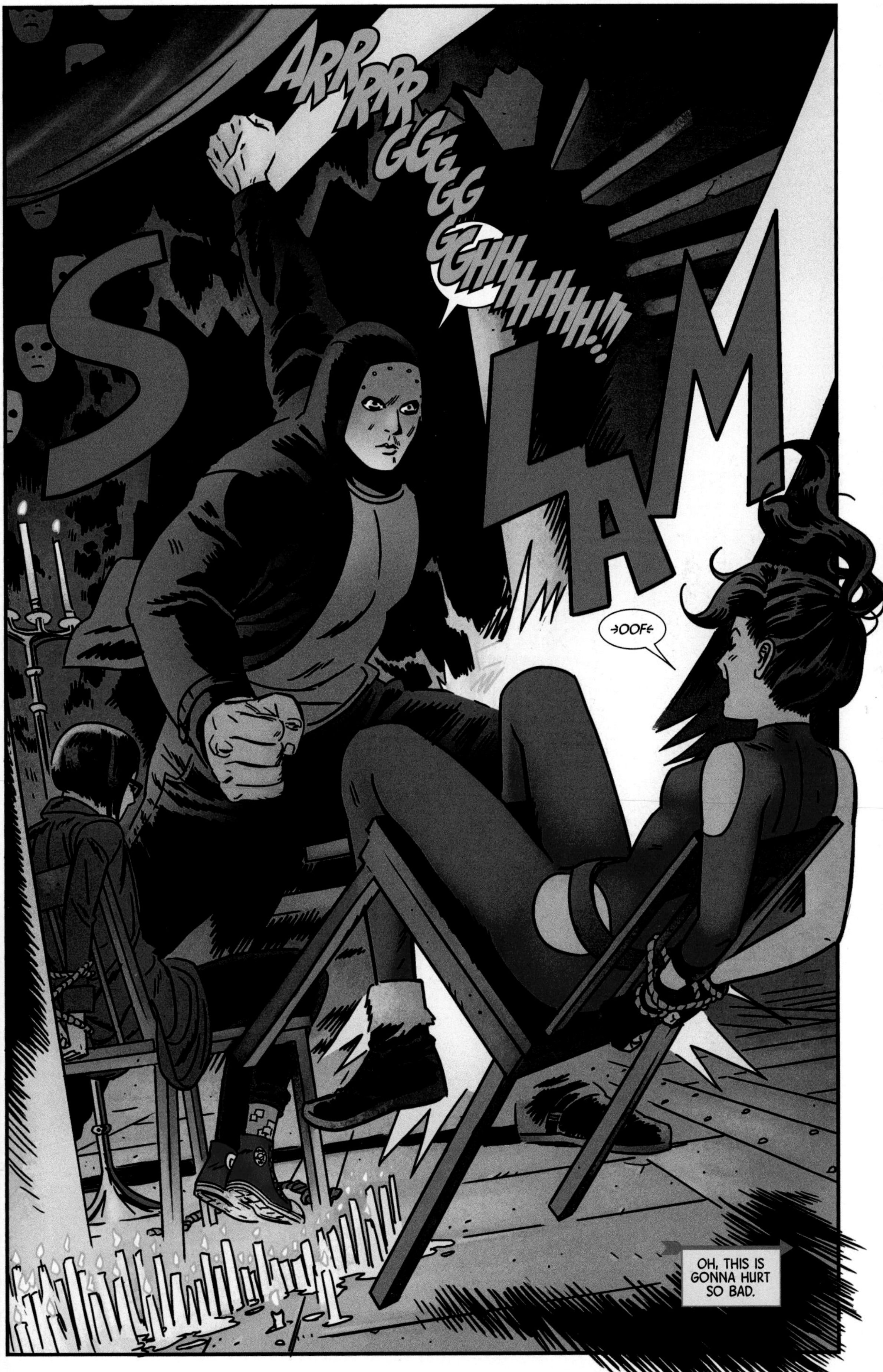
ARRRRRGGGGGGGHHHHHHH!!!
SLAM
OOF
OH, THIS IS GONNA HURT SO BAD.

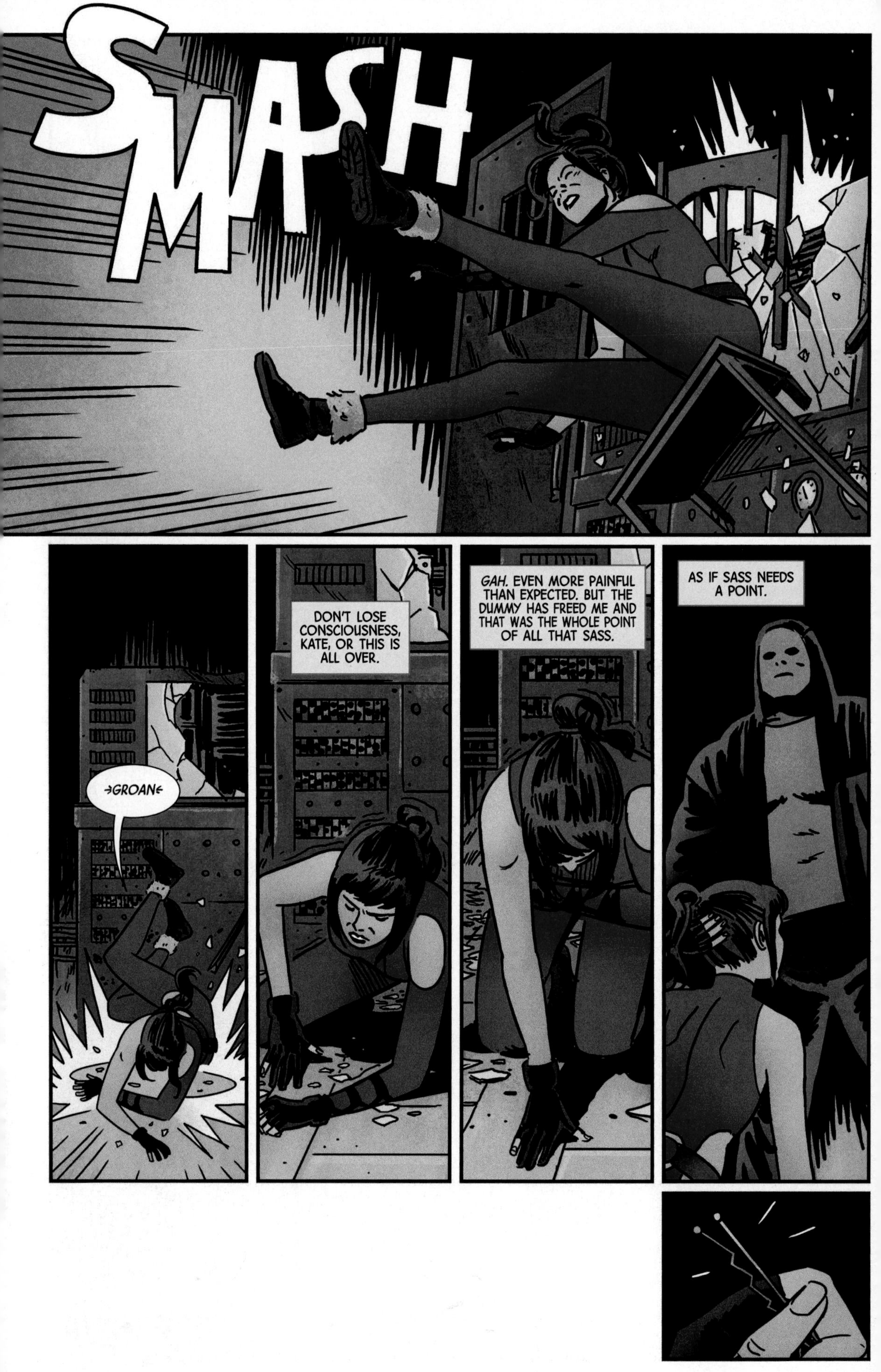
SMASH
→GROAN←
DON'T LOSE CONSCIOUSNESS, KATE, OR THIS IS ALL OVER.
GAH. EVEN MORE PAINFUL THAN EXPECTED. BUT THE DUMMY HAS FREED ME AND THAT WAS THE WHOLE POINT OF ALL THAT SASS.
AS IF SASS NEEDS A POINT.

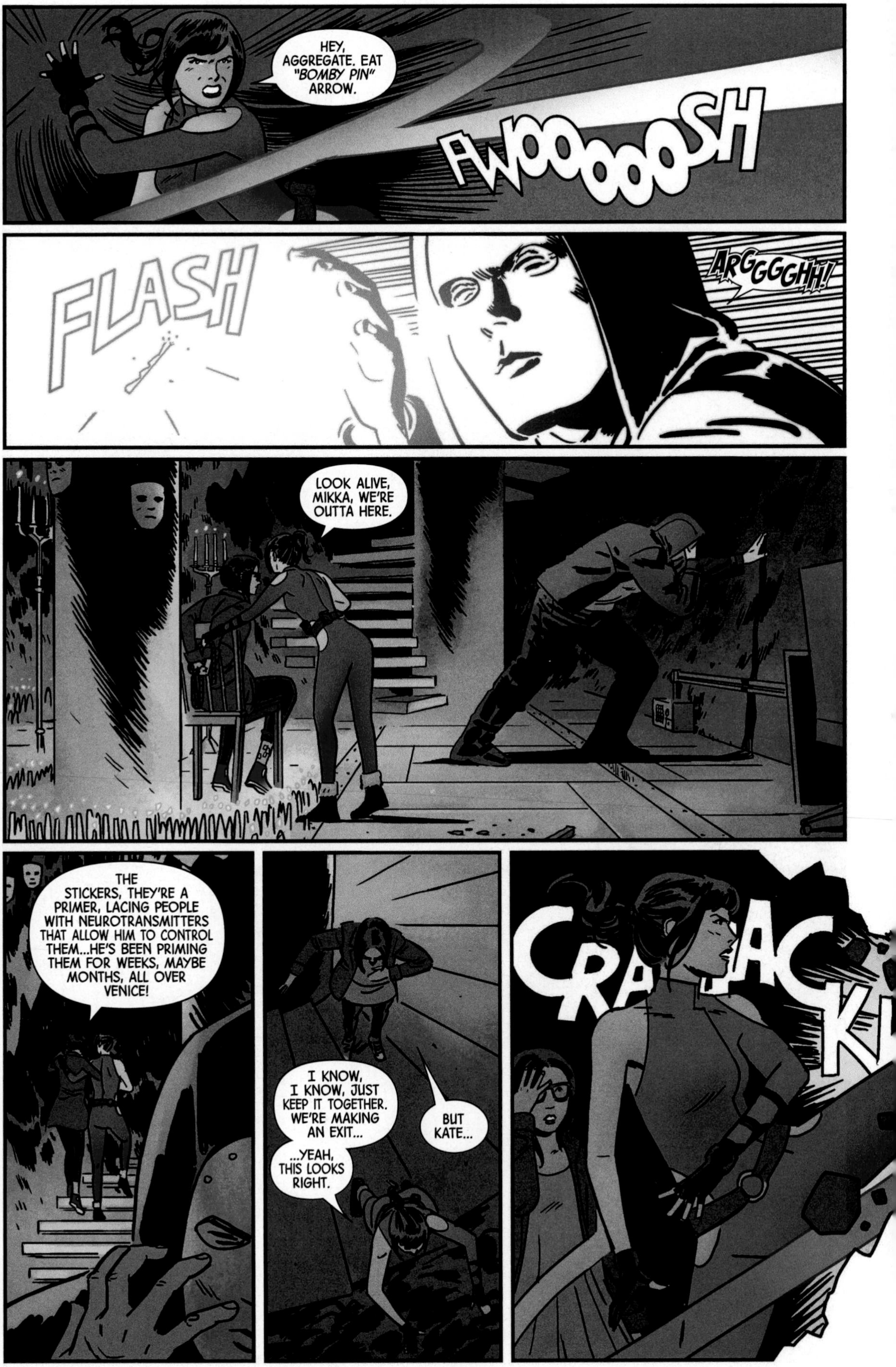

HEY, AGGREGATE. EAT "BOMBY PIN" ARROW.
AWOOOOOOSH
FLASH
ARGGGGHH!
LOOK ALIVE, MIKKA, WE'RE OUTTA HERE.
THE STICKERS, THEY'RE A PRIMER, LACING PEOPLE WITH NEUROTRANSMITTERS THAT ALLOW HIM TO CONTROL THEM...HE'S BEEN PRIMING THEM FOR WEEKS, MAYBE MONTHS, ALL OVER VENICE!
I KNOW, I KNOW, JUST KEEP IT TOGETHER. WE'RE MAKING AN EXIT...
...YEAH, THIS LOOKS RIGHT.
BUT KATE...

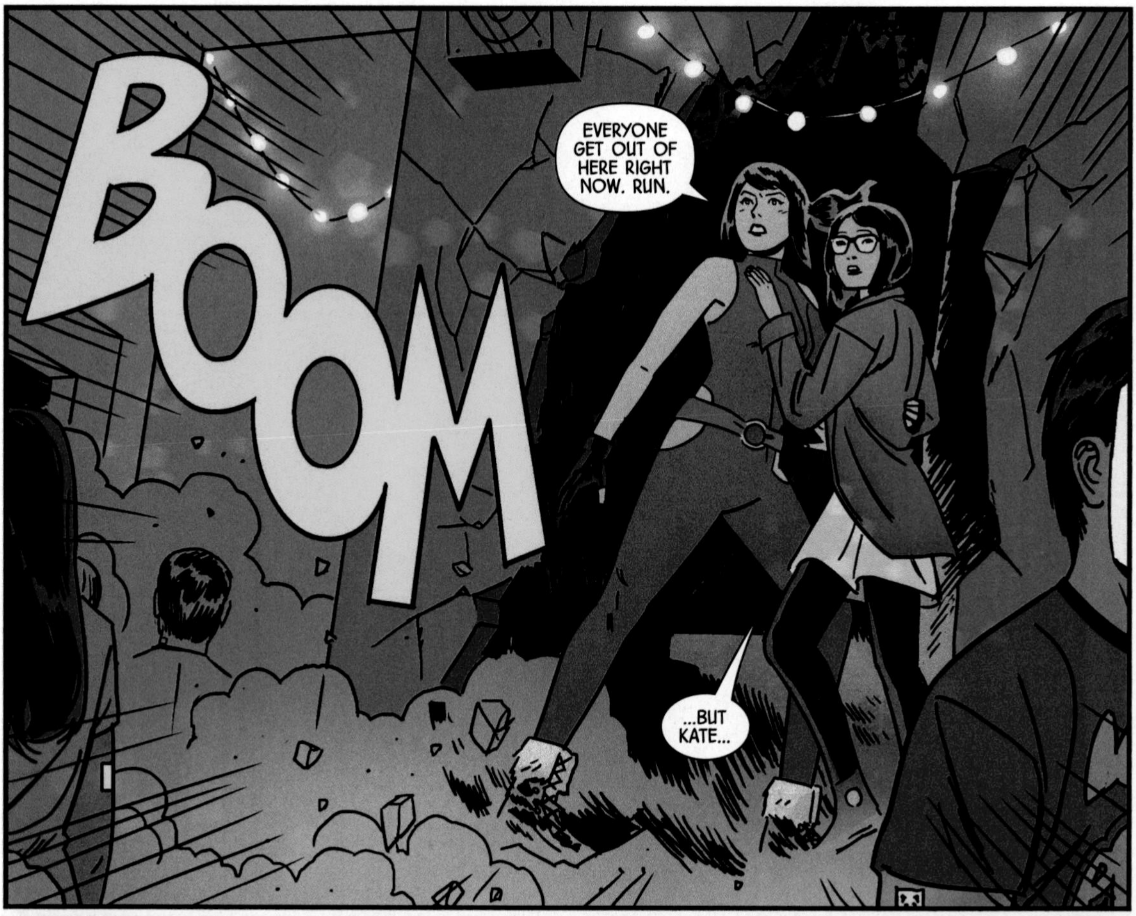
BOOM
EVERYONE GET OUT OF HERE RIGHT NOW. RUN.
...BUT KATE...

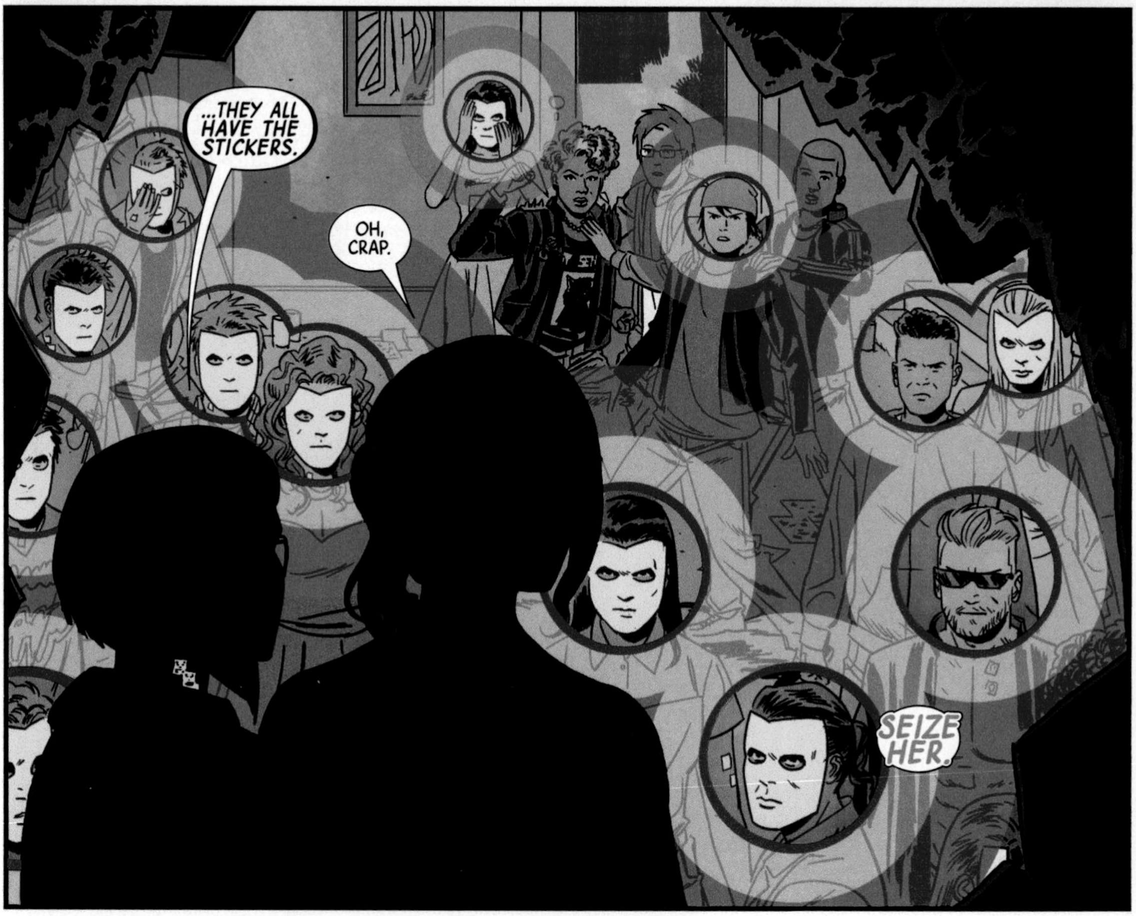
...THEY ALL HAVE THE STICKERS.
OH, CRAP.
SEIZE HER.

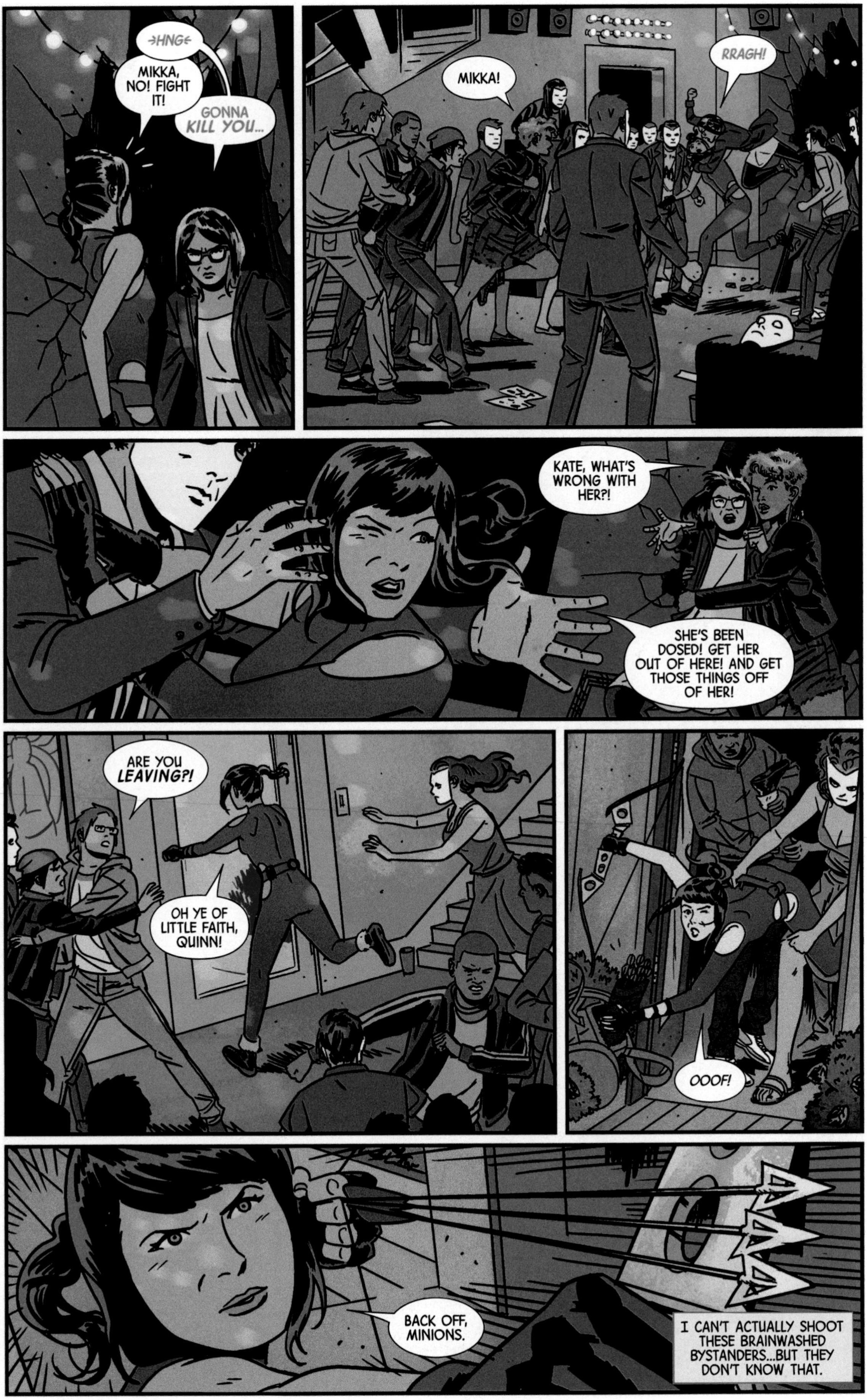

HNG
MIKKA, NO! FIGHT IT!
GONNA KILL YOU...
MIKKA!
RRAGH!
KATE, WHAT'S WRONG WITH HER?!
SHE'S BEEN DOSED! GET HER OUT OF HERE! AND GET THOSE THINGS OFF OF HER!
ARE YOU LEAVING?!
OH YE OF LITTLE FAITH, QUINN!
OOOF!
BACK OFF, MINIONS.
I CAN'T ACTUALLY SHOOT THESE BRAINWASHED BYSTANDERS...BUT THEY DON'T KNOW THAT.

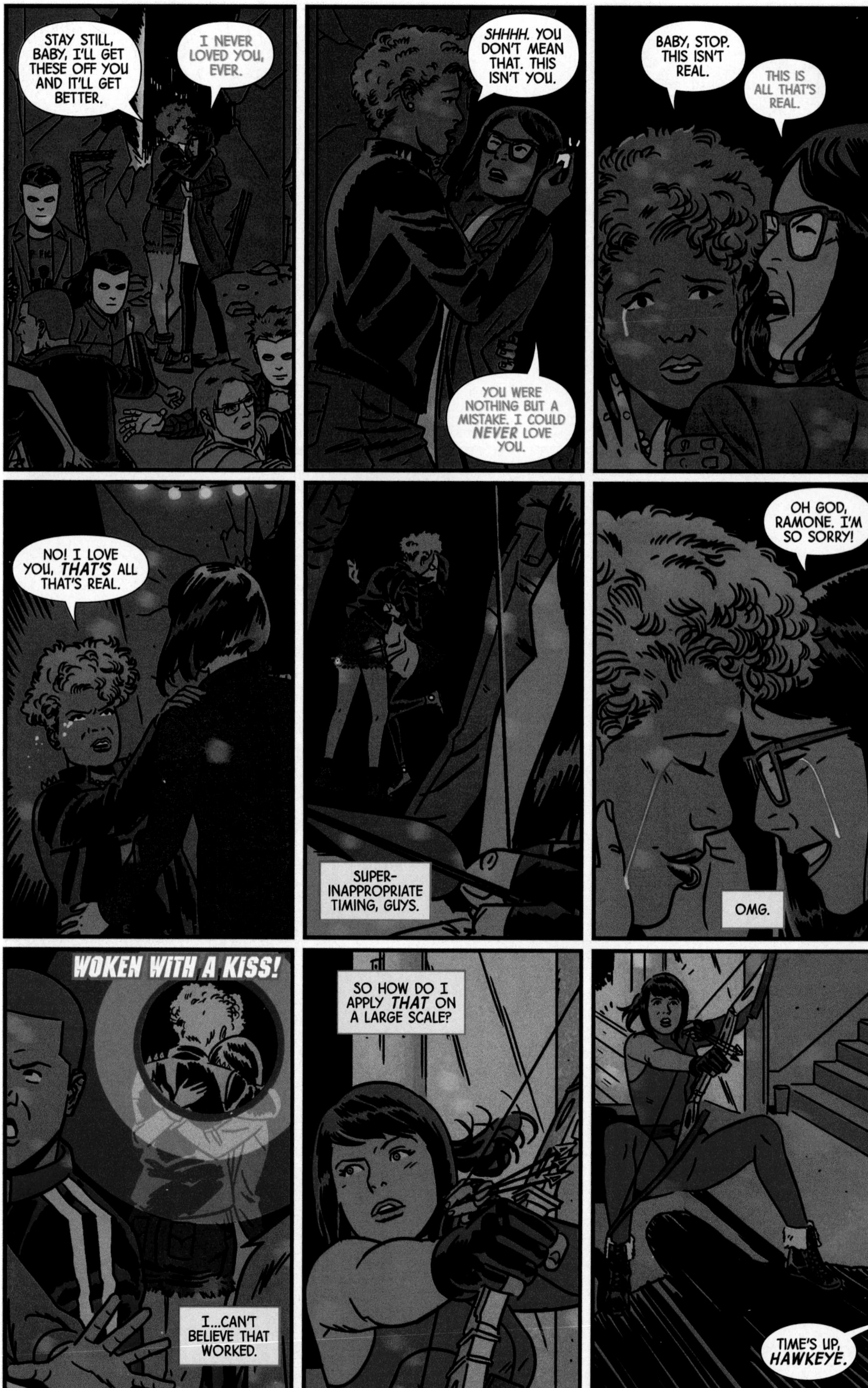
STAY STILL, BABY, I'LL GET THESE OFF YOU AND IT'LL GET BETTER.
I NEVER LOVED YOU, EVER.
SHHHH. YOU DON'T MEAN THAT. THIS ISN'T YOU.
YOU WERE NOTHING BUT A MISTAKE. I COULD NEVER LOVE YOU.
BABY, STOP. THIS ISN'T REAL.
THIS IS ALL THAT'S REAL.
NO! I LOVE YOU, THAT'S ALL THAT'S REAL.
SUPER-INAPPROPRIATE TIMING, GUYS.
OH GOD, RAMONE. I'M SO SORRY!
OMG.
WOKEN WITH A KISS!
I...CAN'T BELIEVE THAT WORKED.
SO HOW DO I APPLY THAT ON A LARGE SCALE?
TIME'S UP, HAWKEYE.

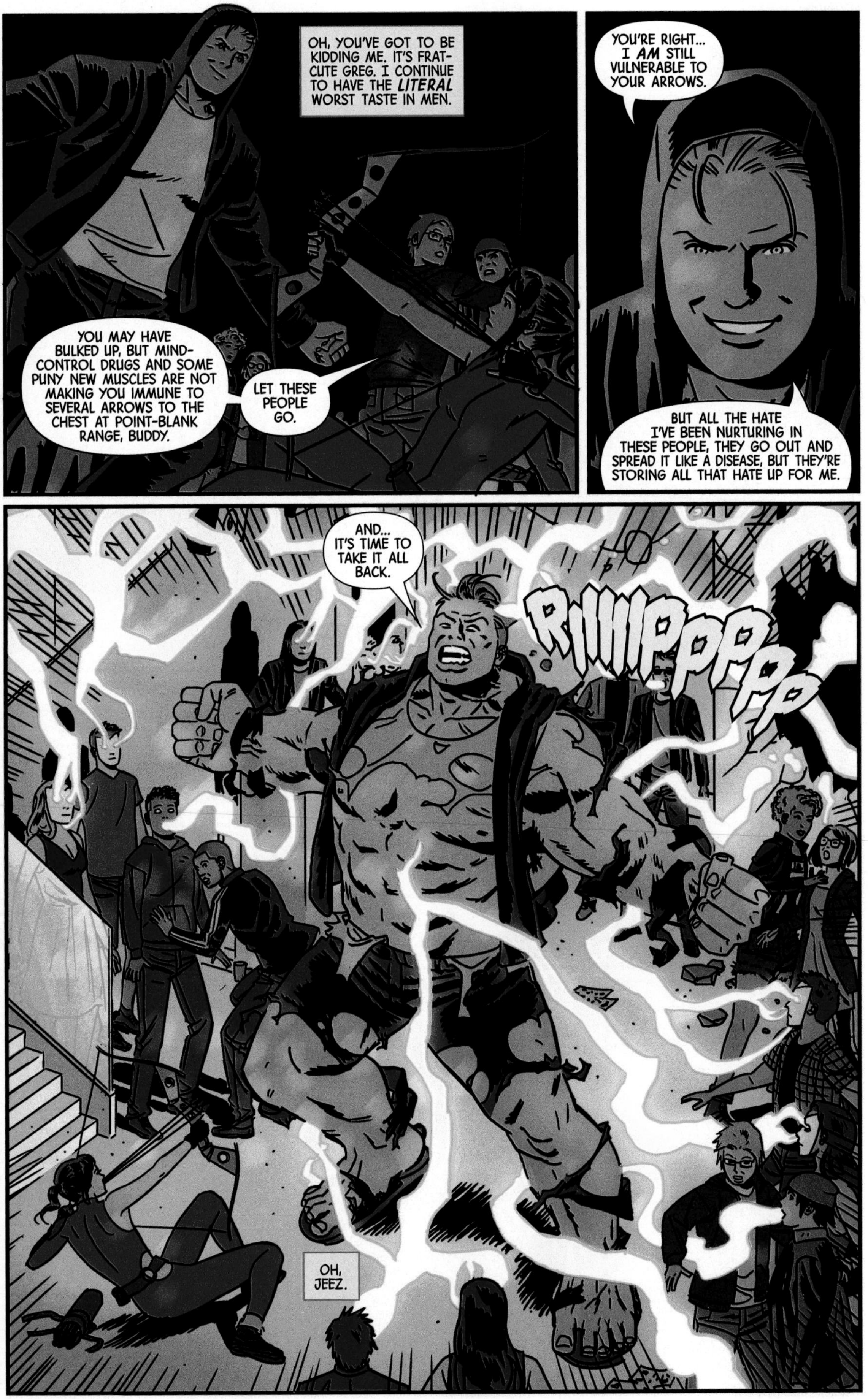

OH, YOU'VE GOT TO BE KIDDING ME. IT'S FRAT-CUTE GREG. I CONTINUE TO HAVE THE *LITERAL* WORST TASTE IN MEN.
YOU MAY HAVE BULKED UP, BUT MIND-CONTROL DRUGS AND SOME PUNY NEW MUSCLES ARE NOT MAKING YOU IMMUNE TO SEVERAL ARROWS TO THE CHEST AT POINT-BLANK RANGE, BUDDY.
LET THESE PEOPLE GO.
YOU'RE RIGHT... I *AM* STILL VULNERABLE TO YOUR ARROWS.
BUT ALL THE HATE I'VE BEEN NURTURING IN THESE PEOPLE, THEY GO OUT AND SPREAD IT LIKE A DISEASE, BUT THEY'RE STORING ALL THAT HATE UP FOR ME.
AND... IT'S TIME TO TAKE IT ALL BACK.
RIIIIIPPPPP
OH, JEEZ.

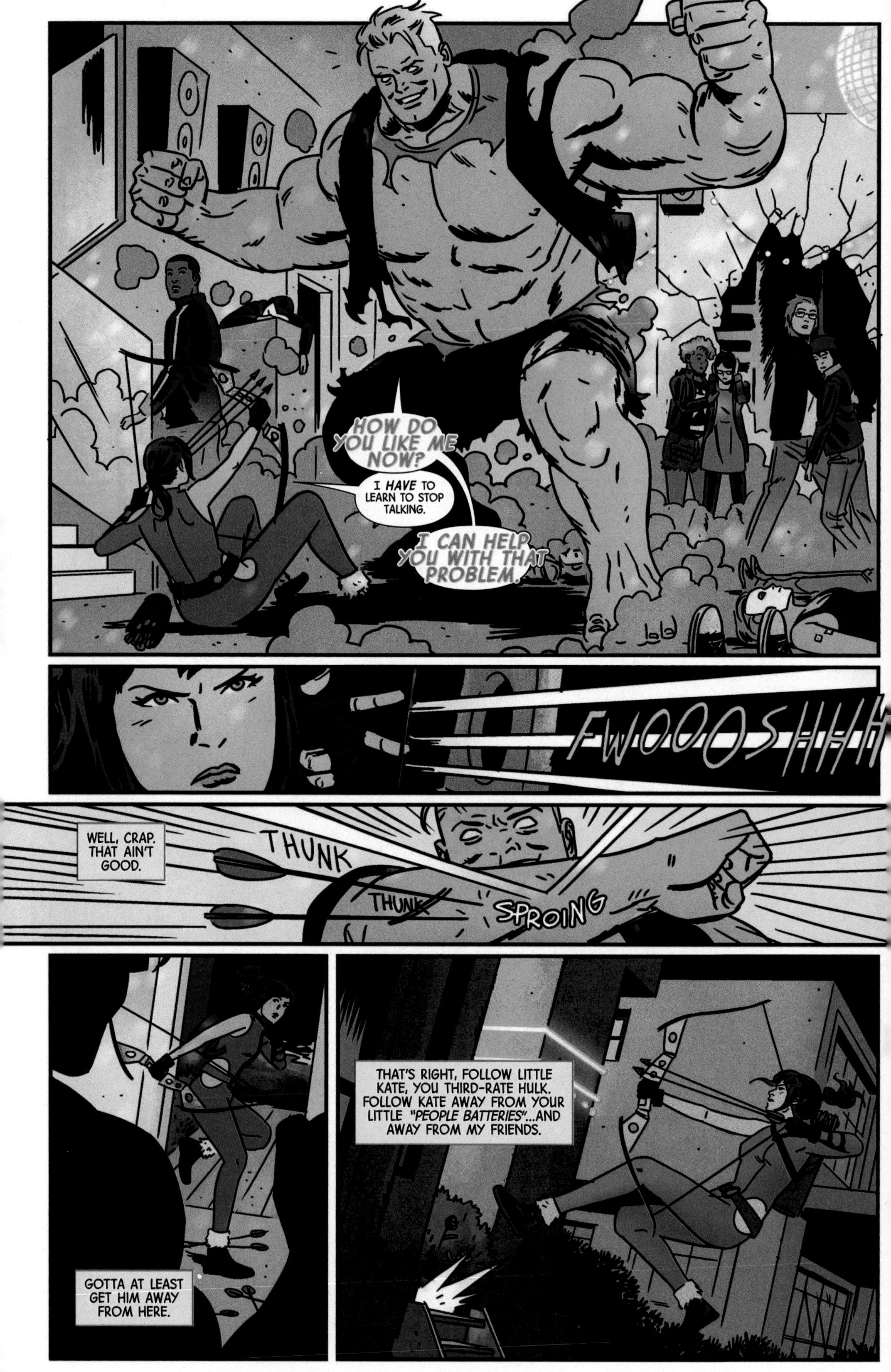
HOW DO YOU LIKE ME NOW?
I HAVE TO LEARN TO STOP TALKING.
I CAN HELP YOU WITH THAT PROBLEM.
FWOOOSHHH
WELL, CRAP. THAT AIN'T GOOD.
THUNK
THUNK
SPROING
GOTTA AT LEAST GET HIM AWAY FROM HERE.
THAT'S RIGHT, FOLLOW LITTLE KATE, YOU THIRD-RATE HULK. FOLLOW KATE AWAY FROM YOUR LITTLE "PEOPLE BATTERIES"...AND AWAY FROM MY FRIENDS.

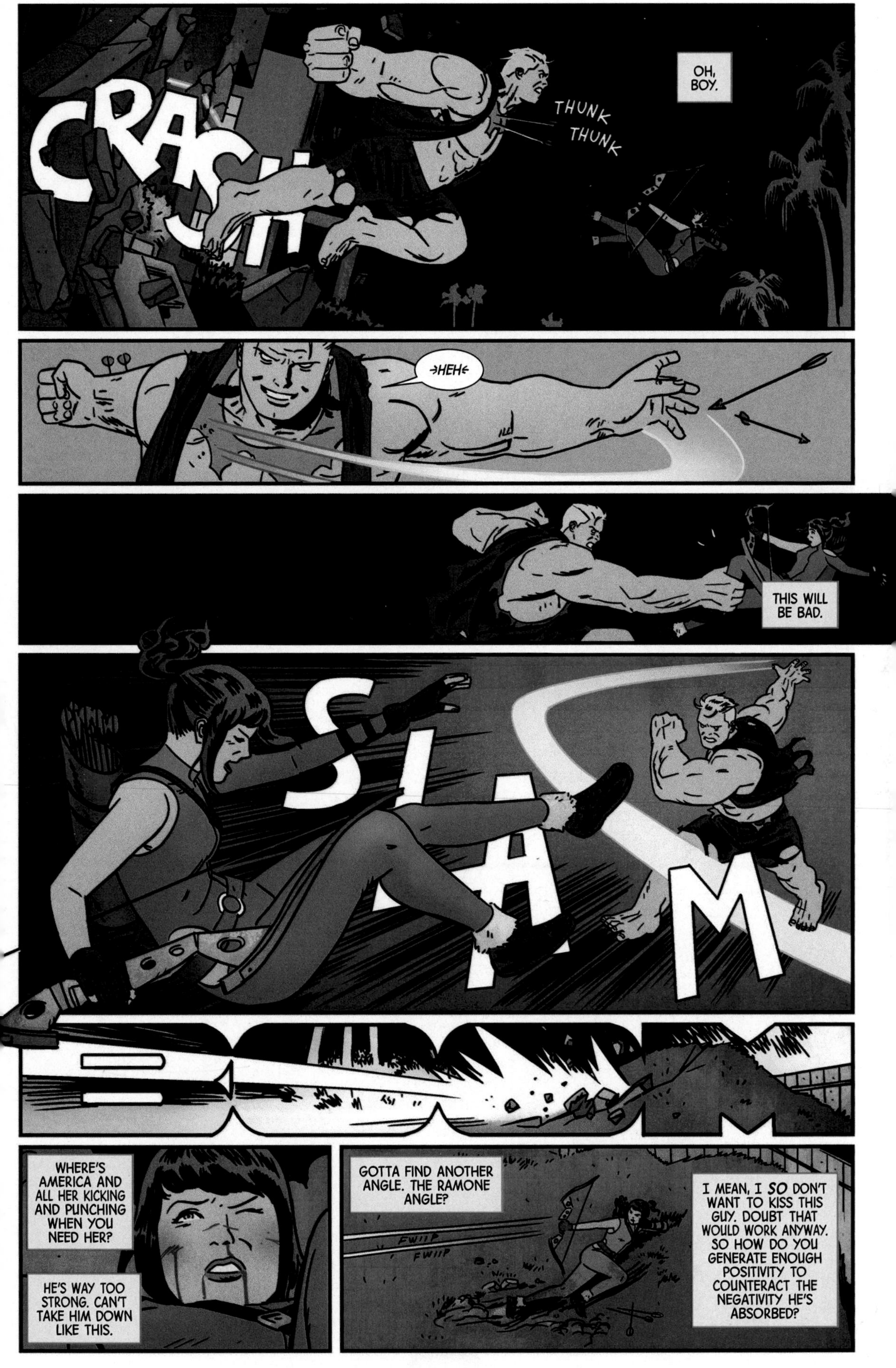
CRASH
THUNK
THUNK
OH, BOY.
HEH
THIS WILL BE BAD.
SLAM
BOOM
WHERE'S AMERICA AND ALL HER KICKING AND PUNCHING WHEN YOU NEED HER?
HE'S WAY TOO STRONG. CAN'T TAKE HIM DOWN LIKE THIS.
GOTTA FIND ANOTHER ANGLE. THE RAMONE ANGLE?
FWIIP
FWIIP
I MEAN, I SO DON'T WANT TO KISS THIS GUY. DOUBT THAT WOULD WORK ANYWAY. SO HOW DO YOU GENERATE ENOUGH POSITIVITY TO COUNTERACT THE NEGATIVITY HE'S ABSORBED?

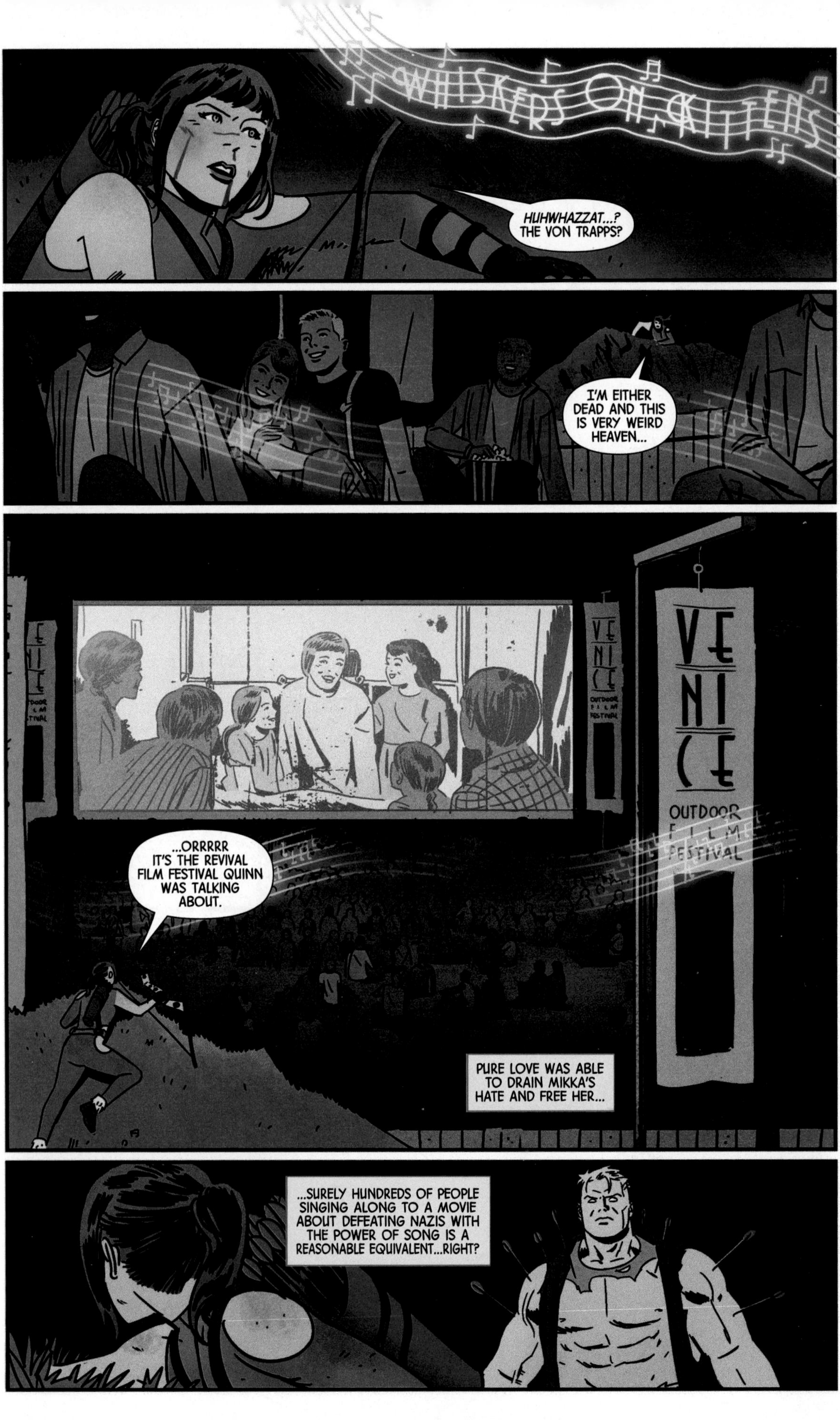
WHISKERS ON KITTENS
HUHWHAZZAT...? THE VON TRAPPS?
I'M EITHER DEAD AND THIS IS VERY WEIRD HEAVEN...
VENICE OUTDOOR FILM FESTIVAL
...ORRRRR IT'S THE REVIVAL FILM FESTIVAL QUINN WAS TALKING ABOUT.
PURE LOVE WAS ABLE TO DRAIN MIKKA'S HATE AND FREE HER...
...SURELY HUNDREDS OF PEOPLE SINGING ALONG TO A MOVIE ABOUT DEFEATING NAZIS WITH THE POWER OF SONG IS A REASONABLE EQUIVALENT...RIGHT?

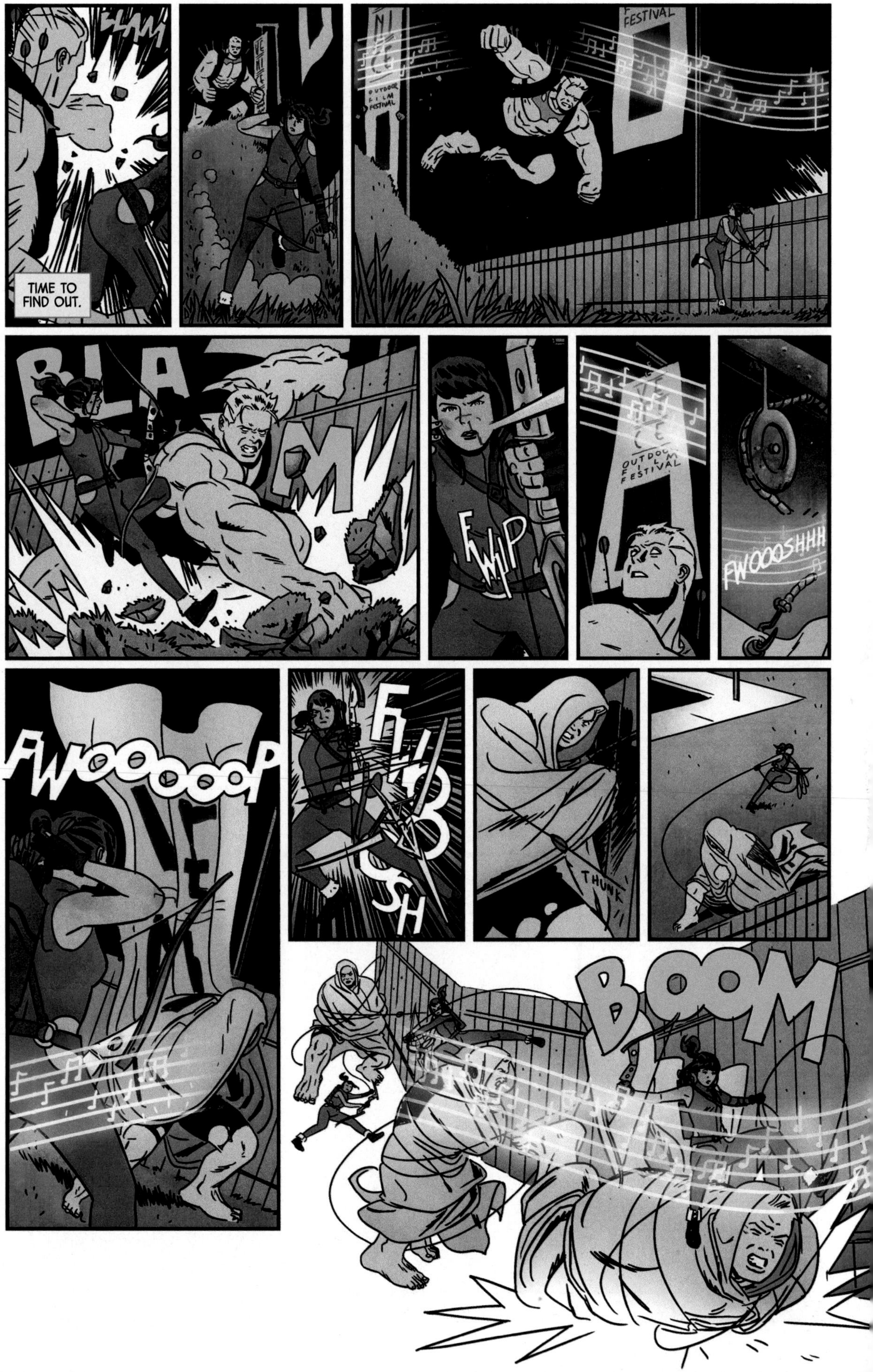
BLAM
TIME TO FIND OUT.
FESTIVAL
OUTDOOR FILM FESTIVAL
BLAM
FWIP
OUTDOOR FILM FESTIVAL
FWOOOSHHH
FWOOOOOOP
FWOOSH
THUNK
BOOM

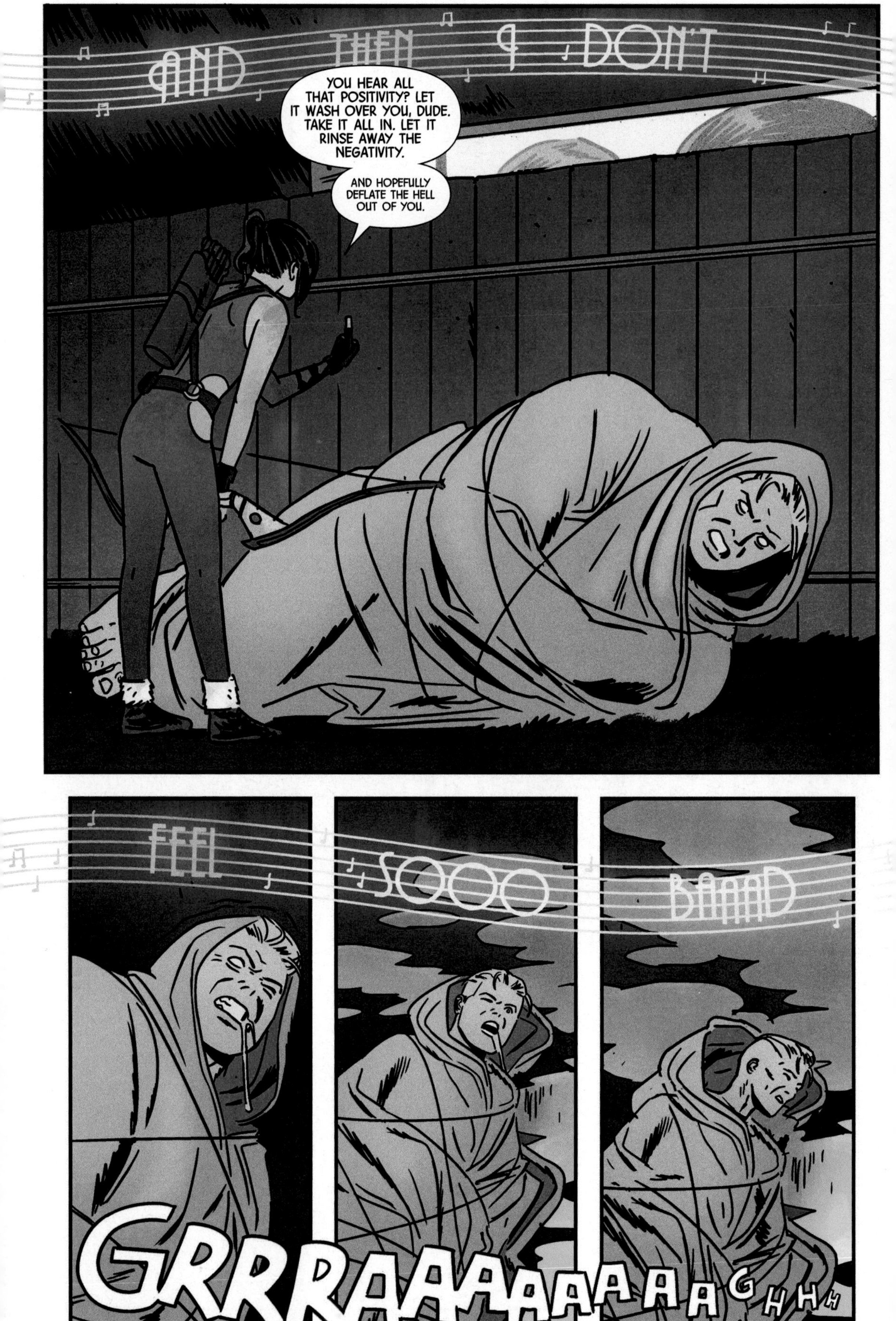

AND THEN I DON'T
YOU HEAR ALL THAT POSITIVITY? LET IT WASH OVER YOU, DUDE. TAKE IT ALL IN. LET IT RINSE AWAY THE NEGATIVITY.
AND HOPEFULLY DEFLATE THE HELL OUT OF YOU.
FEEL
SOOO
BAAAD
GRRRAAAAAAAAAGHHH

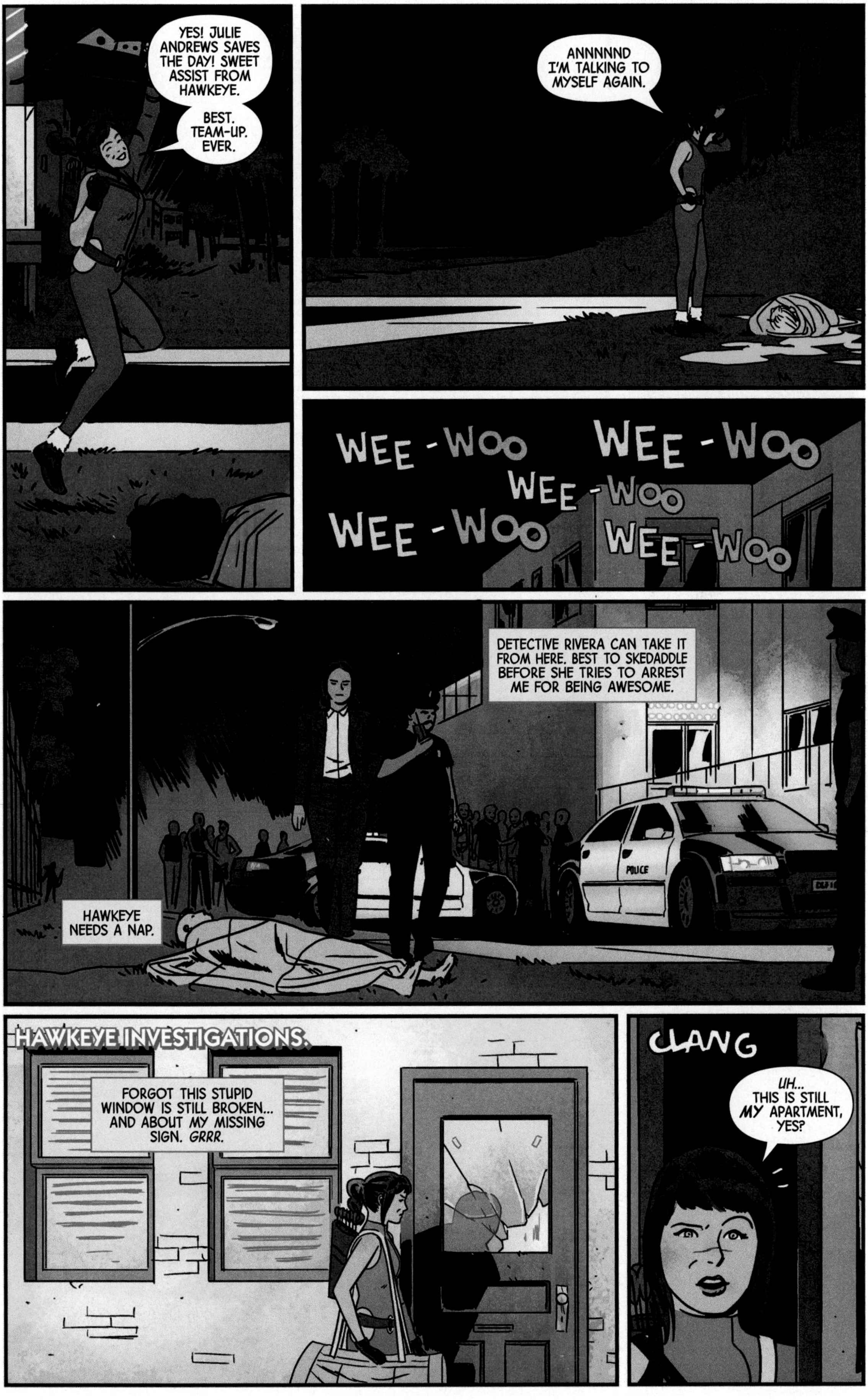
YES! JULIE ANDREWS SAVES THE DAY! SWEET ASSIST FROM HAWKEYE.
BEST. TEAM-UP. EVER.
ANNNNND I'M TALKING TO MYSELF AGAIN.
WEE-WOO WEE-WOO WEE-WOO WEE-WOO WEE-WOO
DETECTIVE RIVERA CAN TAKE IT FROM HERE. BEST TO SKEDADDLE BEFORE SHE TRIES TO ARREST ME FOR BEING AWESOME.
POLICE
HAWKEYE NEEDS A NAP.
HAWKEYE INVESTIGATIONS.
FORGOT THIS STUPID WINDOW IS STILL BROKEN... AND ABOUT MY MISSING SIGN. *GRRR.*
CLANG
UH... THIS IS STILL *MY* APARTMENT, YES?

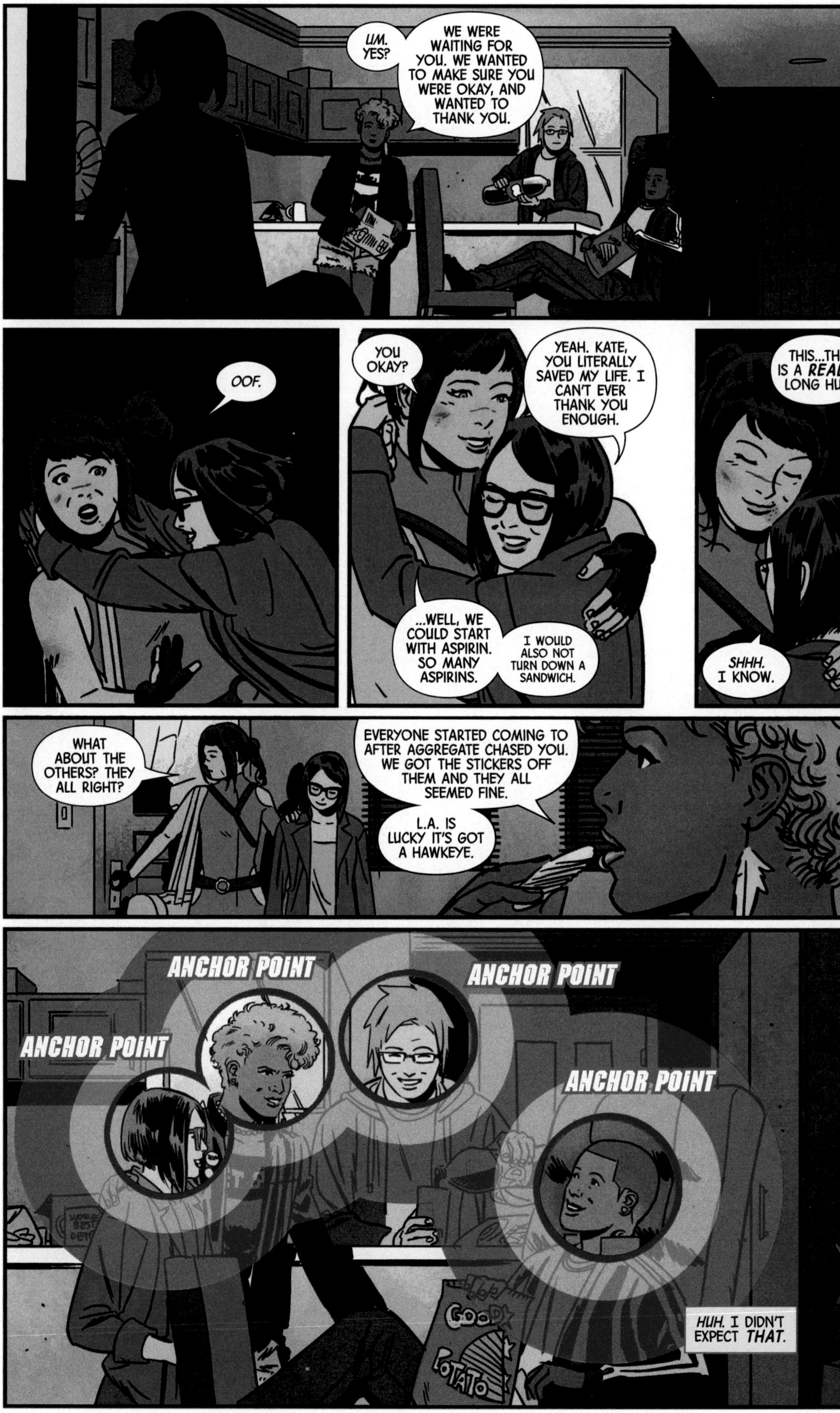
UM. YES?
WE WERE WAITING FOR YOU. WE WANTED TO MAKE SURE YOU WERE OKAY, AND WANTED TO THANK YOU.
OOF.
YOU OKAY?
YEAH. KATE, YOU LITERALLY SAVED MY LIFE. I CAN'T EVER THANK YOU ENOUGH.
...WELL, WE COULD START WITH ASPIRIN. SO MANY ASPIRINS.
I WOULD ALSO NOT TURN DOWN A SANDWICH.
THIS...THIS IS A REALLY LONG HUG.
SHHH. I KNOW.
WHAT ABOUT THE OTHERS? THEY ALL RIGHT?
EVERYONE STARTED COMING TO AFTER AGGREGATE CHASED YOU. WE GOT THE STICKERS OFF THEM AND THEY ALL SEEMED FINE.
L.A. IS LUCKY IT'S GOT A HAWKEYE.
ANCHOR POINT
ANCHOR POINT
ANCHOR POINT
ANCHOR POINT
GOOD POTATO
HUH. I DIDN'T EXPECT THAT.

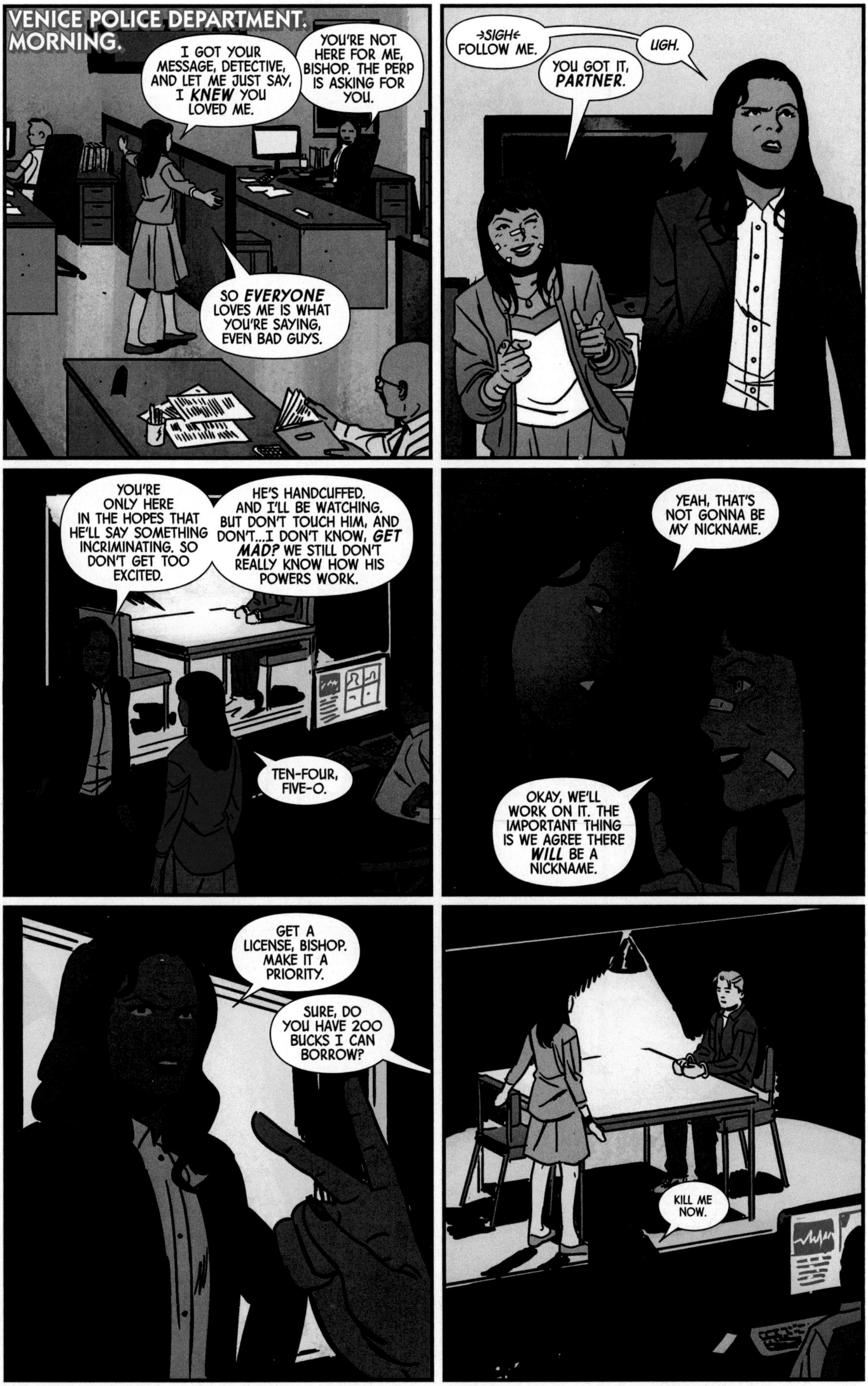
VENICE POLICE DEPARTMENT. MORNING.
I GOT YOUR MESSAGE, DETECTIVE, AND LET ME JUST SAY, I KNEW YOU LOVED ME.
YOU'RE NOT HERE FOR ME, BISHOP. THE PERP IS ASKING FOR YOU.
SO EVERYONE LOVES ME IS WHAT YOU'RE SAYING, EVEN BAD GUYS.
→SIGH← FOLLOW ME.
UGH.
YOU GOT IT, PARTNER.
YOU'RE ONLY HERE IN THE HOPES THAT HE'LL SAY SOMETHING INCRIMINATING. SO DON'T GET TOO EXCITED.
HE'S HANDCUFFED. AND I'LL BE WATCHING. BUT DON'T TOUCH HIM, AND DON'T...I DON'T KNOW, GET MAD? WE STILL DON'T REALLY KNOW HOW HIS POWERS WORK.
TEN-FOUR, FIVE-O.
YEAH, THAT'S NOT GONNA BE MY NICKNAME.
OKAY, WE'LL WORK ON IT. THE IMPORTANT THING IS WE AGREE THERE WILL BE A NICKNAME.
GET A LICENSE, BISHOP. MAKE IT A PRIORITY.
SURE, DO YOU HAVE 200 BUCKS I CAN BORROW?
KILL ME NOW.

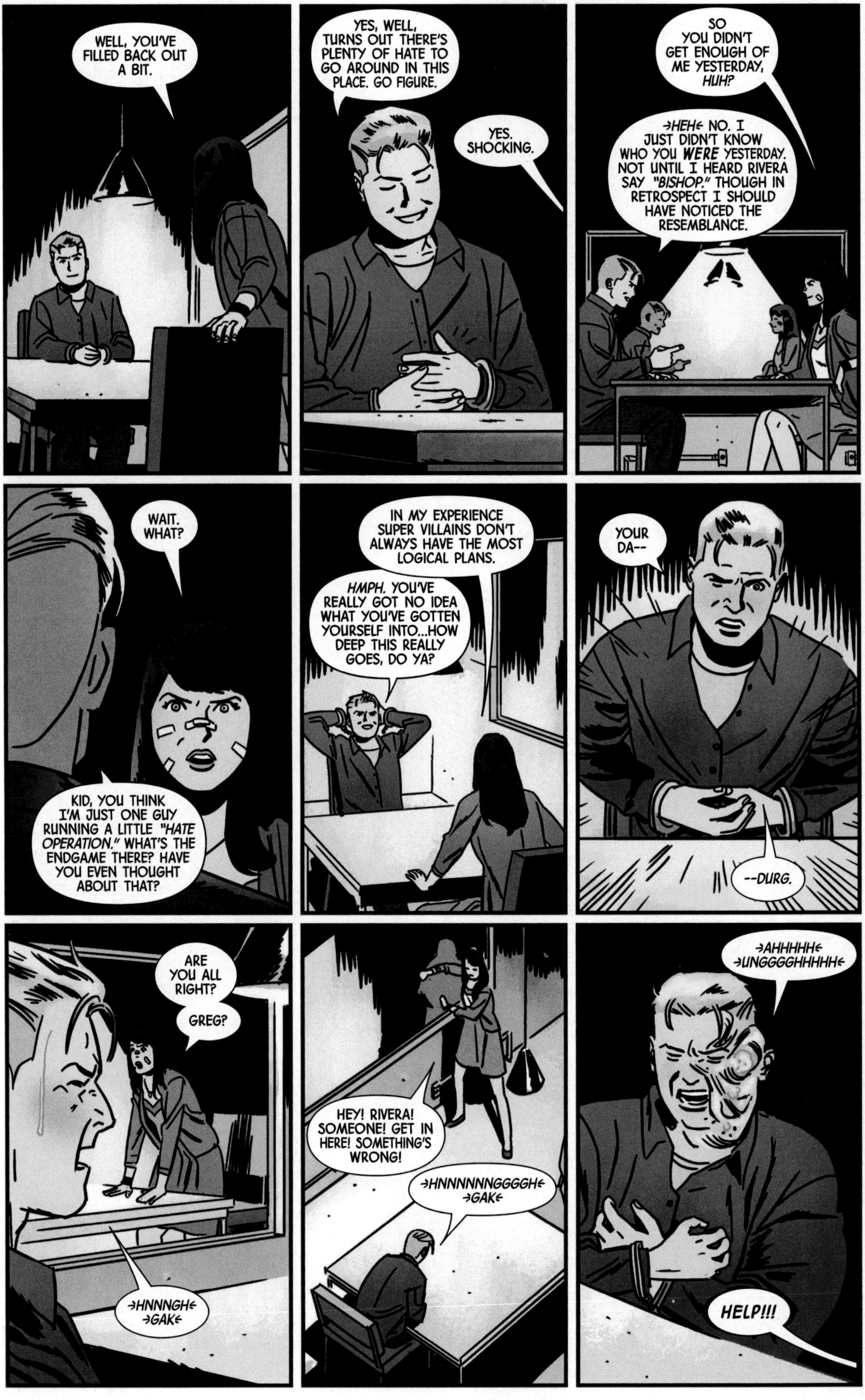
WELL, YOU'VE FILLED BACK OUT A BIT.
YES, WELL, TURNS OUT THERE'S PLENTY OF HATE TO GO AROUND IN THIS PLACE. GO FIGURE.
YES. SHOCKING.
SO YOU DIDN'T GET ENOUGH OF ME YESTERDAY, HUH?
HEH NO. I JUST DIDN'T KNOW WHO YOU WERE YESTERDAY. NOT UNTIL I HEARD RIVERA SAY "BISHOP." THOUGH IN RETROSPECT I SHOULD HAVE NOTICED THE RESEMBLANCE.
WAIT. WHAT?
KID, YOU THINK I'M JUST ONE GUY RUNNING A LITTLE "HATE OPERATION." WHAT'S THE ENDGAME THERE? HAVE YOU EVEN THOUGHT ABOUT THAT?
IN MY EXPERIENCE SUPER VILLAINS DON'T ALWAYS HAVE THE MOST LOGICAL PLANS.
HMPH. YOU'VE REALLY GOT NO IDEA WHAT YOU'VE GOTTEN YOURSELF INTO...HOW DEEP THIS REALLY GOES, DO YA?
YOUR DA--
--DURG.
ARE YOU ALL RIGHT?
GREG?
HNNNGH GAK
HEY! RIVERA! SOMEONE! GET IN HERE! SOMETHING'S WRONG!
HNNNNNNGGGGH GAK
AHHHHHH UNGGGGHHHHHH
HELP!!!

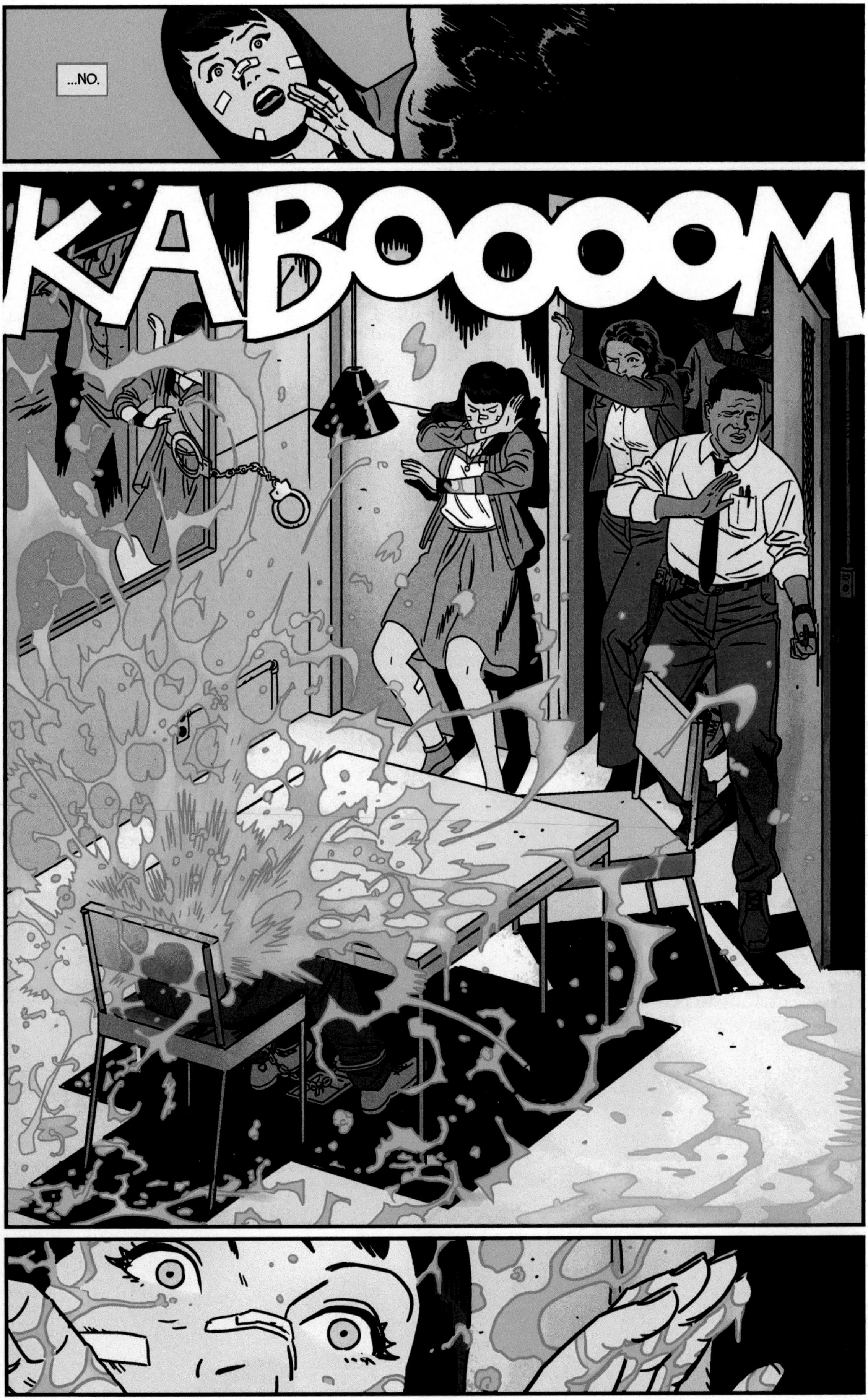
...NO.
KABOOOOM

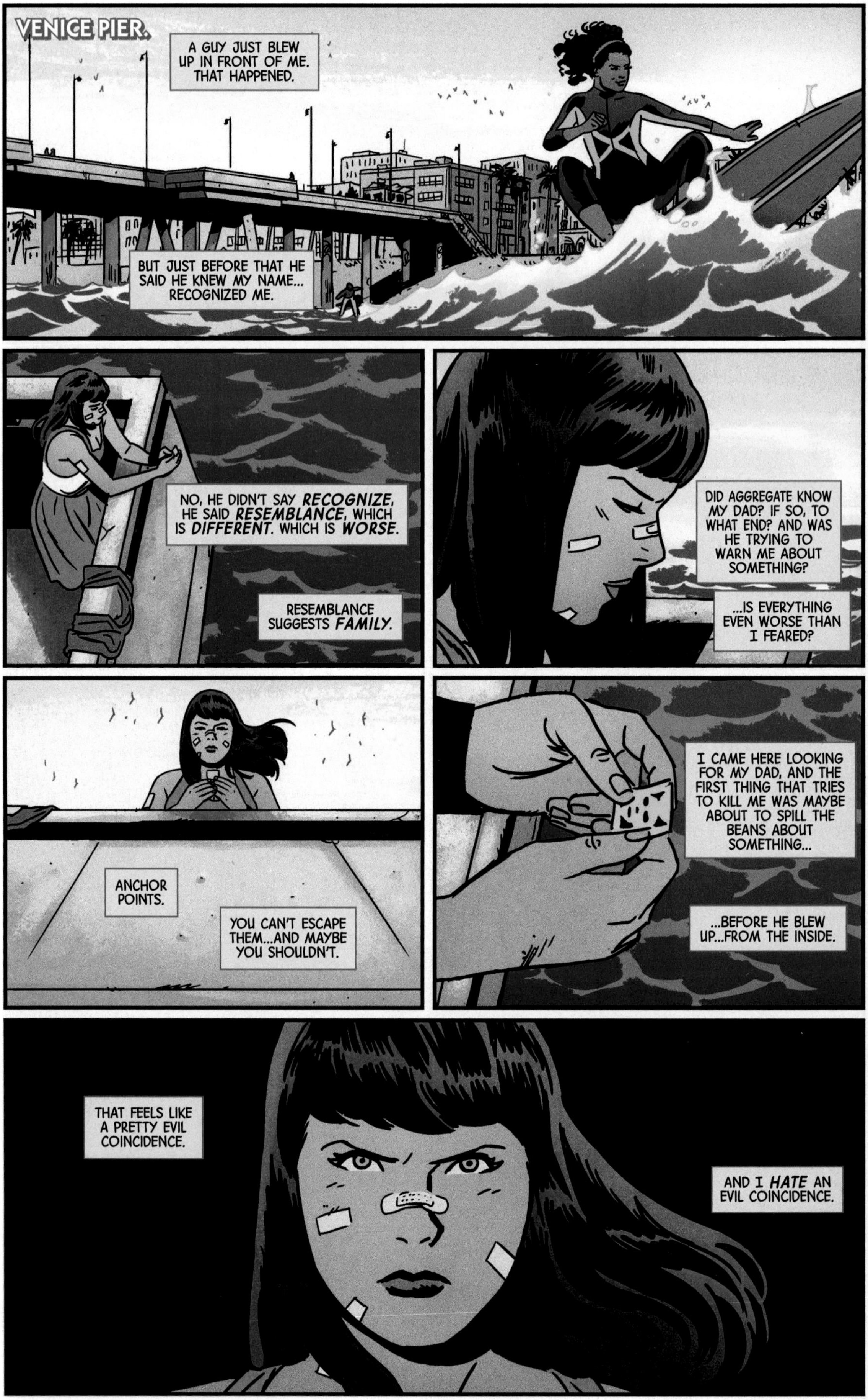
VENICE PIER.
A GUY JUST BLEW UP IN FRONT OF ME. THAT HAPPENED.
BUT JUST BEFORE THAT HE SAID HE KNEW MY NAME... RECOGNIZED ME.
NO, HE DIDN'T SAY RECOGNIZE, HE SAID RESEMBLANCE, WHICH IS DIFFERENT. WHICH IS WORSE.
RESEMBLANCE SUGGESTS FAMILY.
DID AGGREGATE KNOW MY DAD? IF SO, TO WHAT END? AND WAS HE TRYING TO WARN ME ABOUT SOMETHING?
...IS EVERYTHING EVEN WORSE THAN I FEARED?
ANCHOR POINTS.
YOU CAN'T ESCAPE THEM...AND MAYBE YOU SHOULDN'T.
I CAME HERE LOOKING FOR MY DAD, AND THE FIRST THING THAT TRIES TO KILL ME WAS MAYBE ABOUT TO SPILL THE BEANS ABOUT SOMETHING...
...BEFORE HE BLEW UP...FROM THE INSIDE.
THAT FEELS LIKE A PRETTY EVIL COINCIDENCE.
AND I HATE AN EVIL COINCIDENCE.

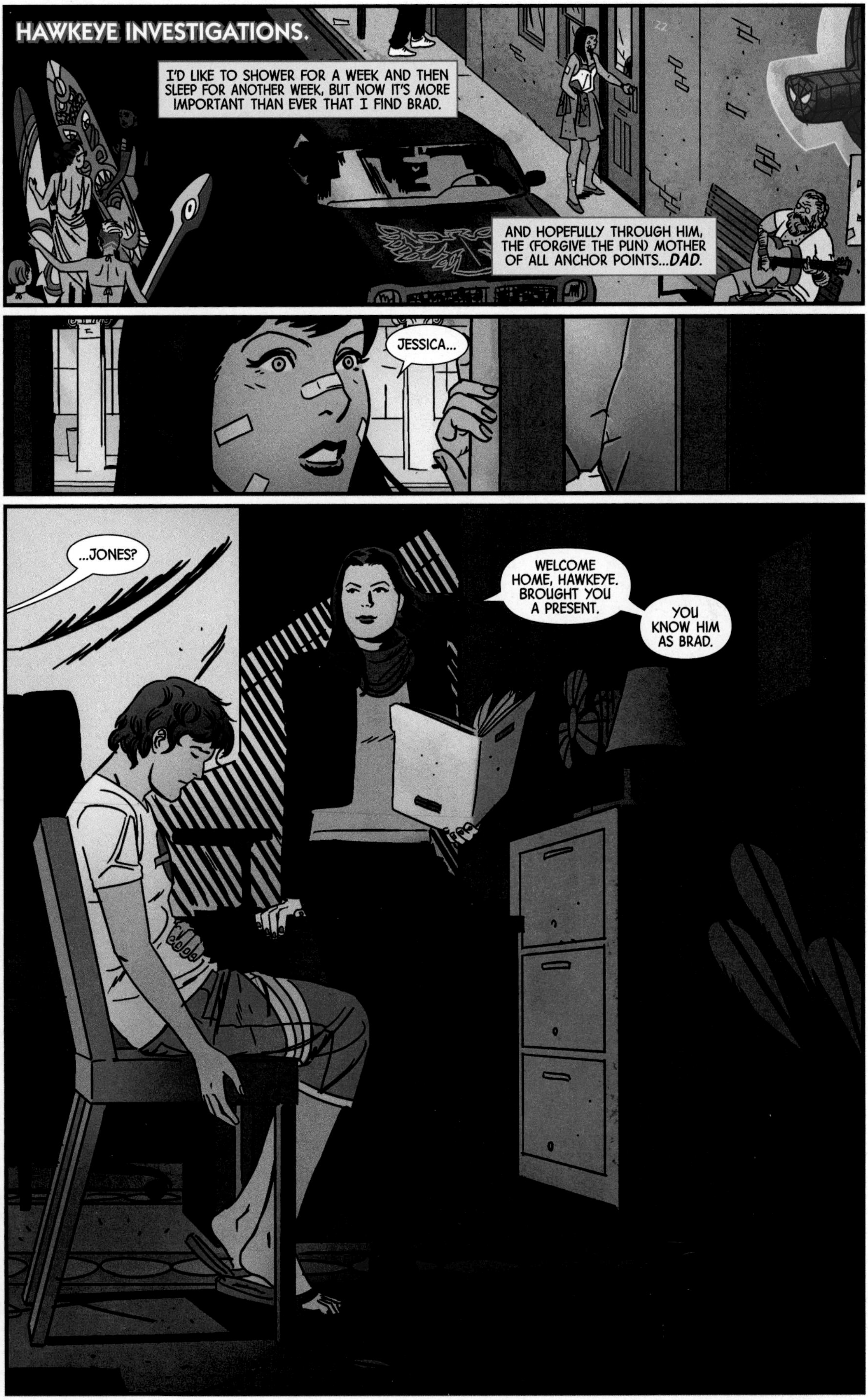
HAWKEYE INVESTIGATIONS.
I'D LIKE TO SHOWER FOR A WEEK AND THEN SLEEP FOR ANOTHER WEEK, BUT NOW IT'S MORE IMPORTANT THAN EVER THAT I FIND BRAD.
AND HOPEFULLY THROUGH HIM, THE (FORGIVE THE PUN) MOTHER OF ALL ANCHOR POINTS...DAD.
JESSICA...
...JONES?
WELCOME HOME, HAWKEYE. BROUGHT YOU A PRESENT.
YOU KNOW HIM AS BRAD.

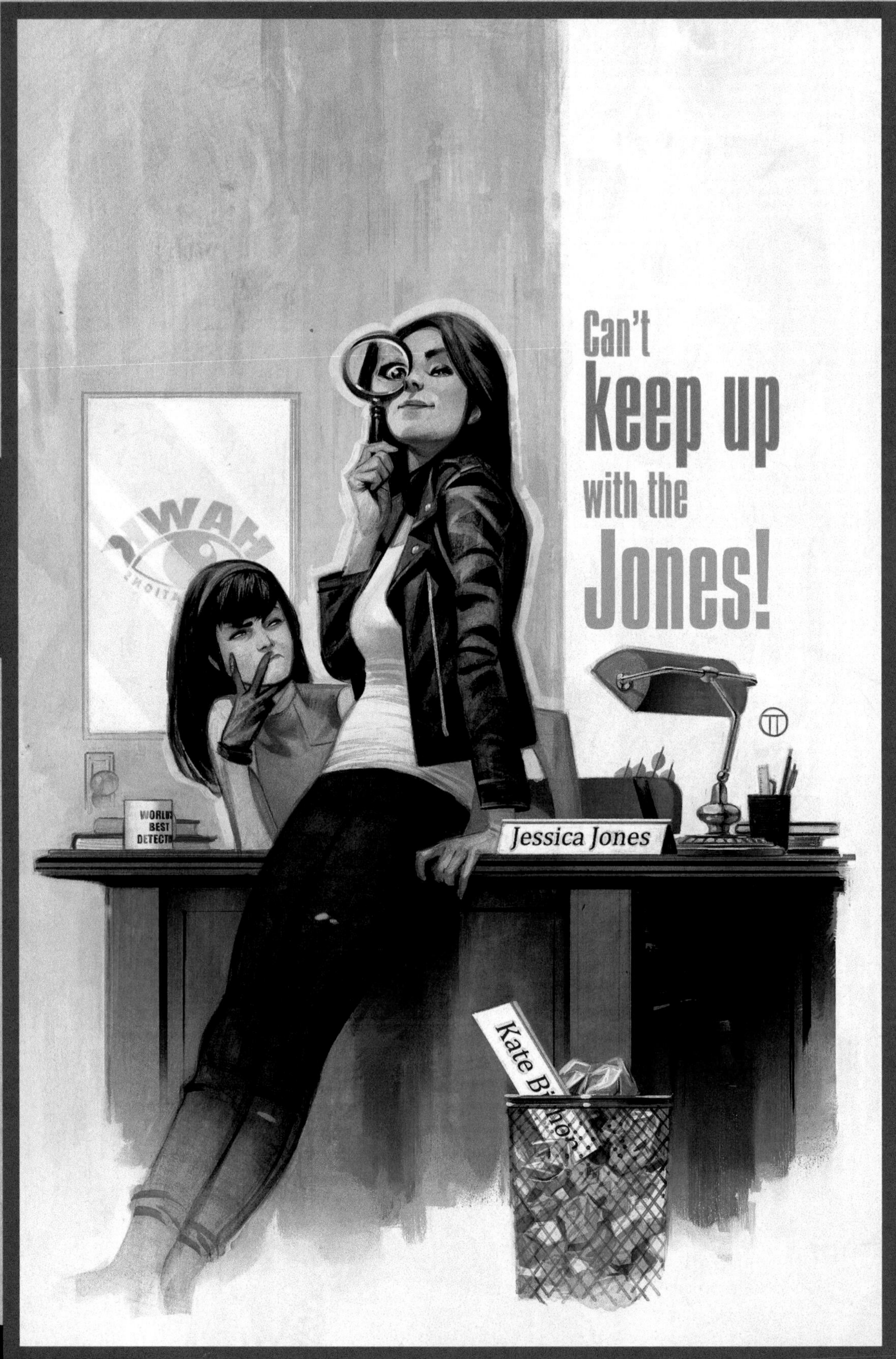
Can't
keep up
with the
Jones!
WORLD'S
BEST
DETECT
Jessica Jones
Kate Bi

5

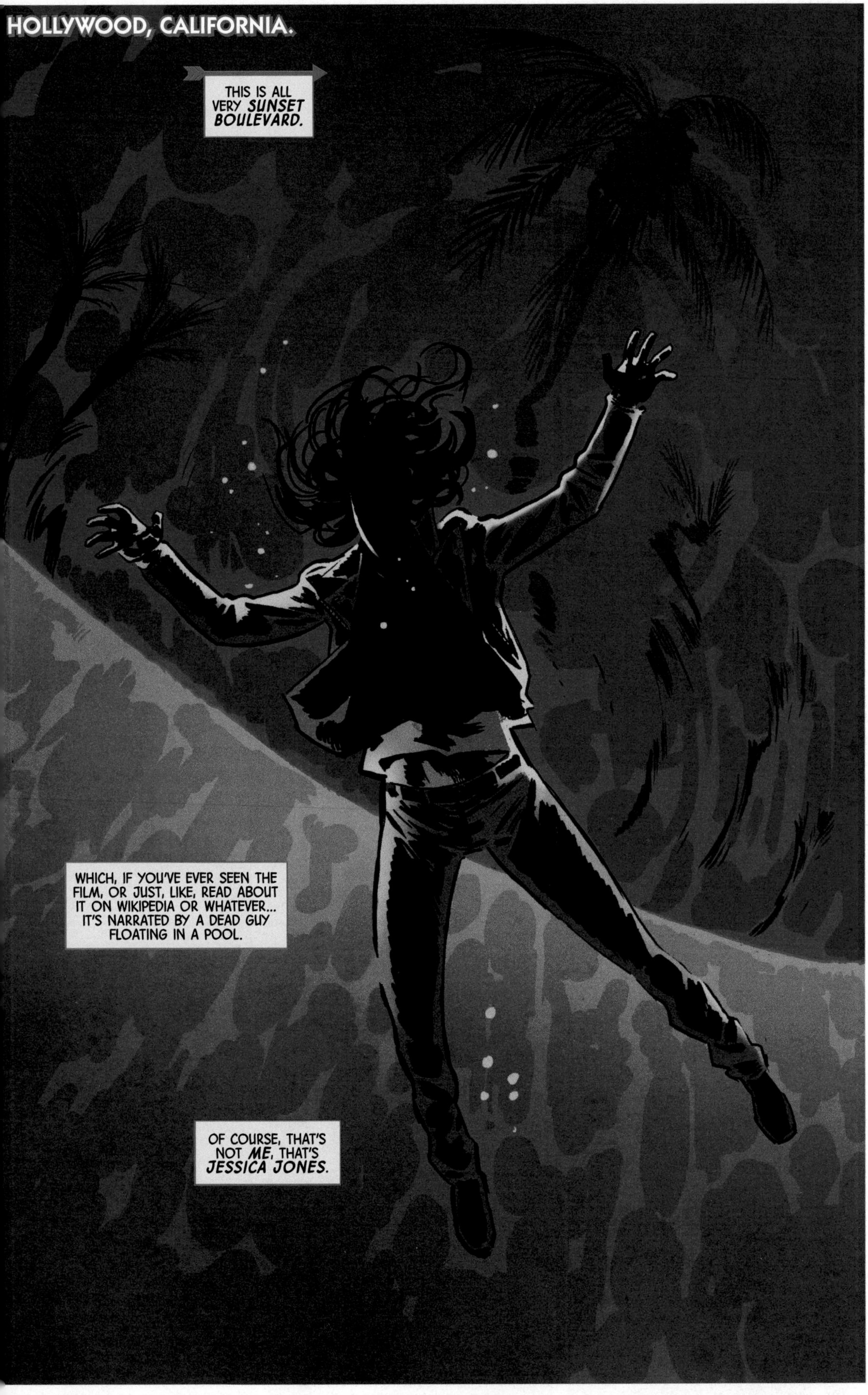
HOLLYWOOD, CALIFORNIA.
THIS IS ALL VERY SUNSET BOULEVARD.
WHICH, IF YOU'VE EVER SEEN THE FILM, OR JUST, LIKE, READ ABOUT IT ON WIKIPEDIA OR WHATEVER... IT'S NARRATED BY A DEAD GUY FLOATING IN A POOL.
OF COURSE, THAT'S NOT ME, THAT'S JESSICA JONES.

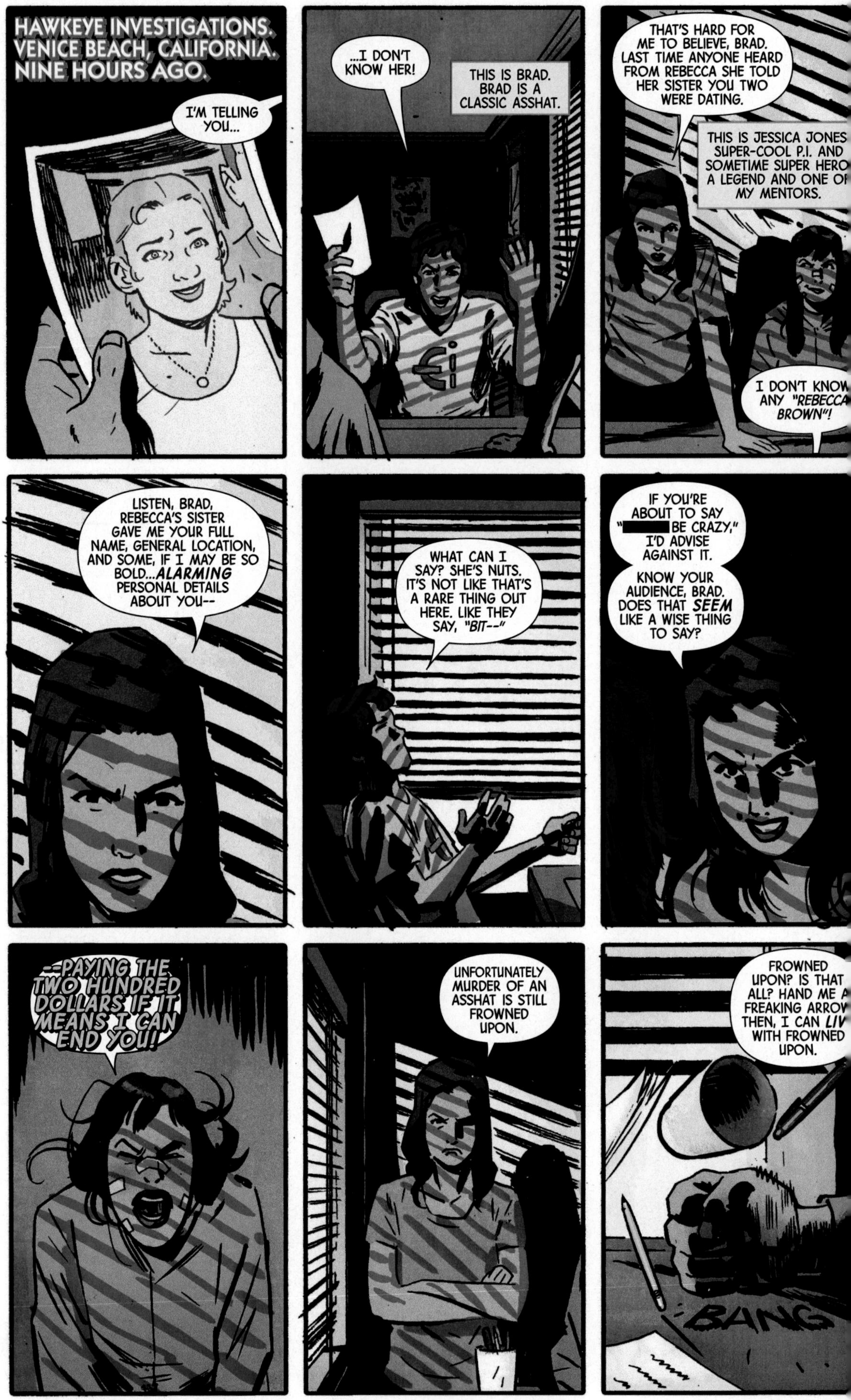

HAWKEYE INVESTIGATIONS. VENICE BEACH, CALIFORNIA. NINE HOURS AGO.
I'M TELLING YOU...
...I DON'T KNOW HER!
THIS IS BRAD. BRAD IS A CLASSIC ASSHAT.
THAT'S HARD FOR ME TO BELIEVE, BRAD. LAST TIME ANYONE HEARD FROM REBECCA SHE TOLD HER SISTER YOU TWO WERE DATING.
THIS IS JESSICA JONES SUPER-COOL P.I. AND SOMETIME SUPER HERO A LEGEND AND ONE OF MY MENTORS.
I DON'T KNOW ANY "REBECCA BROWN"!
LISTEN, BRAD, REBECCA'S SISTER GAVE ME YOUR FULL NAME, GENERAL LOCATION, AND SOME, IF I MAY BE SO BOLD...ALARMING PERSONAL DETAILS ABOUT YOU--
WHAT CAN I SAY? SHE'S NUTS. IT'S NOT LIKE THAT'S A RARE THING OUT HERE. LIKE THEY SAY, "BIT--"
IF YOU'RE ABOUT TO SAY "[redacted] BE CRAZY," I'D ADVISE AGAINST IT.
KNOW YOUR AUDIENCE, BRAD. DOES THAT SEEM LIKE A WISE THING TO SAY?
--PAYING THE TWO HUNDRED DOLLARS IF IT MEANS I CAN END YOU!
UNFORTUNATELY MURDER OF AN ASSHAT IS STILL FROWNED UPON.
FROWNED UPON? IS THAT ALL? HAND ME A FREAKING ARROW THEN, I CAN LIVE WITH FROWNED UPON.
BANG

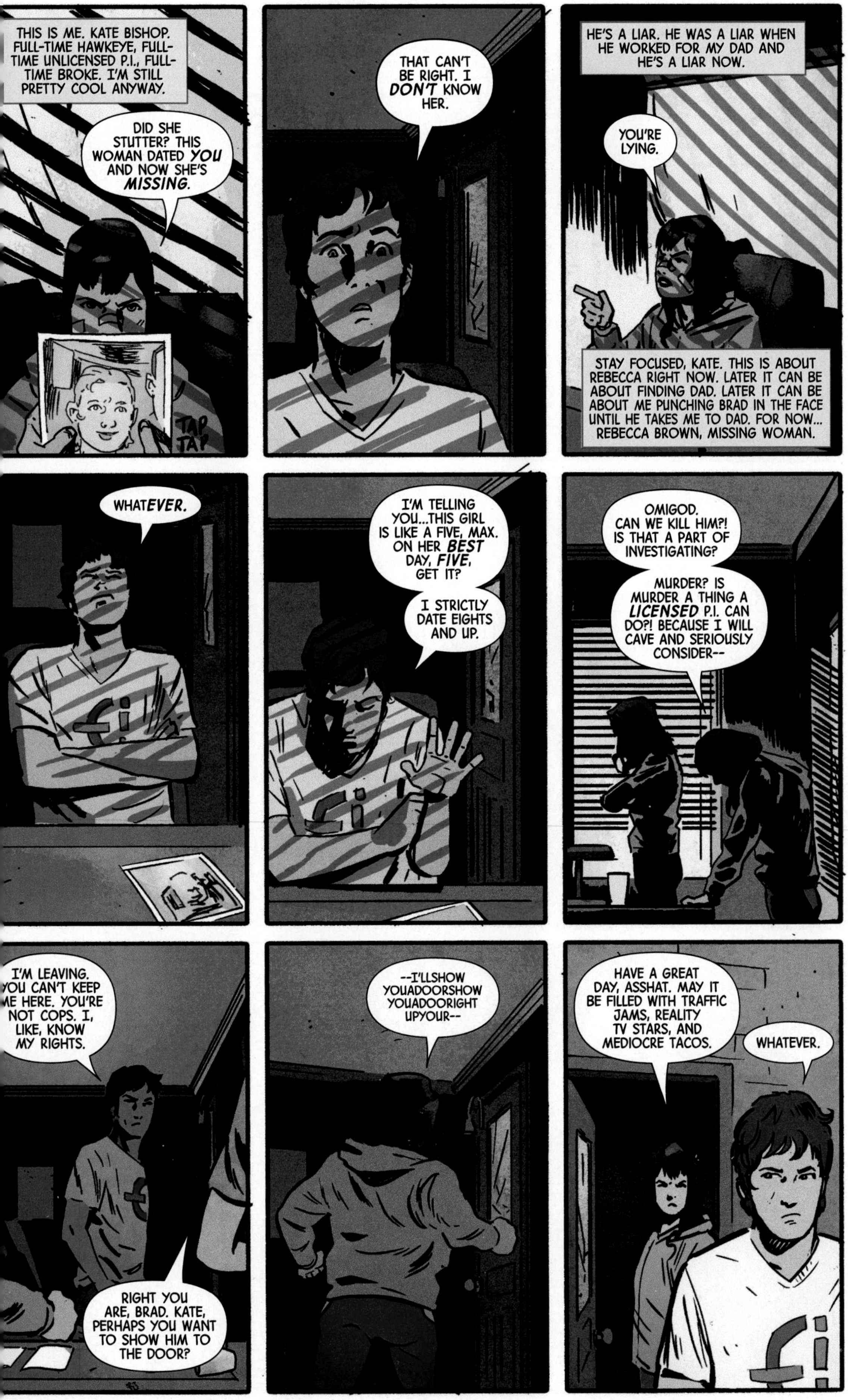
THIS IS ME. KATE BISHOP. FULL-TIME HAWKEYE, FULL-TIME UNLICENSED P.I., FULL-TIME BROKE. I'M STILL PRETTY COOL ANYWAY.
DID SHE STUTTER? THIS WOMAN DATED YOU AND NOW SHE'S MISSING.
TAP TAP
THAT CAN'T BE RIGHT. I DON'T KNOW HER.
HE'S A LIAR. HE WAS A LIAR WHEN HE WORKED FOR MY DAD AND HE'S A LIAR NOW.
YOU'RE LYING.
STAY FOCUSED, KATE. THIS IS ABOUT REBECCA RIGHT NOW. LATER IT CAN BE ABOUT FINDING DAD. LATER IT CAN BE ABOUT ME PUNCHING BRAD IN THE FACE UNTIL HE TAKES ME TO DAD. FOR NOW... REBECCA BROWN, MISSING WOMAN.
WHATEVER.
I'M TELLING YOU...THIS GIRL IS LIKE A FIVE, MAX. ON HER BEST DAY, FIVE, GET IT?
I STRICTLY DATE EIGHTS AND UP.
OMIGOD. CAN WE KILL HIM?! IS THAT A PART OF INVESTIGATING?
MURDER? IS MURDER A THING A LICENSED P.I. CAN DO?! BECAUSE I WILL CAVE AND SERIOUSLY CONSIDER--
I'M LEAVING. YOU CAN'T KEEP ME HERE. YOU'RE NOT COPS. I, LIKE, KNOW MY RIGHTS.
RIGHT YOU ARE, BRAD. KATE, PERHAPS YOU WANT TO SHOW HIM TO THE DOOR?
--I'LLSHOW YOUADOORSHOW YOUADOORIGHT UPYOUR--
HAVE A GREAT DAY, ASSHAT. MAY IT BE FILLED WITH TRAFFIC JAMS, REALITY TV STARS, AND MEDIOCRE TACOS.
WHATEVER.

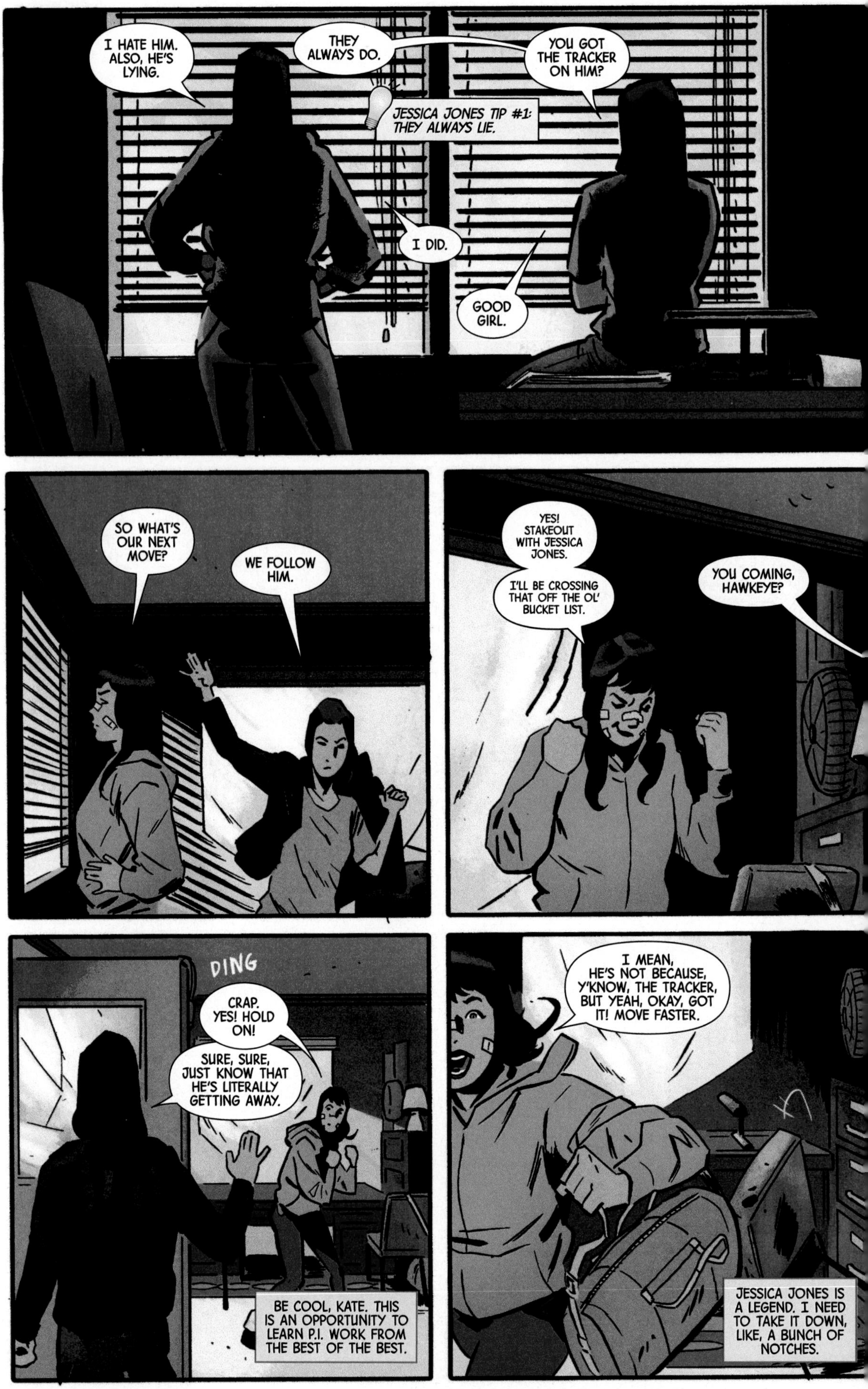
I HATE HIM. ALSO, HE'S LYING.
THEY ALWAYS DO.
YOU GOT THE TRACKER ON HIM?
JESSICA JONES TIP #1: THEY ALWAYS LIE.
I DID.
GOOD GIRL.
SO WHAT'S OUR NEXT MOVE?
WE FOLLOW HIM.
YES! STAKEOUT WITH JESSICA JONES.
I'LL BE CROSSING THAT OFF THE OL' BUCKET LIST.
YOU COMING, HAWKEYE?
DING
CRAP. YES! HOLD ON!
SURE, SURE, JUST KNOW THAT HE'S LITERALLY GETTING AWAY.
BE COOL, KATE. THIS IS AN OPPORTUNITY TO LEARN P.I. WORK FROM THE BEST OF THE BEST.
I MEAN, HE'S NOT BECAUSE, Y'KNOW, THE TRACKER, BUT YEAH, OKAY, GOT IT! MOVE FASTER.
JESSICA JONES IS A LEGEND. I NEED TO TAKE IT DOWN, LIKE, A BUNCH OF NOTCHES.

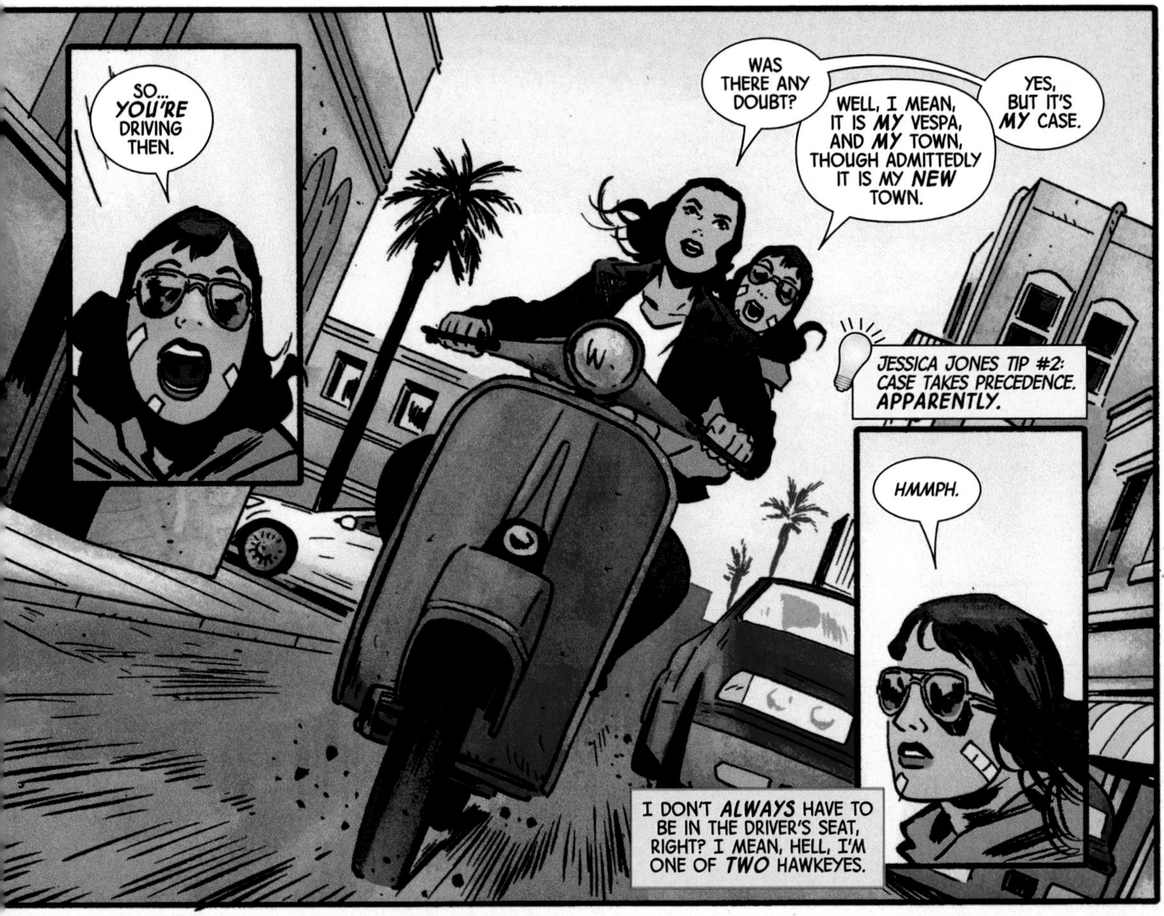
SO... YOU'RE DRIVING THEN.
WAS THERE ANY DOUBT?
WELL, I MEAN, IT IS MY VESPA, AND MY TOWN, THOUGH ADMITTEDLY IT IS MY NEW TOWN.
YES, BUT IT'S MY CASE.
JESSICA JONES TIP #2: CASE TAKES PRECEDENCE. APPARENTLY.
HMMPH.
I DON'T ALWAYS HAVE TO BE IN THE DRIVER'S SEAT, RIGHT? I MEAN, HELL, I'M ONE OF TWO HAWKEYES.

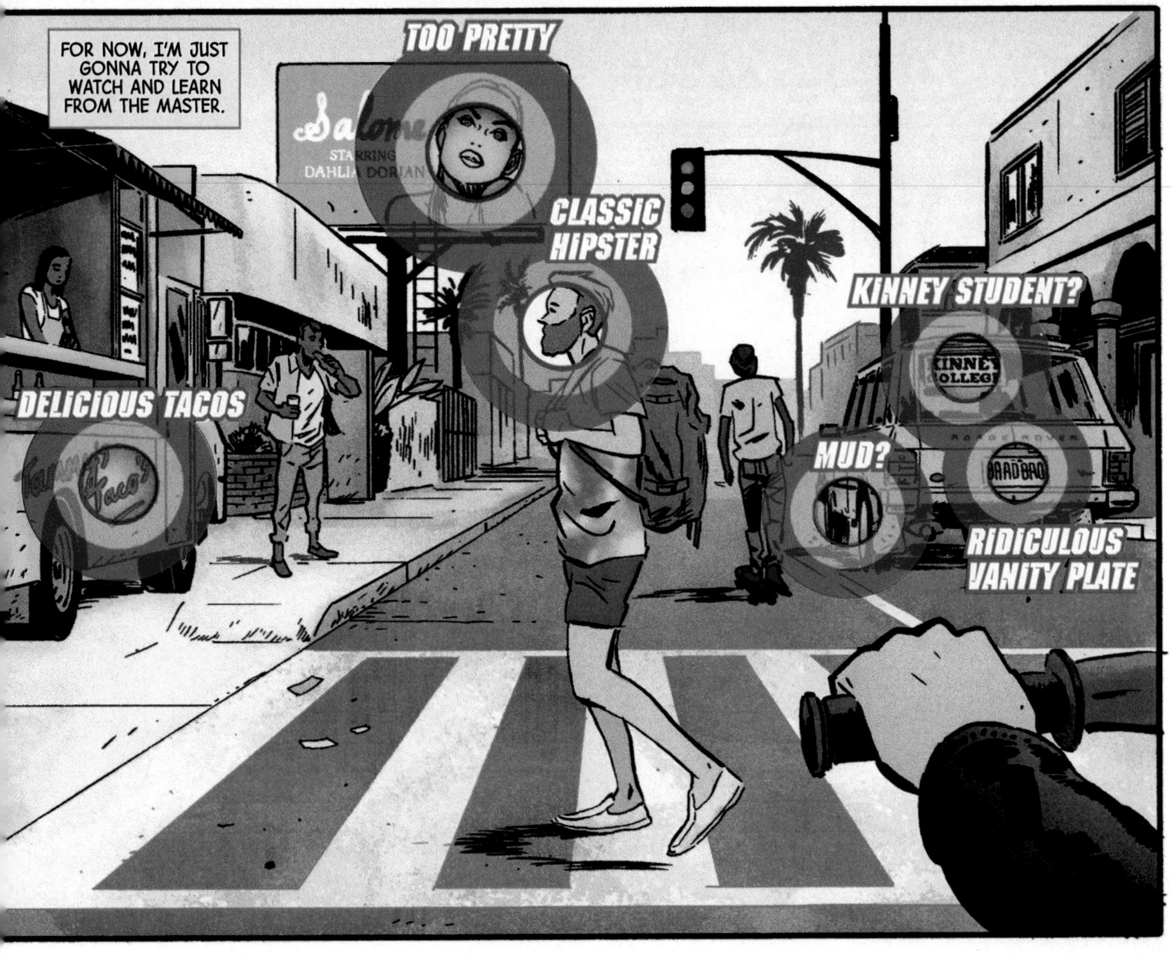
FOR NOW, I'M JUST GONNA TRY TO WATCH AND LEARN FROM THE MASTER.
TOO PRETTY
STARRING DAHLIA DORIAN
CLASSIC HIPSTER
KINNEY STUDENT?
DELICIOUS TACOS
MUD?
RIDICULOUS VANITY PLATE

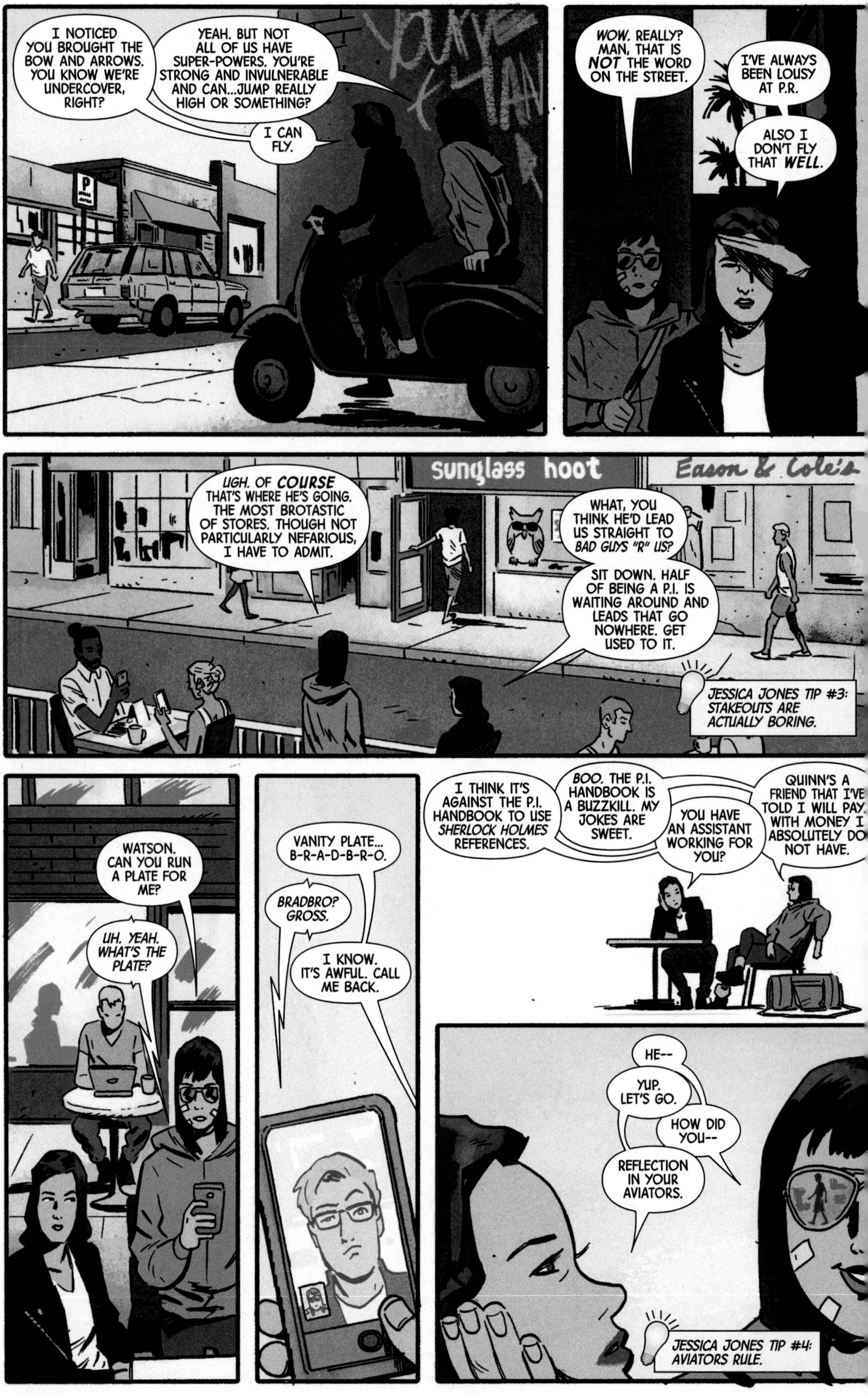
I NOTICED YOU BROUGHT THE BOW AND ARROWS. YOU KNOW WE'RE UNDERCOVER, RIGHT?
YEAH. BUT NOT ALL OF US HAVE SUPER-POWERS. YOU'RE STRONG AND INVULNERABLE AND CAN...JUMP REALLY HIGH OR SOMETHING?
I CAN FLY.
WOW. REALLY? MAN, THAT IS NOT THE WORD ON THE STREET.
I'VE ALWAYS BEEN LOUSY AT P.R.
ALSO I DON'T FLY THAT WELL.
sunglass hoot
Eason & Cole's
UGH. OF COURSE THAT'S WHERE HE'S GOING. THE MOST BROTASTIC OF STORES. THOUGH NOT PARTICULARLY NEFARIOUS, I HAVE TO ADMIT.
WHAT, YOU THINK HE'D LEAD US STRAIGHT TO BAD GUYS "R" US?
SIT DOWN. HALF OF BEING A P.I. IS WAITING AROUND AND LEADS THAT GO NOWHERE. GET USED TO IT.
JESSICA JONES TIP #3: STAKEOUTS ARE ACTUALLY BORING.
WATSON. CAN YOU RUN A PLATE FOR ME?
UH. YEAH. WHAT'S THE PLATE?
VANITY PLATE... B-R-A-D-B-R-O.
BRADBRO? GROSS.
I KNOW. IT'S AWFUL. CALL ME BACK.
I THINK IT'S AGAINST THE P.I. HANDBOOK TO USE SHERLOCK HOLMES REFERENCES.
BOO. THE P.I. HANDBOOK IS A BUZZKILL. MY JOKES ARE SWEET.
YOU HAVE AN ASSISTANT WORKING FOR YOU?
QUINN'S A FRIEND THAT I'VE TOLD I WILL PAY. WITH MONEY I ABSOLUTELY DO NOT HAVE.
HE--
YUP. LET'S GO.
HOW DID YOU--
REFLECTION IN YOUR AVIATORS.
JESSICA JONES TIP #4: AVIATORS RULE.

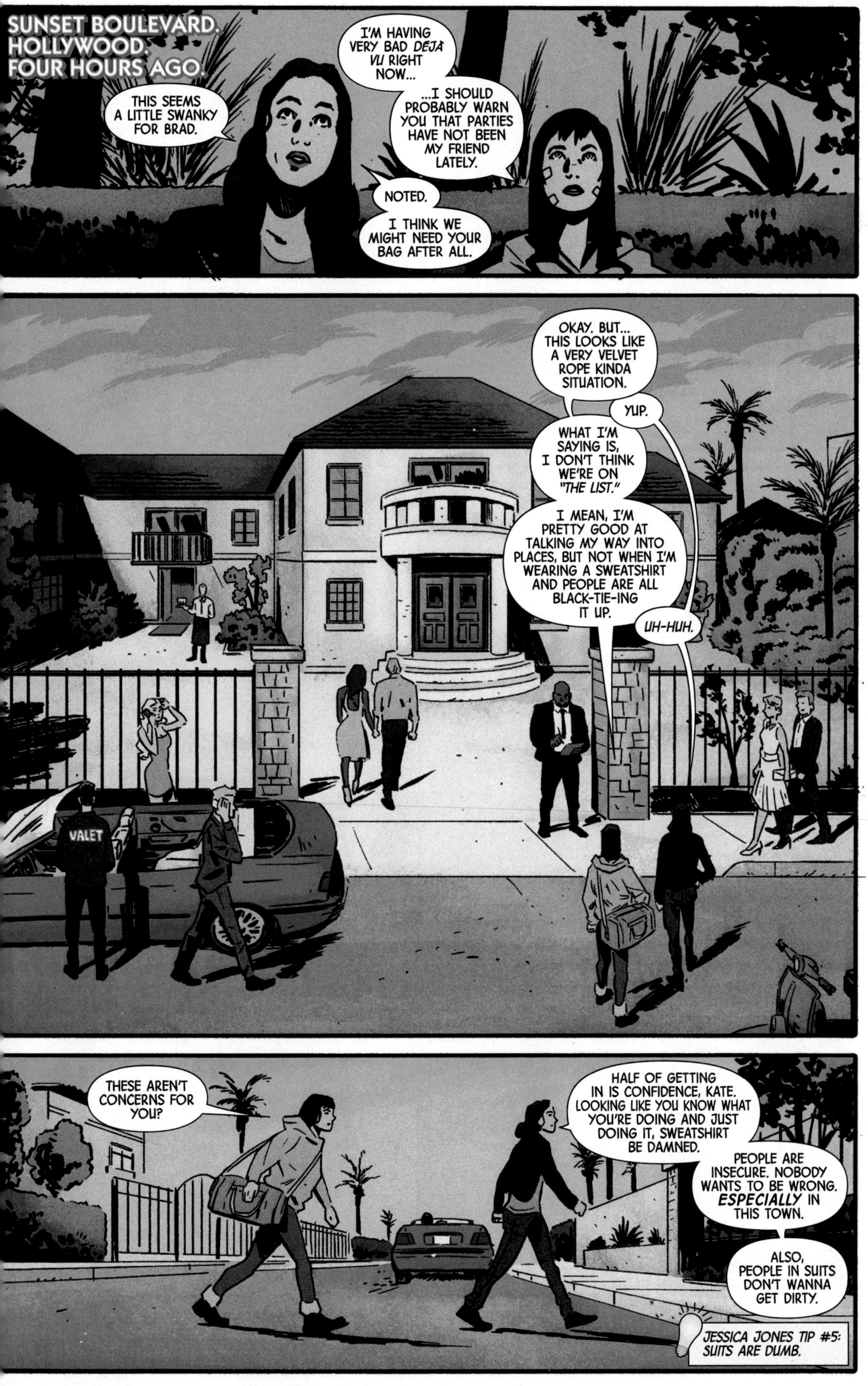
SUNSET BOULEVARD. HOLLYWOOD. FOUR HOURS AGO.
THIS SEEMS A LITTLE SWANKY FOR BRAD.
I'M HAVING VERY BAD DÉJÀ VU RIGHT NOW...
...I SHOULD PROBABLY WARN YOU THAT PARTIES HAVE NOT BEEN MY FRIEND LATELY.
NOTED.
I THINK WE MIGHT NEED YOUR BAG AFTER ALL.
OKAY. BUT... THIS LOOKS LIKE A VERY VELVET ROPE KINDA SITUATION.
YUP.
WHAT I'M SAYING IS, I DON'T THINK WE'RE ON "THE LIST."
I MEAN, I'M PRETTY GOOD AT TALKING MY WAY INTO PLACES, BUT NOT WHEN I'M WEARING A SWEATSHIRT AND PEOPLE ARE ALL BLACK-TIE-ING IT UP.
UH-HUH.
VALET
THESE AREN'T CONCERNS FOR YOU?
HALF OF GETTING IN IS CONFIDENCE, KATE. LOOKING LIKE YOU KNOW WHAT YOU'RE DOING AND JUST DOING IT, SWEATSHIRT BE DAMNED.
PEOPLE ARE INSECURE. NOBODY WANTS TO BE WRONG. ESPECIALLY IN THIS TOWN.
ALSO, PEOPLE IN SUITS DON'T WANNA GET DIRTY.
JESSICA JONES TIP #5: SUITS ARE DUMB.

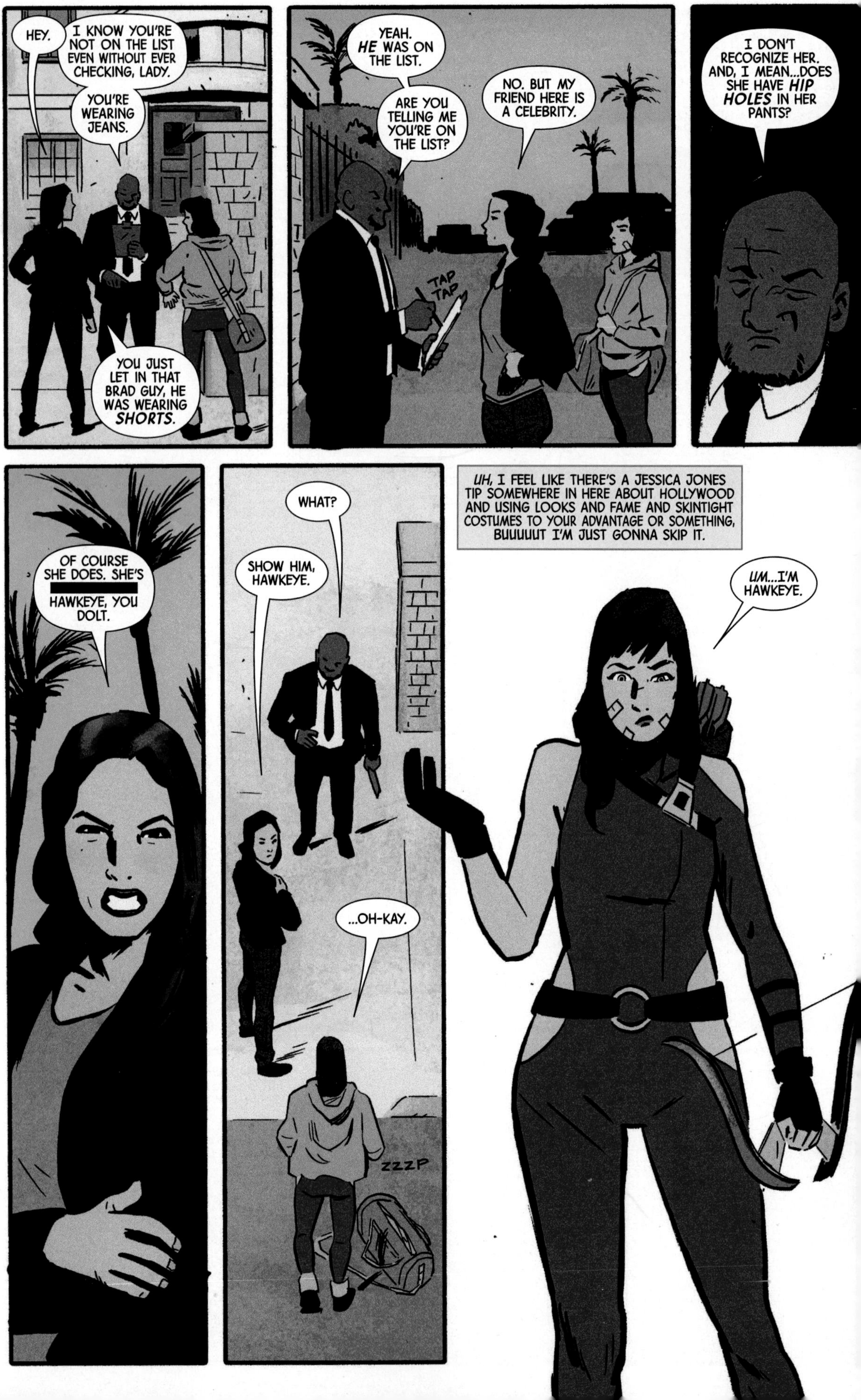
HEY.
I KNOW YOU'RE NOT ON THE LIST EVEN WITHOUT EVER CHECKING, LADY.
YOU'RE WEARING JEANS.
YOU JUST LET IN THAT BRAD GUY, HE WAS WEARING SHORTS.
YEAH. HE WAS ON THE LIST.
ARE YOU TELLING ME YOU'RE ON THE LIST?
NO. BUT MY FRIEND HERE IS A CELEBRITY.
TAP TAP
I DON'T RECOGNIZE HER. AND, I MEAN...DOES SHE HAVE HIP HOLES IN HER PANTS?
OF COURSE SHE DOES. SHE'S [redacted] HAWKEYE, YOU DOLT.
WHAT?
SHOW HIM, HAWKEYE.
...OH-KAY.
ZZZP
UH, I FEEL LIKE THERE'S A JESSICA JONES TIP SOMEWHERE IN HERE ABOUT HOLLYWOOD AND USING LOOKS AND FAME AND SKINTIGHT COSTUMES TO YOUR ADVANTAGE OR SOMETHING, BUUUUUT I'M JUST GONNA SKIP IT.
UM...I'M HAWKEYE.

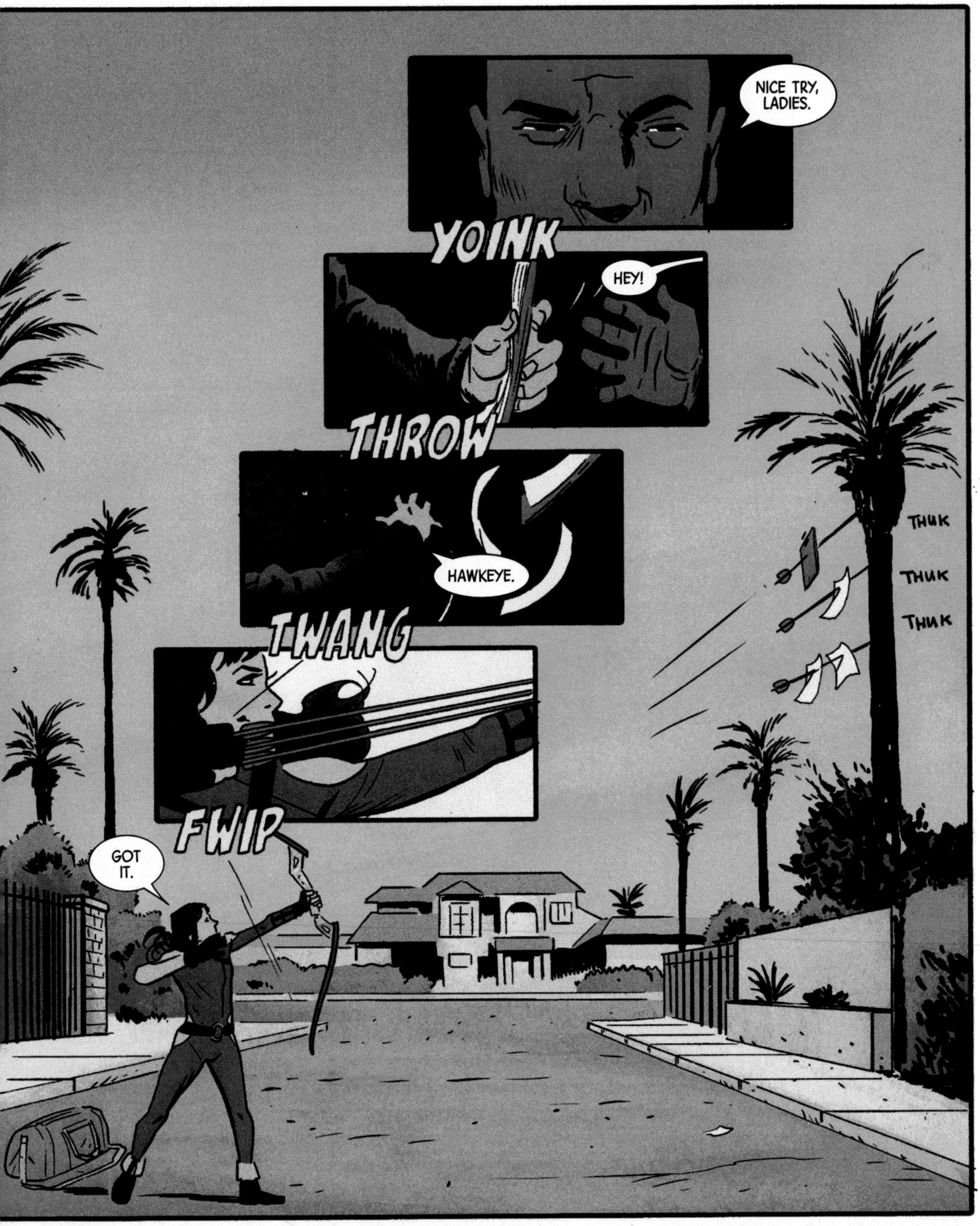
NICE TRY, LADIES.
YOINK
HEY!
THROW
HAWKEYE.
TWANG
FWIP
THUK
THUK
THUK
GOT IT.

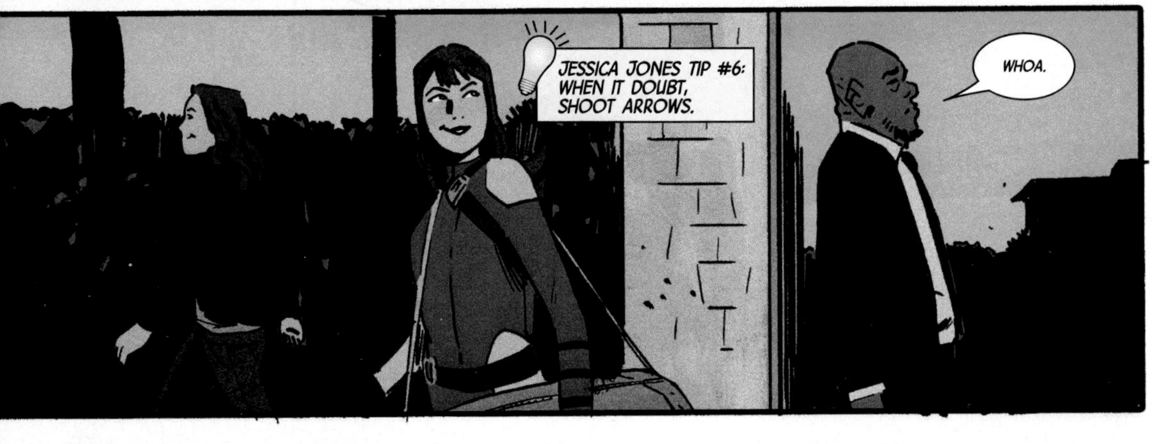
JESSICA JONES TIP #6: WHEN IT DOUBT, SHOOT ARROWS.
WHOA.

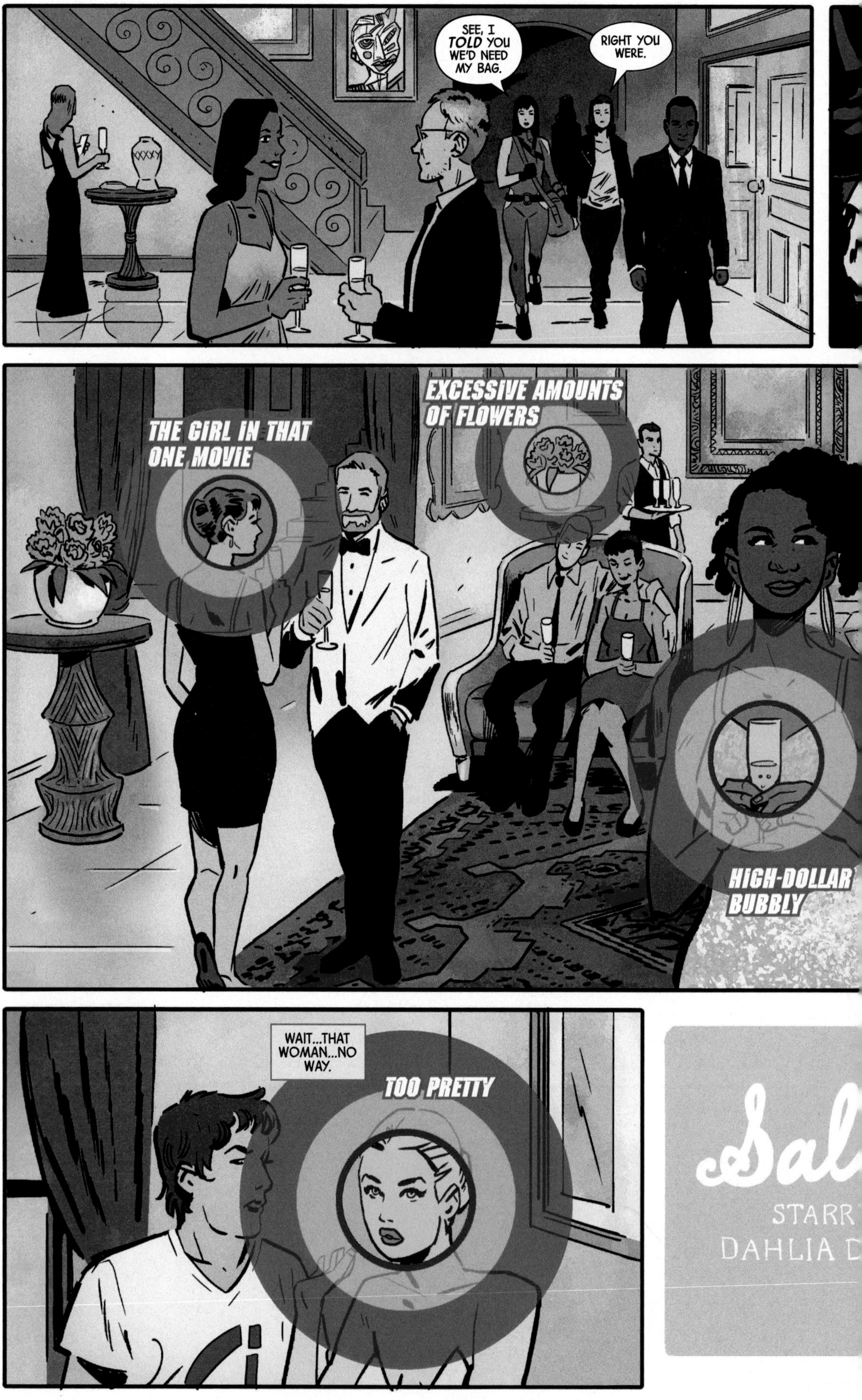
SEE, I TOLD YOU WE'D NEED MY BAG.
RIGHT YOU WERE.
THE GIRL IN THAT ONE MOVIE
EXCESSIVE AMOUNTS OF FLOWERS
HIGH-DOLLAR BUBBLY
WAIT...THAT WOMAN...NO WAY.
TOO PRETTY

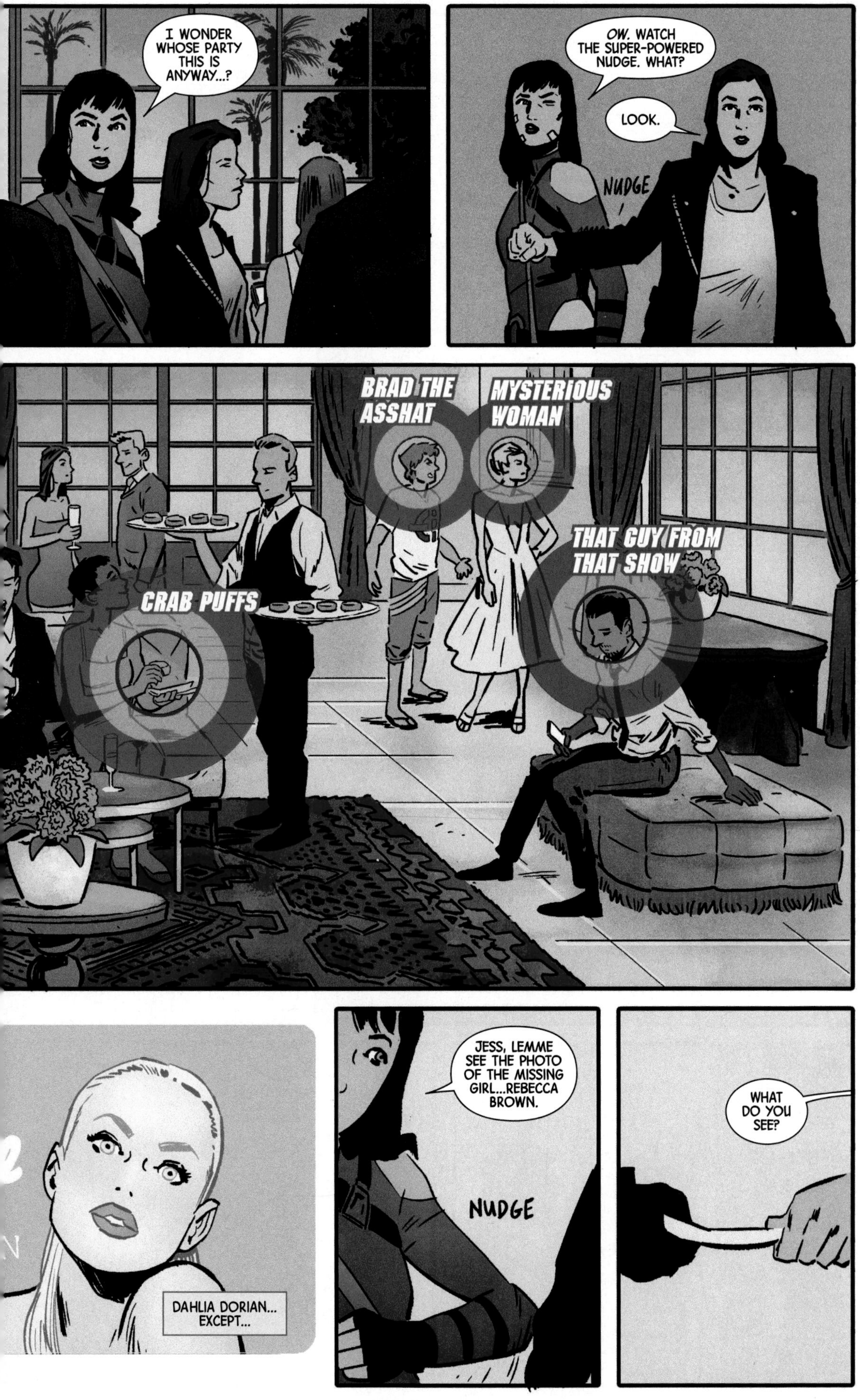
I WONDER WHOSE PARTY THIS IS ANYWAY...?
OW. WATCH THE SUPER-POWERED NUDGE. WHAT?
LOOK.
NUDGE
BRAD THE ASSHAT
MYSTERIOUS WOMAN
THAT GUY FROM THAT SHOW
CRAB PUFFS
DAHLIA DORIAN... EXCEPT...
JESS, LEMME SEE THE PHOTO OF THE MISSING GIRL...REBECCA BROWN.
NUDGE
WHAT DO YOU SEE?

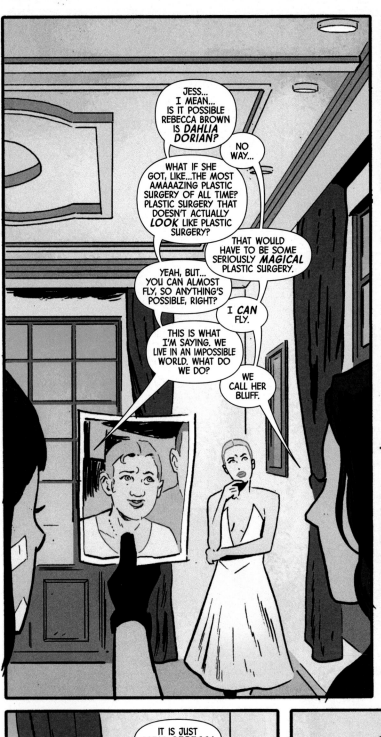

JESS... I MEAN... IS IT POSSIBLE REBECCA BROWN IS *DAHLIA DORIAN?*

NO WAY...

WHAT IF SHE GOT, LIKE...THE MOST AMAAAZING PLASTIC SURGERY OF ALL TIME? PLASTIC SURGERY THAT DOESN'T ACTUALLY *LOOK* LIKE PLASTIC SURGERY?

THAT WOULD HAVE TO BE SOME SERIOUSLY *MAGICAL* PLASTIC SURGERY.

YEAH, BUT... YOU CAN ALMOST FLY, SO ANYTHING'S POSSIBLE, RIGHT?

I *CAN* FLY.

THIS IS WHAT I'M SAYING. WE LIVE IN AN IMPOSSIBLE WORLD. WHAT DO WE DO?

WE CALL HER BLUFF.

OHMIGOD. SO *CUTE!* YOU'RE DRESSED AS *HAWKEYE!* HE'S MY FAVORITE SUPER HERO! SO GREAT!

YEAH. GREAT.

IT IS JUST GREAT, *REBECCA BROWN.*

WE'LL CALL THAT FACE A CONFIRMATION.

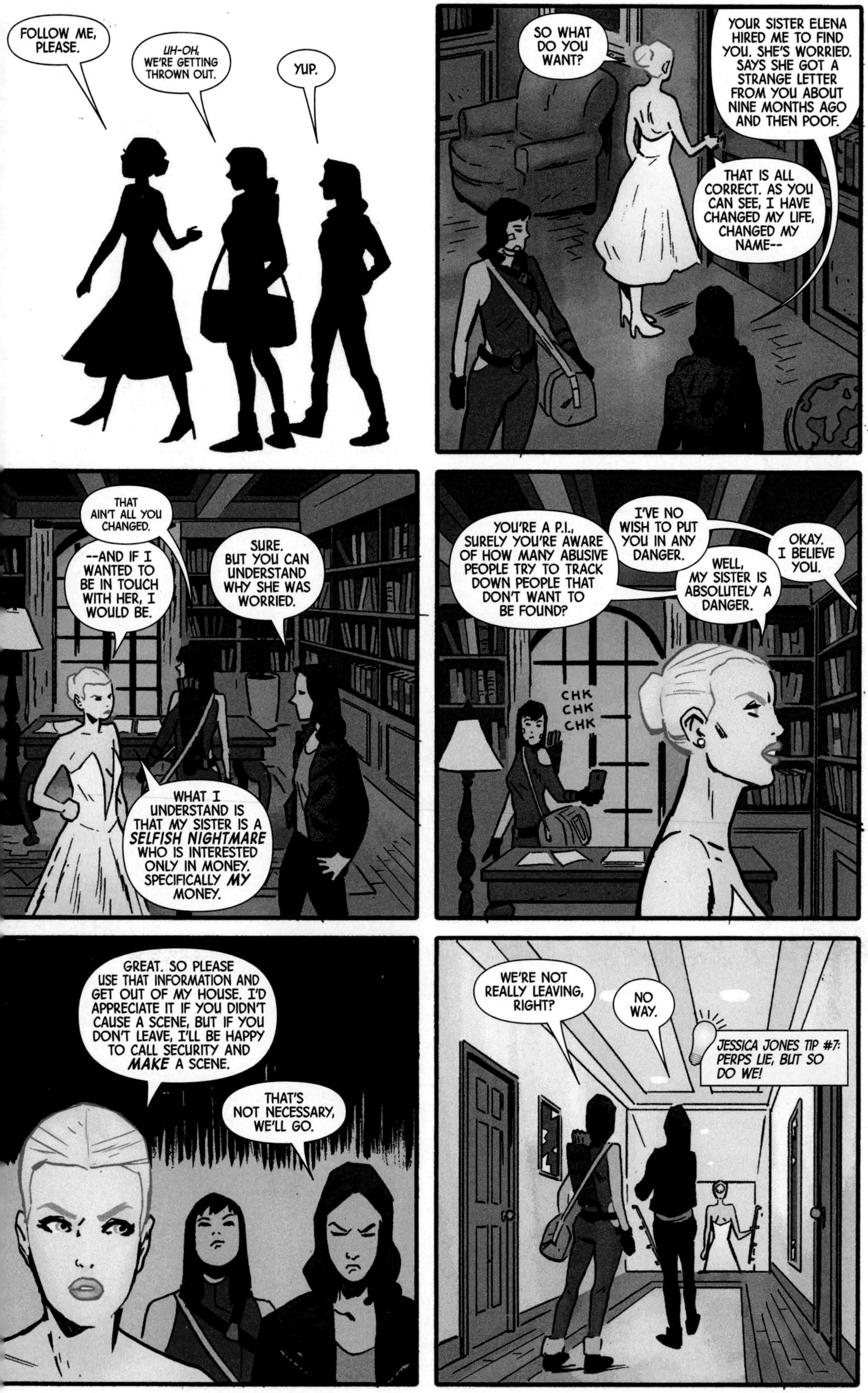
FOLLOW ME, PLEASE.
UH-OH, WE'RE GETTING THROWN OUT.
YUP.
SO WHAT DO YOU WANT?
YOUR SISTER ELENA HIRED ME TO FIND YOU. SHE'S WORRIED. SAYS SHE GOT A STRANGE LETTER FROM YOU ABOUT NINE MONTHS AGO AND THEN POOF.
THAT IS ALL CORRECT. AS YOU CAN SEE, I HAVE CHANGED MY LIFE, CHANGED MY NAME--
THAT AIN'T ALL YOU CHANGED.
--AND IF I WANTED TO BE IN TOUCH WITH HER, I WOULD BE.
SURE. BUT YOU CAN UNDERSTAND WHY SHE WAS WORRIED.
WHAT I UNDERSTAND IS THAT MY SISTER IS A SELFISH NIGHTMARE WHO IS INTERESTED ONLY IN MONEY. SPECIFICALLY MY MONEY.
YOU'RE A P.I., SURELY YOU'RE AWARE OF HOW MANY ABUSIVE PEOPLE TRY TO TRACK DOWN PEOPLE THAT DON'T WANT TO BE FOUND?
I'VE NO WISH TO PUT YOU IN ANY DANGER.
OKAY. I BELIEVE YOU.
WELL, MY SISTER IS ABSOLUTELY A DANGER.
CHK CHK CHK
GREAT. SO PLEASE USE THAT INFORMATION AND GET OUT OF MY HOUSE. I'D APPRECIATE IT IF YOU DIDN'T CAUSE A SCENE, BUT IF YOU DON'T LEAVE, I'LL BE HAPPY TO CALL SECURITY AND MAKE A SCENE.
THAT'S NOT NECESSARY, WE'LL GO.
WE'RE NOT REALLY LEAVING, RIGHT?
NO WAY.
JESSICA JONES TIP #7: PERPS LIE, BUT SO DO WE!

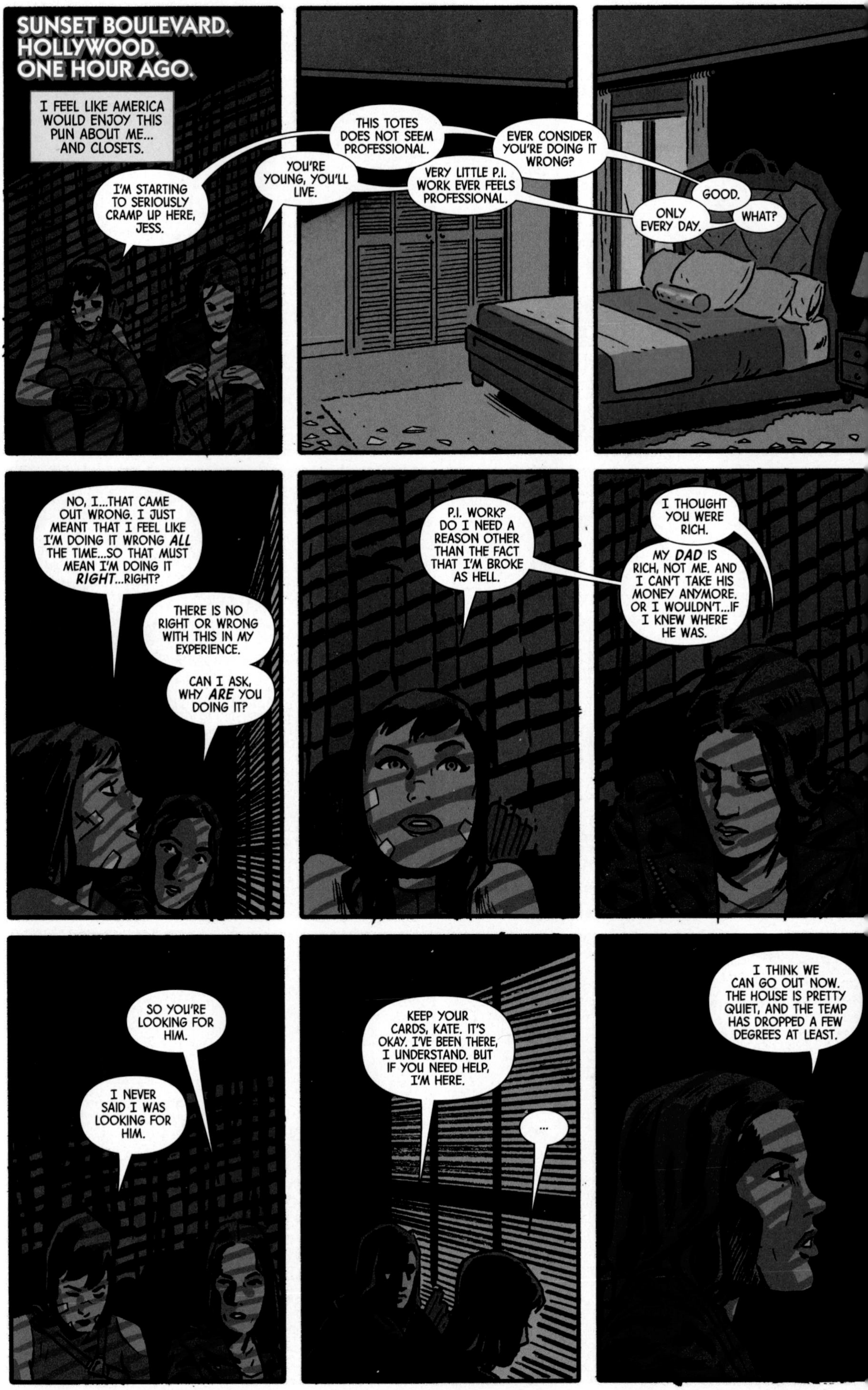
SUNSET BOULEVARD. HOLLYWOOD. ONE HOUR AGO.
I FEEL LIKE AMERICA WOULD ENJOY THIS PUN ABOUT ME... AND CLOSETS.
I'M STARTING TO SERIOUSLY CRAMP UP HERE, JESS.
YOU'RE YOUNG, YOU'LL LIVE.
THIS TOTES DOES NOT SEEM PROFESSIONAL.
VERY LITTLE P.I. WORK EVER FEELS PROFESSIONAL.
EVER CONSIDER YOU'RE DOING IT WRONG?
ONLY EVERY DAY.
GOOD.
WHAT?
NO, I...THAT CAME OUT WRONG. I JUST MEANT THAT I FEEL LIKE I'M DOING IT WRONG ALL THE TIME...SO THAT MUST MEAN I'M DOING IT RIGHT...RIGHT?
THERE IS NO RIGHT OR WRONG WITH THIS IN MY EXPERIENCE.
CAN I ASK, WHY ARE YOU DOING IT?
P.I. WORK? DO I NEED A REASON OTHER THAN THE FACT THAT I'M BROKE AS HELL.
I THOUGHT YOU WERE RICH.
MY DAD IS RICH, NOT ME. AND I CAN'T TAKE HIS MONEY ANYMORE. OR I WOULDN'T...IF I KNEW WHERE HE WAS.
SO YOU'RE LOOKING FOR HIM.
I NEVER SAID I WAS LOOKING FOR HIM.
KEEP YOUR CARDS, KATE. IT'S OKAY. I'VE BEEN THERE, I UNDERSTAND. BUT IF YOU NEED HELP, I'M HERE.
...
I THINK WE CAN GO OUT NOW. THE HOUSE IS PRETTY QUIET, AND THE TEMP HAS DROPPED A FEW DEGREES AT LEAST.

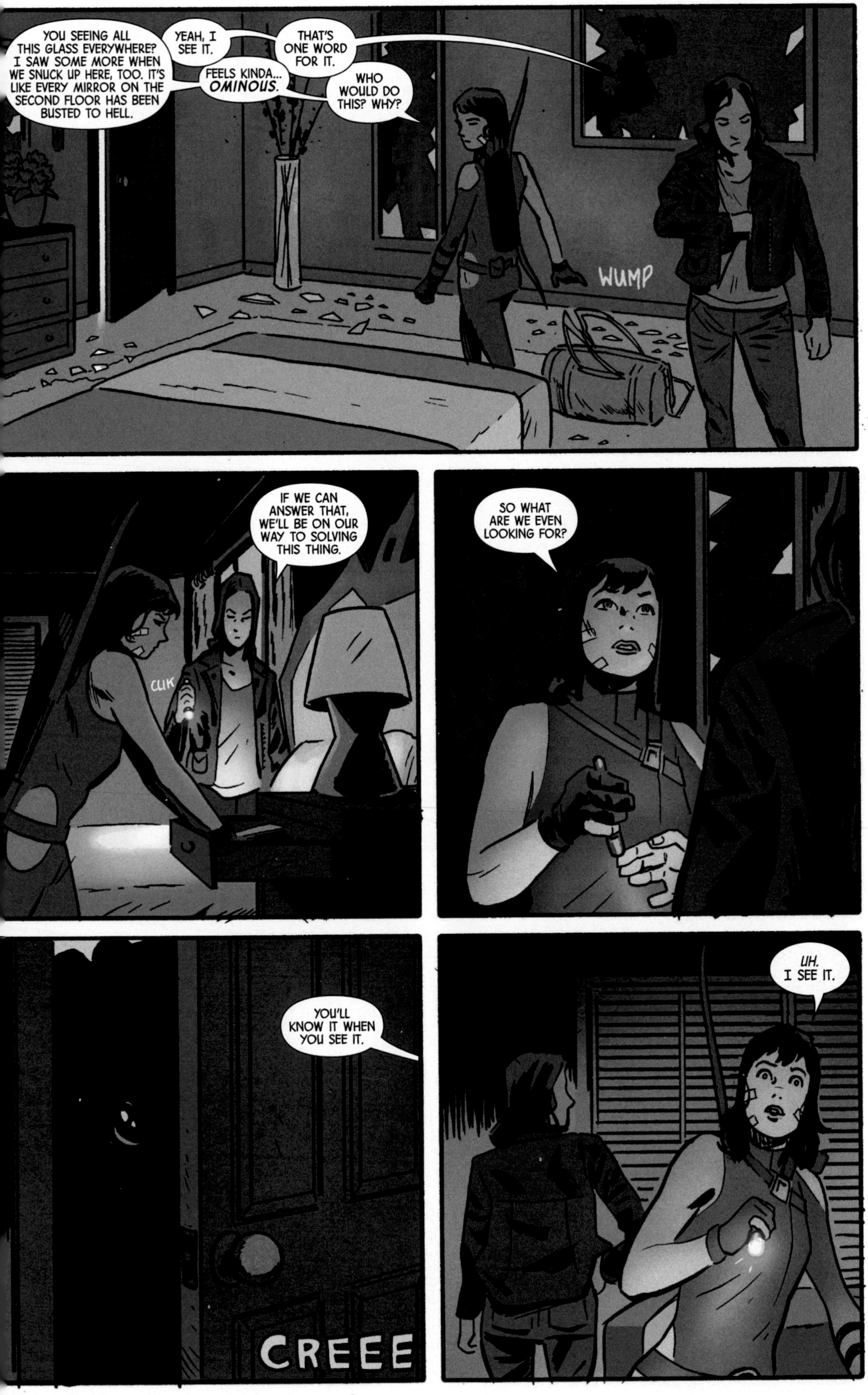
YOU SEEING ALL THIS GLASS EVERYWHERE? I SAW SOME MORE WHEN WE SNUCK UP HERE, TOO. IT'S LIKE EVERY MIRROR ON THE SECOND FLOOR HAS BEEN BUSTED TO HELL.
YEAH, I SEE IT.
FEELS KINDA... *OMINOUS.*
THAT'S ONE WORD FOR IT.
WHO WOULD DO THIS? WHY?
WUMP
IF WE CAN ANSWER THAT, WE'LL BE ON OUR WAY TO SOLVING THIS THING.
CLIK
SO WHAT ARE WE EVEN LOOKING FOR?
YOU'LL KNOW IT WHEN YOU SEE IT.
CREEE
UH. I SEE IT.

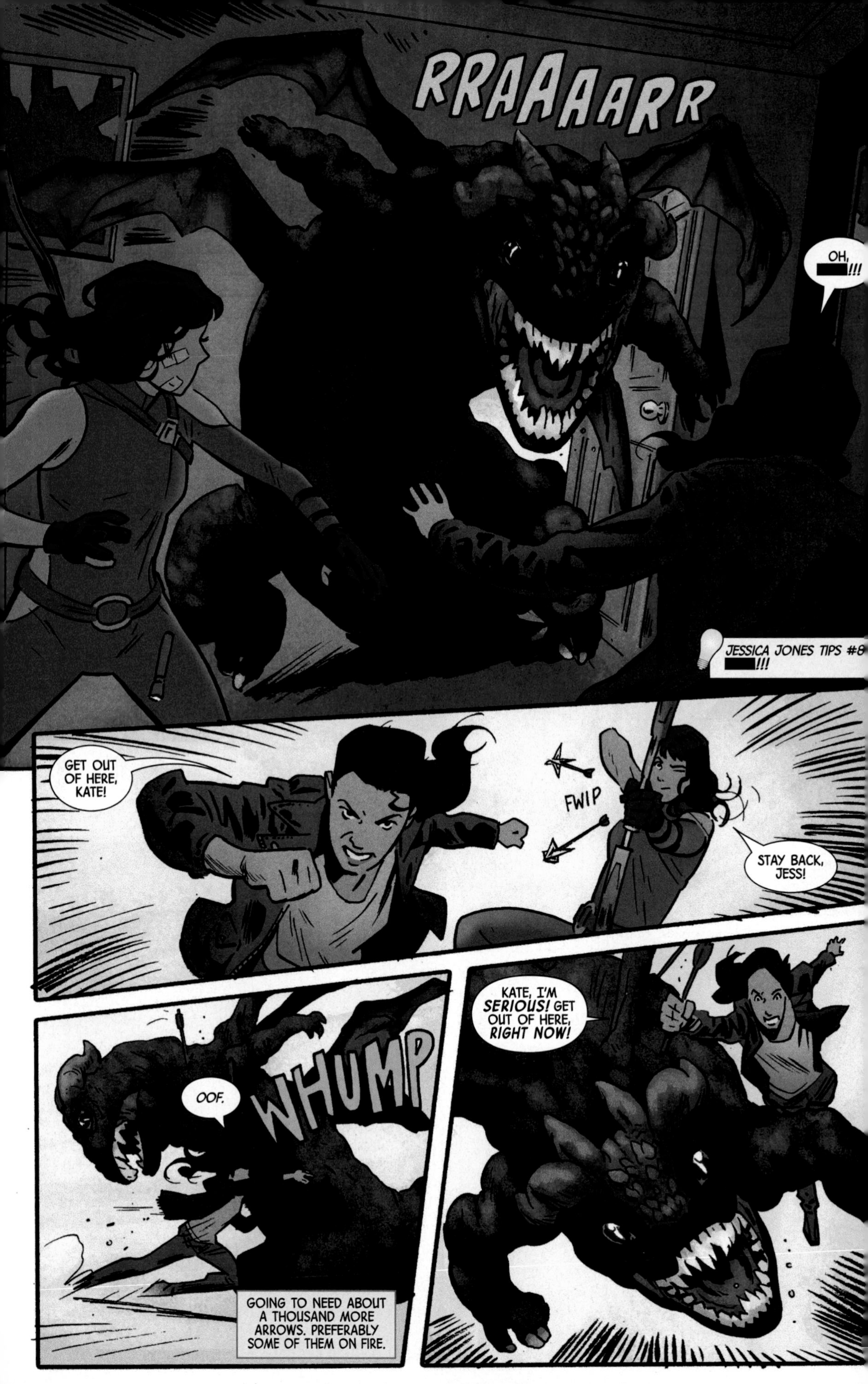
RRAAAARR
OH, [redacted]!!!
JESSICA JONES TIPS #8
[redacted]!!!
GET OUT OF HERE, KATE!
FWIP
STAY BACK, JESS!
OOF.
WHUMP
GOING TO NEED ABOUT A THOUSAND MORE ARROWS. PREFERABLY SOME OF THEM ON FIRE.
KATE, I'M SERIOUS! GET OUT OF HERE, RIGHT NOW!

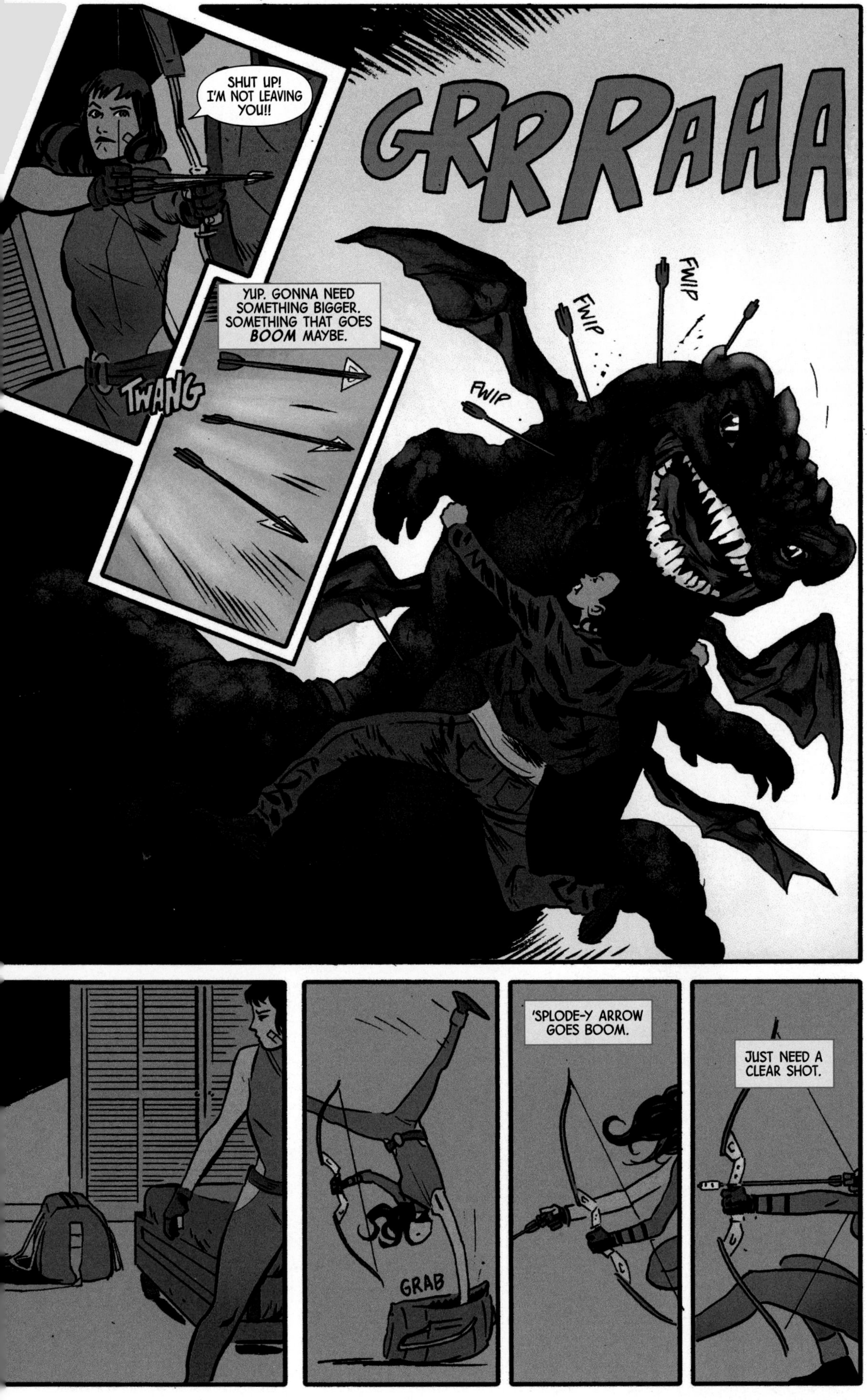
SHUT UP! I'M NOT LEAVING YOU!!
GRRRAAA
YUP. GONNA NEED SOMETHING BIGGER. SOMETHING THAT GOES BOOM MAYBE.
TWANG
FWIP
FWIP
FWIP
GRAB
'SPLODE-Y ARROW GOES BOOM.
JUST NEED A CLEAR SHOT.

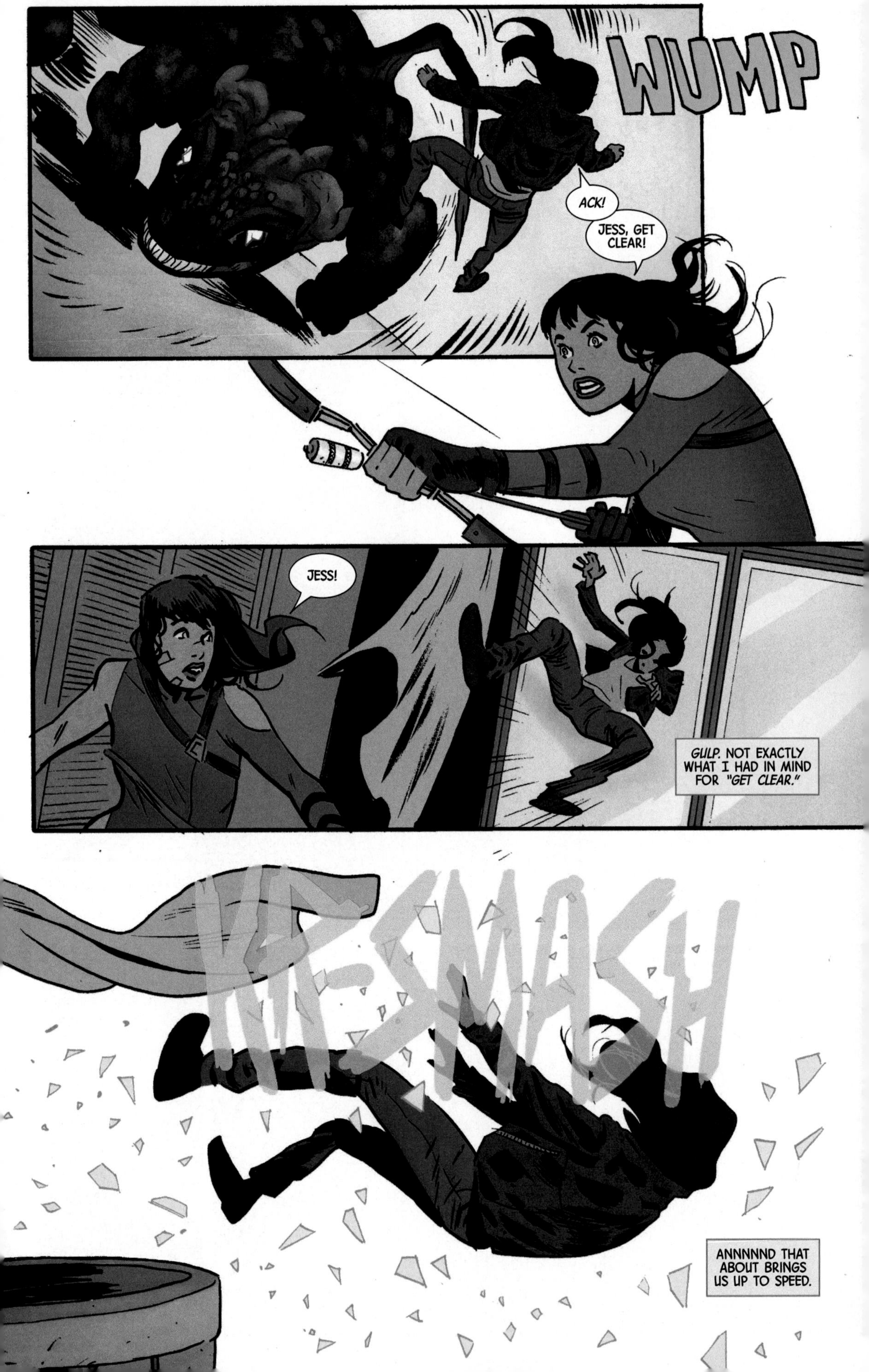
WUMP
ACK!
JESS, GET CLEAR!
JESS!
GULP. NOT EXACTLY WHAT I HAD IN MIND FOR "GET CLEAR."
KR-SMASH
ANNNNND THAT ABOUT BRINGS US UP TO SPEED.

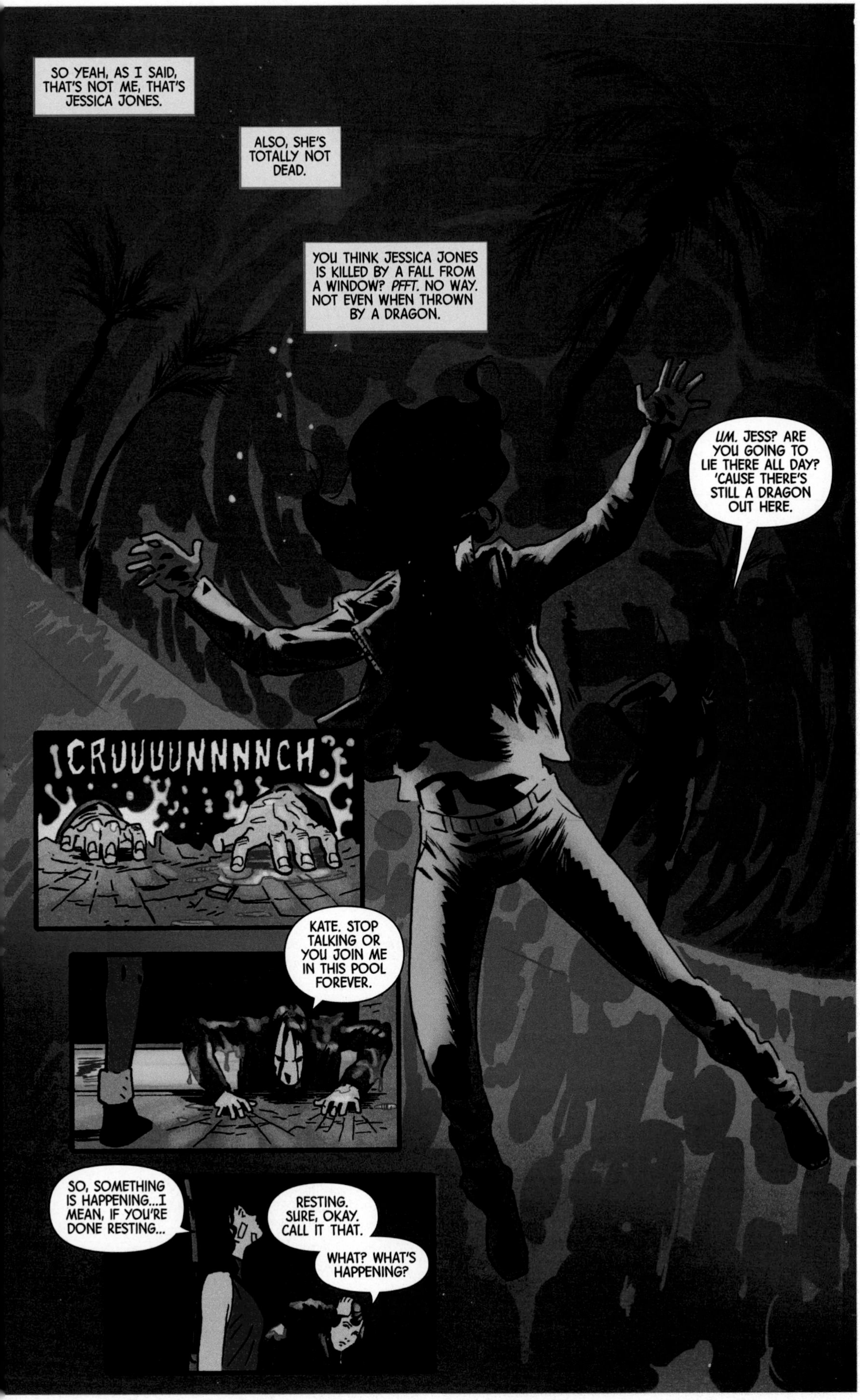
SO YEAH, AS I SAID, THAT'S NOT ME, THAT'S JESSICA JONES.
ALSO, SHE'S TOTALLY NOT DEAD.
YOU THINK JESSICA JONES IS KILLED BY A FALL FROM A WINDOW? PFFT. NO WAY. NOT EVEN WHEN THROWN BY A DRAGON.
UM. JESS? ARE YOU GOING TO LIE THERE ALL DAY? 'CAUSE THERE'S STILL A DRAGON OUT HERE.
CRUUUUNNNNCH
KATE. STOP TALKING OR YOU JOIN ME IN THIS POOL FOREVER.
SO, SOMETHING IS HAPPENING...I MEAN, IF YOU'RE DONE RESTING...
RESTING. SURE, OKAY. CALL IT THAT.
WHAT? WHAT'S HAPPENING?

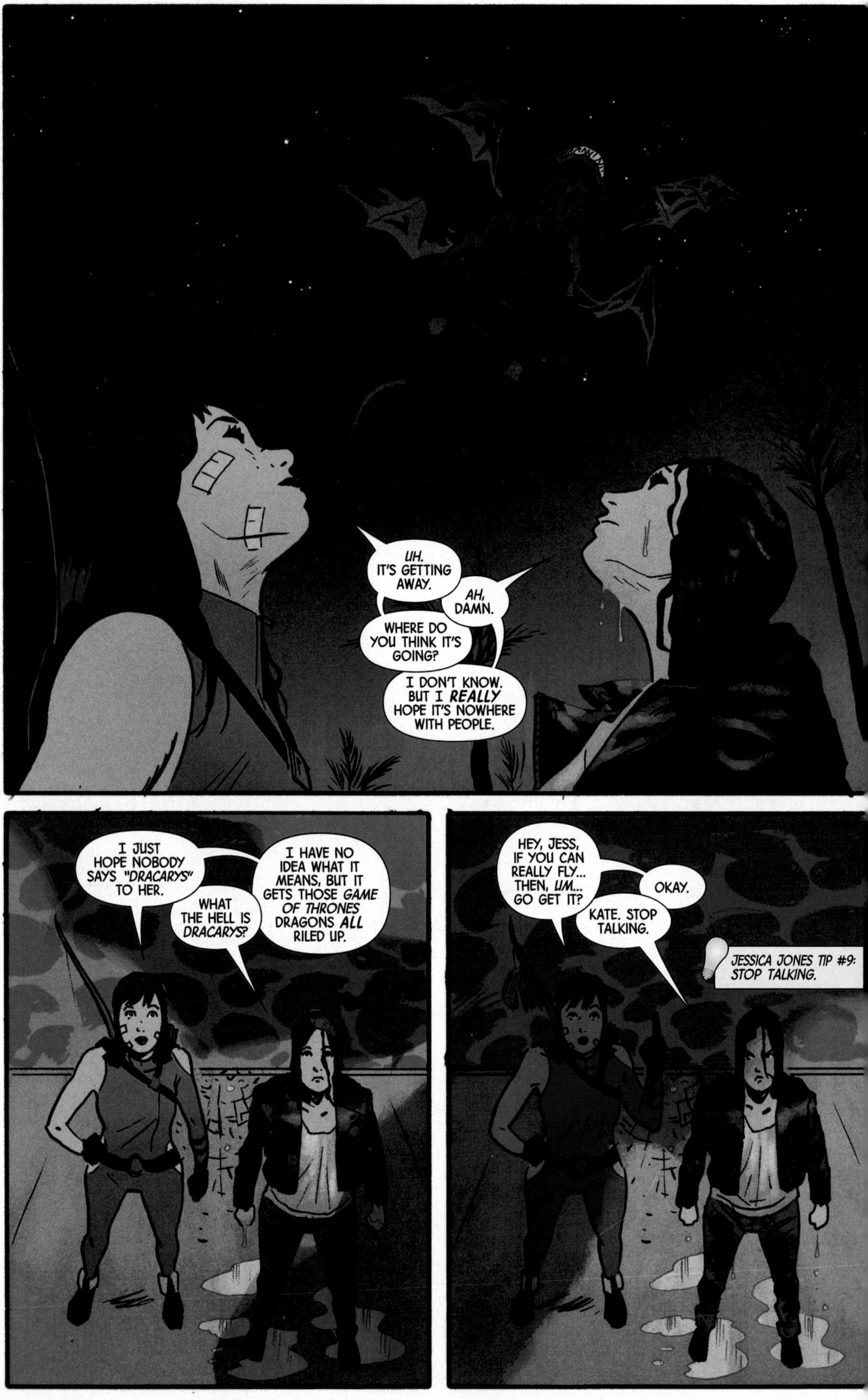

UH. IT'S GETTING AWAY.
AH, DAMN.
WHERE DO YOU THINK IT'S GOING?
I DON'T KNOW. BUT I *REALLY* HOPE IT'S NOWHERE WITH PEOPLE.
I JUST HOPE NOBODY SAYS "*DRACARYS*" TO HER.
WHAT THE HELL IS *DRACARYS*?
I HAVE NO IDEA WHAT IT MEANS, BUT IT GETS THOSE *GAME OF THRONES* DRAGONS *ALL* RILED UP.
HEY, JESS, IF YOU CAN REALLY FLY... THEN, *UM*... GO GET IT?
OKAY.
KATE. STOP TALKING.
JESSICA JONES TIP #9: STOP TALKING.

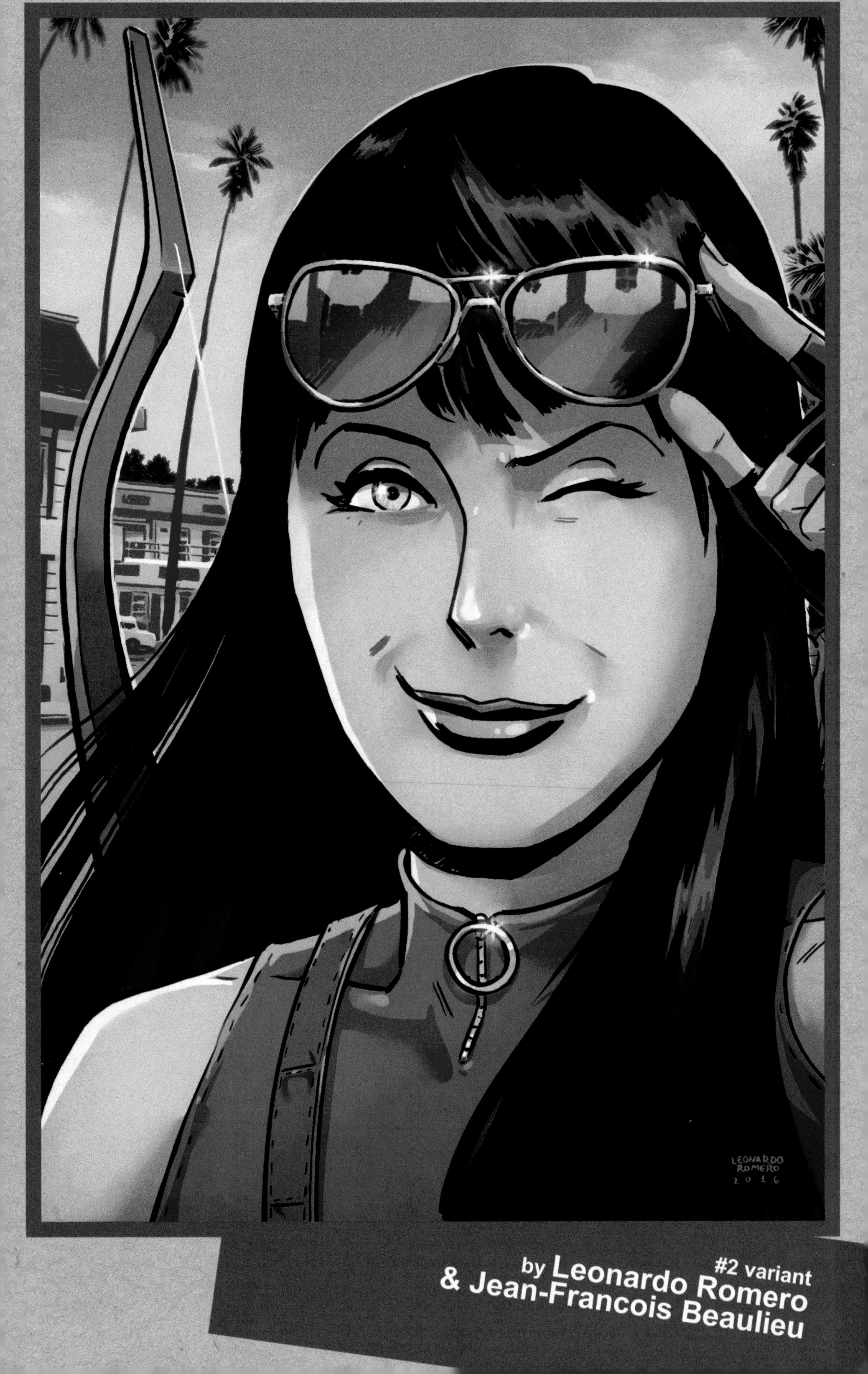
LEONARDO ROMERO 2016

#2 variant
by Leonardo Romero
& Jean-Francois Beaulieu

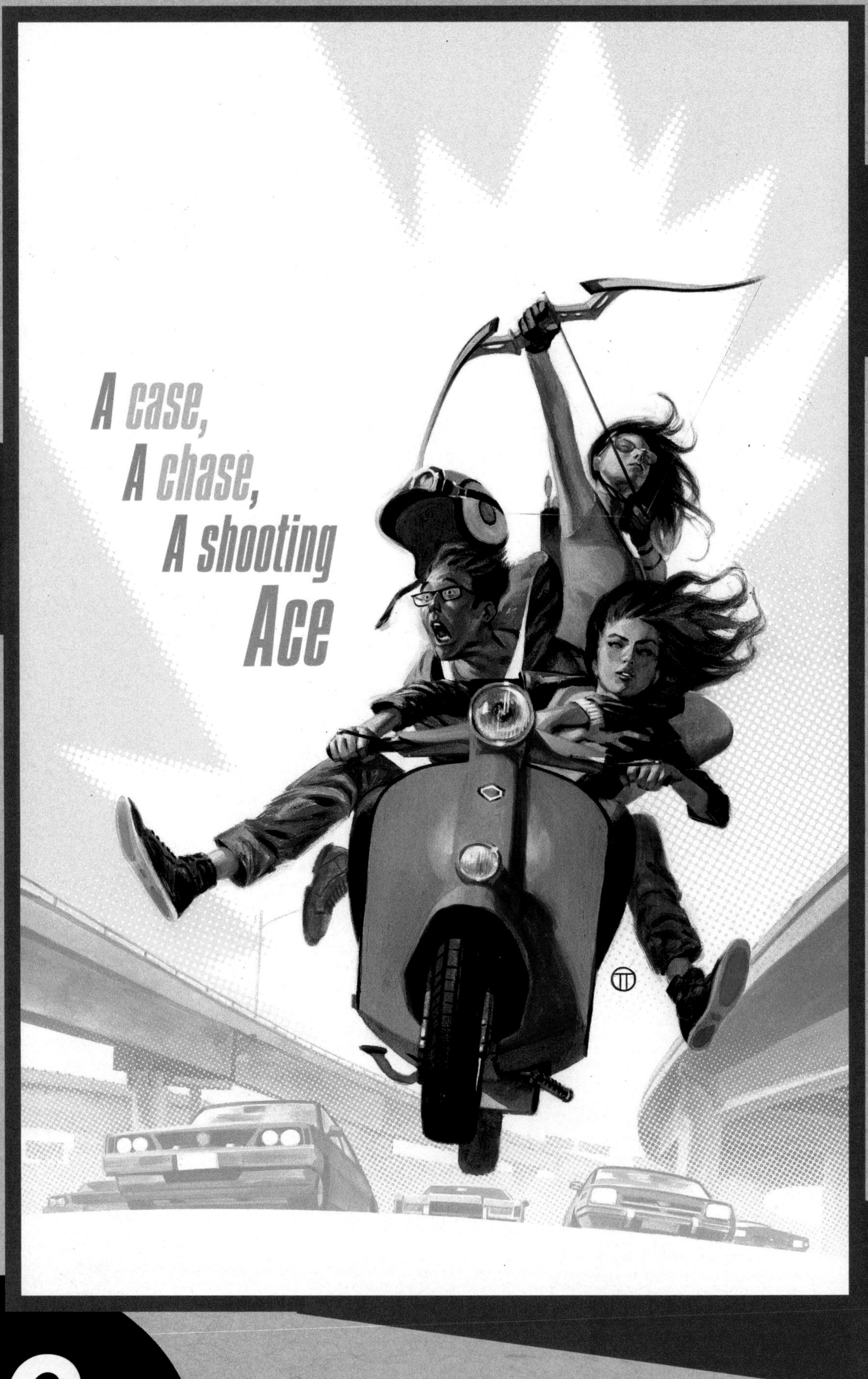
A case,
A chase,
A shooting
Ace

6

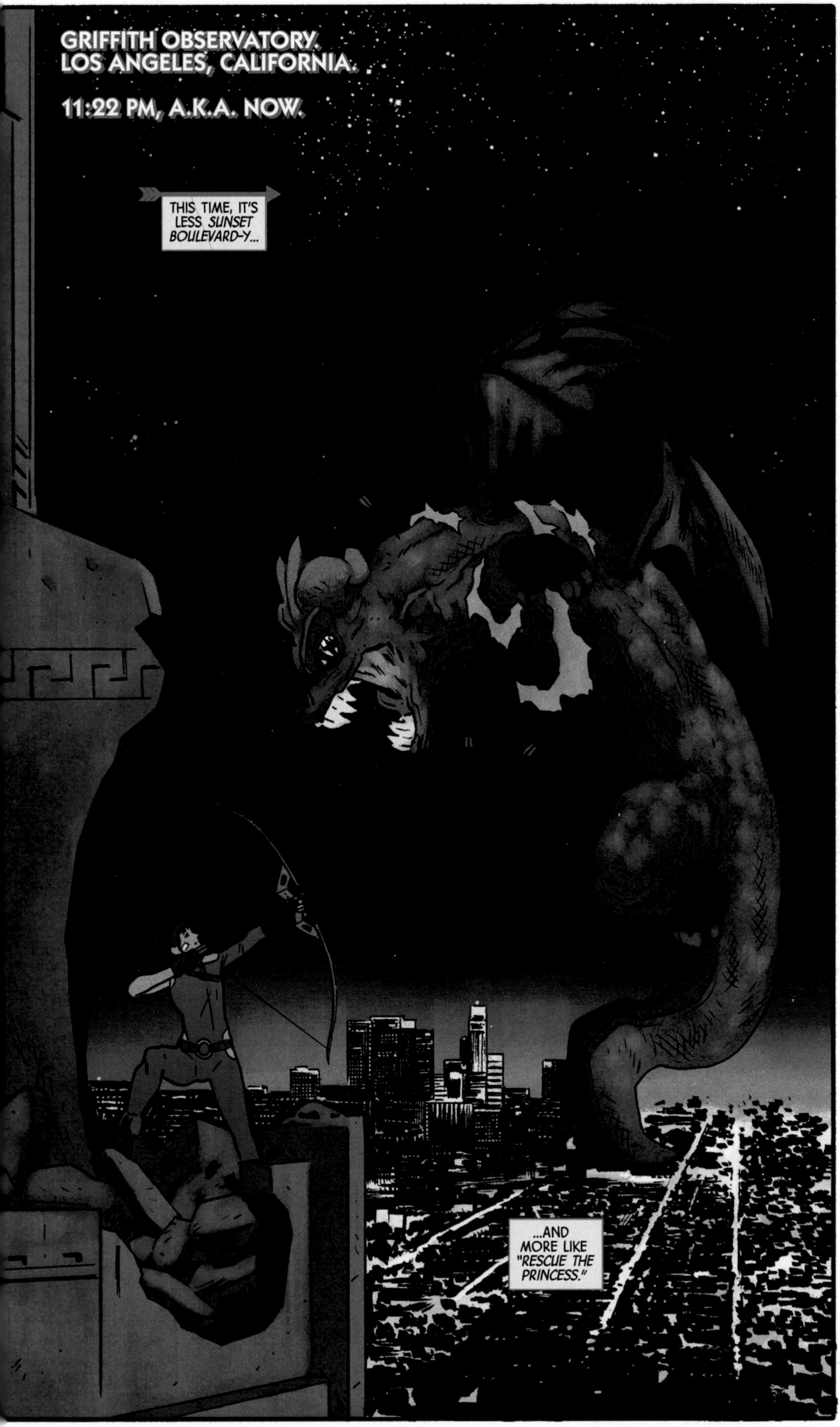
GRIFFITH OBSERVATORY.
LOS ANGELES, CALIFORNIA.
11:22 PM, A.K.A. NOW.
THIS TIME, IT'S LESS *SUNSET BOULEVARD*-Y...
...AND MORE LIKE *"RESCUE THE PRINCESS."*

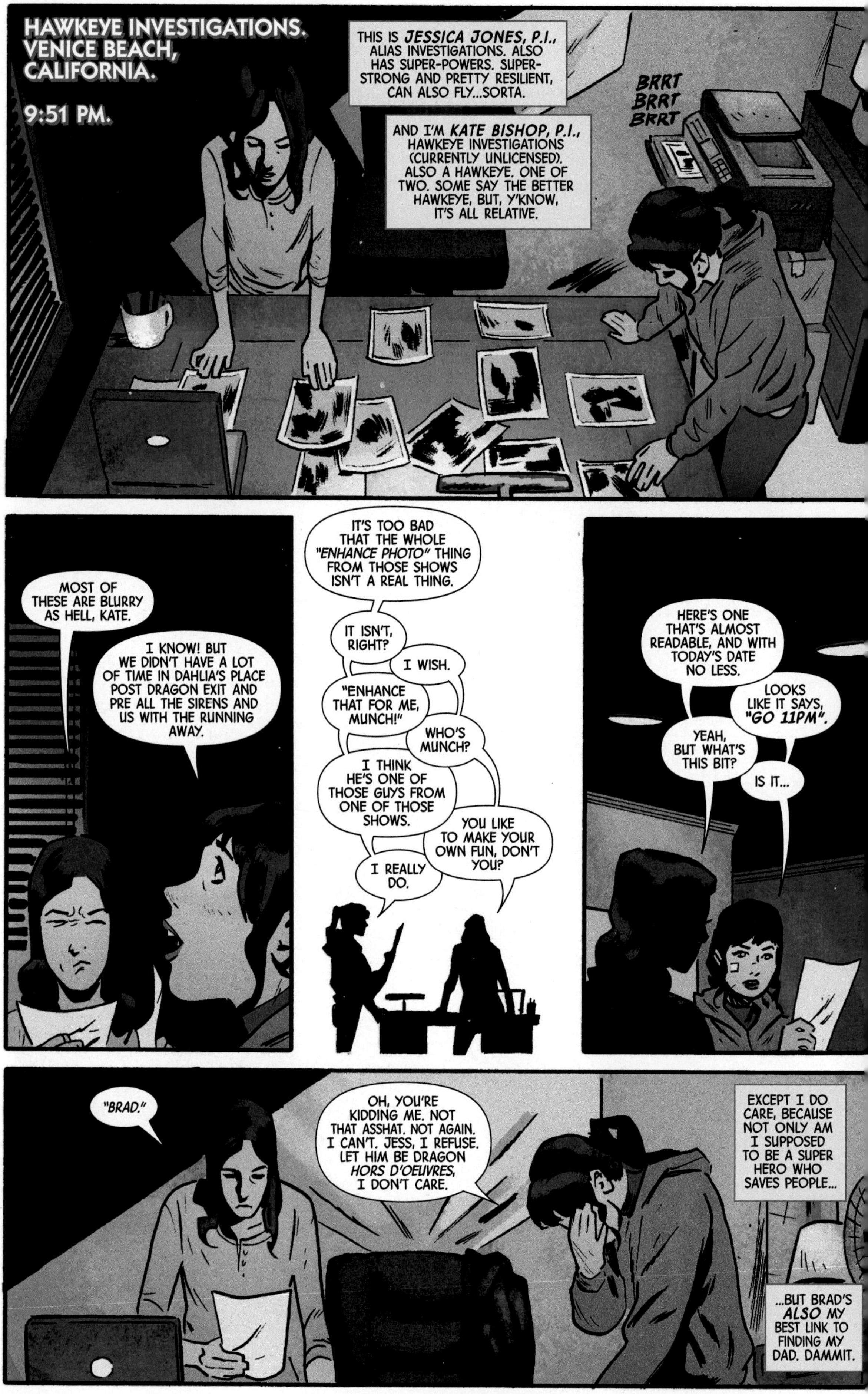
HAWKEYE INVESTIGATIONS. VENICE BEACH, CALIFORNIA.
9:51 PM.
THIS IS JESSICA JONES, P.I., ALIAS INVESTIGATIONS. ALSO HAS SUPER-POWERS. SUPER-STRONG AND PRETTY RESILIENT, CAN ALSO FLY...SORTA.
AND I'M KATE BISHOP, P.I., HAWKEYE INVESTIGATIONS (CURRENTLY UNLICENSED). ALSO A HAWKEYE. ONE OF TWO. SOME SAY THE BETTER HAWKEYE, BUT, Y'KNOW, IT'S ALL RELATIVE.
BRRT BRRT BRRT
MOST OF THESE ARE BLURRY AS HELL, KATE.
I KNOW! BUT WE DIDN'T HAVE A LOT OF TIME IN DAHLIA'S PLACE POST DRAGON EXIT AND PRE ALL THE SIRENS AND US WITH THE RUNNING AWAY.
IT'S TOO BAD THAT THE WHOLE "ENHANCE PHOTO" THING FROM THOSE SHOWS ISN'T A REAL THING.
IT ISN'T, RIGHT?
I WISH.
"ENHANCE THAT FOR ME, MUNCH!"
WHO'S MUNCH?
I THINK HE'S ONE OF THOSE GUYS FROM ONE OF THOSE SHOWS.
YOU LIKE TO MAKE YOUR OWN FUN, DON'T YOU?
I REALLY DO.
HERE'S ONE THAT'S ALMOST READABLE, AND WITH TODAY'S DATE NO LESS.
LOOKS LIKE IT SAYS, "GO 11PM".
YEAH, BUT WHAT'S THIS BIT?
IS IT...
"BRAD."
OH, YOU'RE KIDDING ME. NOT THAT ASSHAT. NOT AGAIN. I CAN'T. JESS, I REFUSE. LET HIM BE DRAGON HORS D'OEUVRES, I DON'T CARE.
EXCEPT I DO CARE, BECAUSE NOT ONLY AM I SUPPOSED TO BE A SUPER HERO WHO SAVES PEOPLE...
...BUT BRAD'S ALSO MY BEST LINK TO FINDING MY DAD. DAMMIT.

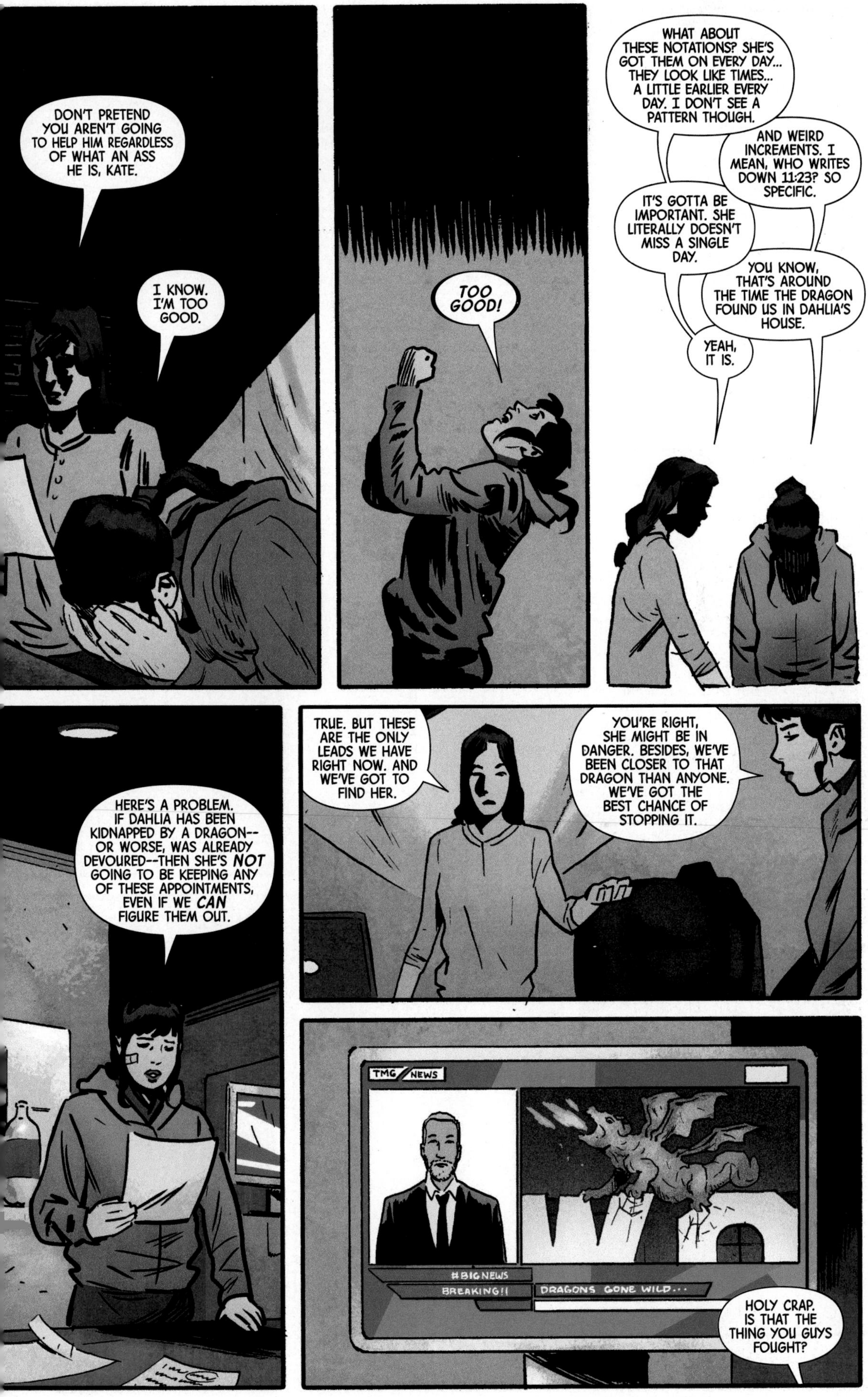
DON'T PRETEND YOU AREN'T GOING TO HELP HIM REGARDLESS OF WHAT AN ASS HE IS, KATE.
I KNOW. I'M TOO GOOD.
TOO GOOD!
WHAT ABOUT THESE NOTATIONS? SHE'S GOT THEM ON EVERY DAY... THEY LOOK LIKE TIMES... A LITTLE EARLIER EVERY DAY. I DON'T SEE A PATTERN THOUGH.
AND WEIRD INCREMENTS. I MEAN, WHO WRITES DOWN 11:23? SO SPECIFIC.
IT'S GOTTA BE IMPORTANT. SHE LITERALLY DOESN'T MISS A SINGLE DAY.
YOU KNOW, THAT'S AROUND THE TIME THE DRAGON FOUND US IN DAHLIA'S HOUSE.
YEAH, IT IS.
HERE'S A PROBLEM. IF DAHLIA HAS BEEN KIDNAPPED BY A DRAGON--OR WORSE, WAS ALREADY DEVOURED--THEN SHE'S NOT GOING TO BE KEEPING ANY OF THESE APPOINTMENTS, EVEN IF WE CAN FIGURE THEM OUT.
TRUE. BUT THESE ARE THE ONLY LEADS WE HAVE RIGHT NOW. AND WE'VE GOT TO FIND HER.
YOU'RE RIGHT, SHE MIGHT BE IN DANGER. BESIDES, WE'VE BEEN CLOSER TO THAT DRAGON THAN ANYONE. WE'VE GOT THE BEST CHANCE OF STOPPING IT.
TMG NEWS
#BIGNEWS
BREAKING!!
DRAGONS GONE WILD...
HOLY CRAP. IS THAT THE THING YOU GUYS FOUGHT?

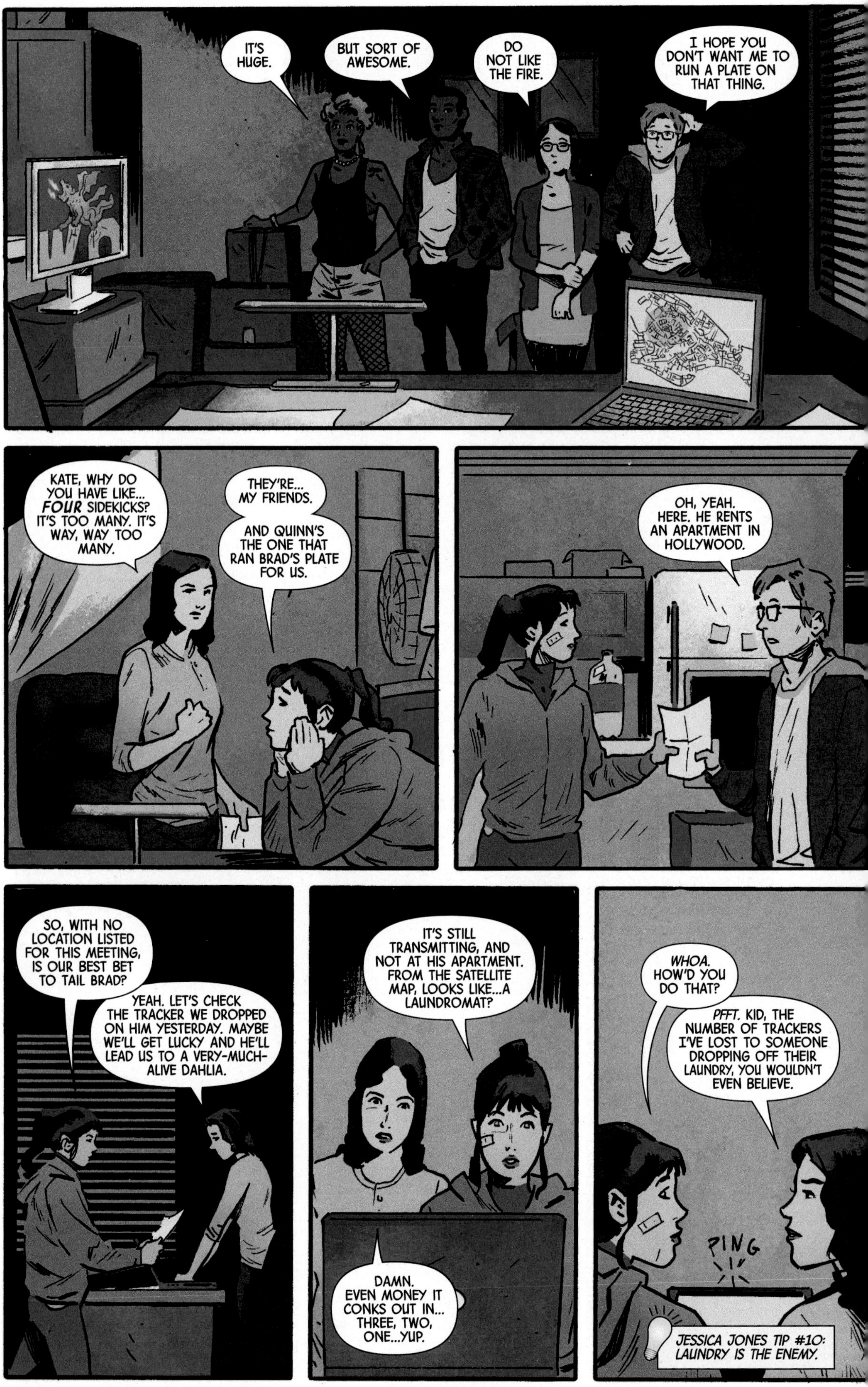
IT'S HUGE.
BUT SORT OF AWESOME.
DO NOT LIKE THE FIRE.
I HOPE YOU DON'T WANT ME TO RUN A PLATE ON THAT THING.
KATE, WHY DO YOU HAVE LIKE... FOUR SIDEKICKS? IT'S TOO MANY. IT'S WAY, WAY TOO MANY.
THEY'RE... MY FRIENDS.
AND QUINN'S THE ONE THAT RAN BRAD'S PLATE FOR US.
OH, YEAH. HERE. HE RENTS AN APARTMENT IN HOLLYWOOD.
SO, WITH NO LOCATION LISTED FOR THIS MEETING, IS OUR BEST BET TO TAIL BRAD?
YEAH. LET'S CHECK THE TRACKER WE DROPPED ON HIM YESTERDAY. MAYBE WE'LL GET LUCKY AND HE'LL LEAD US TO A VERY-MUCH-ALIVE DAHLIA.
IT'S STILL TRANSMITTING, AND NOT AT HIS APARTMENT. FROM THE SATELLITE MAP, LOOKS LIKE...A LAUNDROMAT?
DAMN. EVEN MONEY IT CONKS OUT IN... THREE, TWO, ONE...YUP.
WHOA. HOW'D YOU DO THAT?
PFFT. KID, THE NUMBER OF TRACKERS I'VE LOST TO SOMEONE DROPPING OFF THEIR LAUNDRY, YOU WOULDN'T EVEN BELIEVE.
PING
JESSICA JONES TIP #10: LAUNDRY IS THE ENEMY.

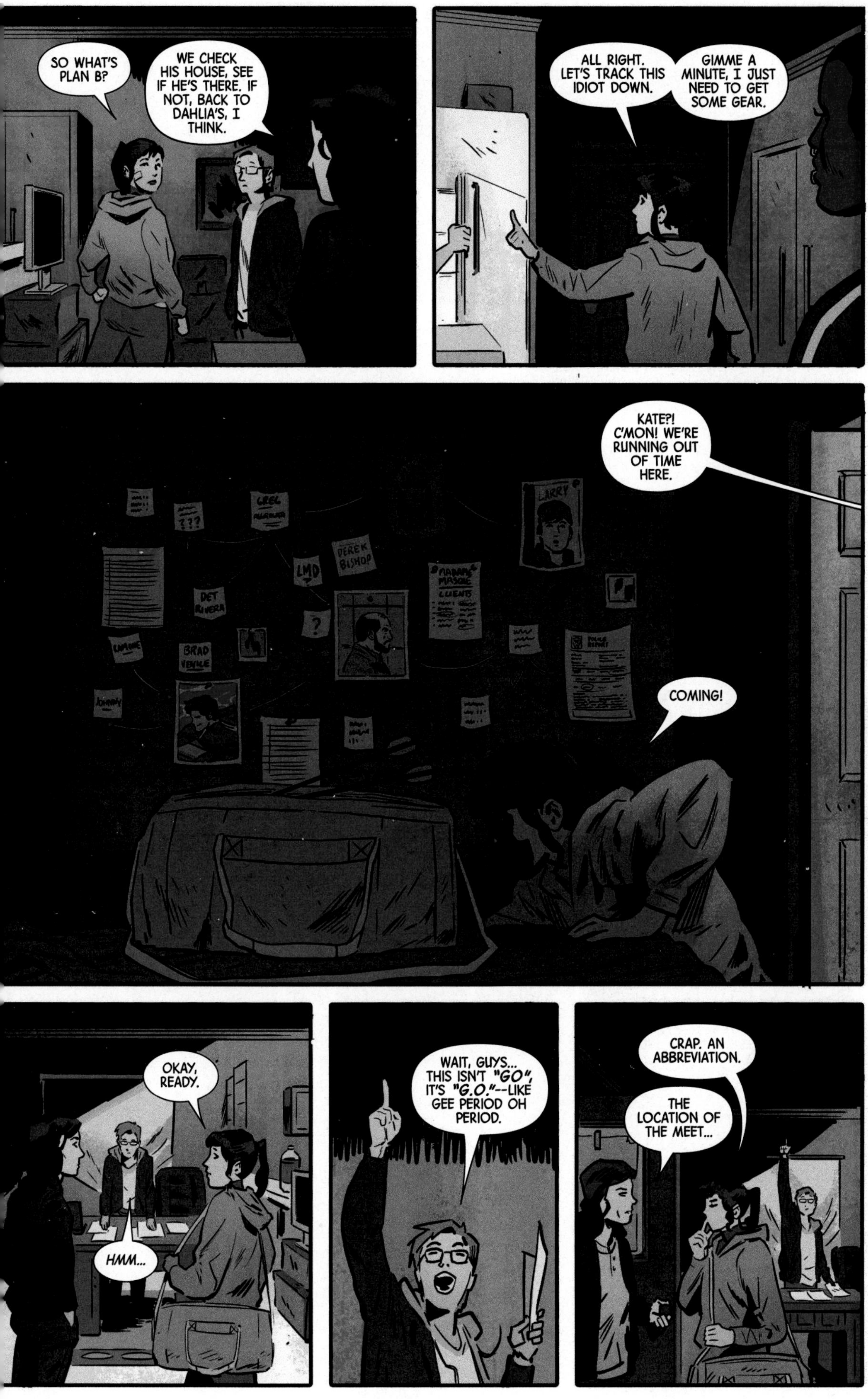
SO WHAT'S PLAN B?
WE CHECK HIS HOUSE, SEE IF HE'S THERE. IF NOT, BACK TO DAHLIA'S, I THINK.
ALL RIGHT. LET'S TRACK THIS IDIOT DOWN.
GIMME A MINUTE, I JUST NEED TO GET SOME GEAR.
KATE?! C'MON! WE'RE RUNNING OUT OF TIME HERE.
COMING!
LARRY
GREG
???
DEREK BISHOP
LMD
DET RIVERA
?
BRAD
MADAME MASQUE CLIENTS
OKAY, READY.
HMM...
WAIT, GUYS... THIS ISN'T "GO", IT'S "G.O."--LIKE GEE PERIOD OH PERIOD.
CRAP. AN ABBREVIATION.
THE LOCATION OF THE MEET...

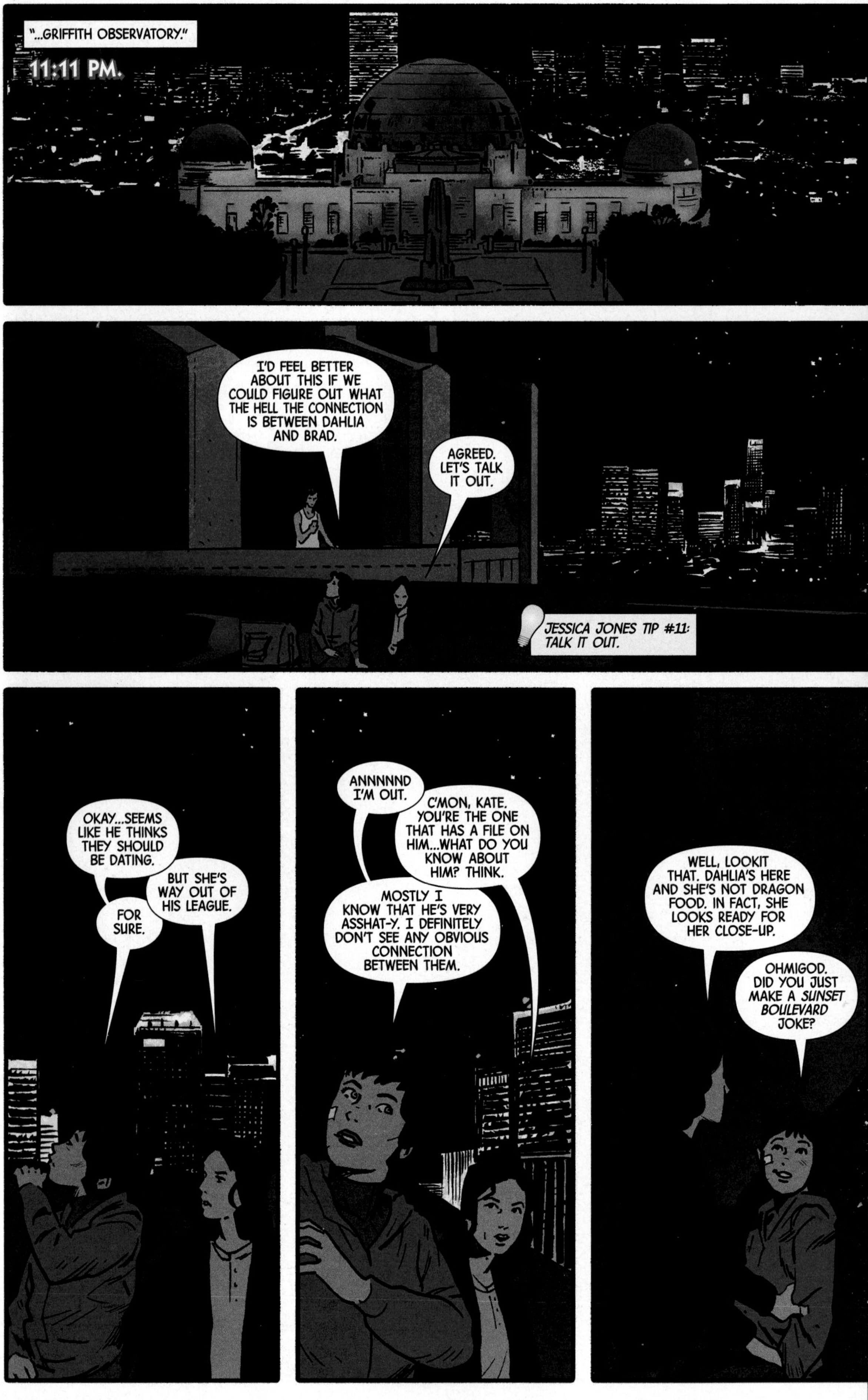
"...GRIFFITH OBSERVATORY."
11:11 PM.
I'D FEEL BETTER ABOUT THIS IF WE COULD FIGURE OUT WHAT THE HELL THE CONNECTION IS BETWEEN DAHLIA AND BRAD.
AGREED. LET'S TALK IT OUT.
JESSICA JONES TIP #11: TALK IT OUT.
OKAY...SEEMS LIKE HE THINKS THEY SHOULD BE DATING.
BUT SHE'S WAY OUT OF HIS LEAGUE.
FOR SURE.
ANNNNND I'M OUT.
C'MON, KATE. YOU'RE THE ONE THAT HAS A FILE ON HIM...WHAT DO YOU KNOW ABOUT HIM? THINK.
MOSTLY I KNOW THAT HE'S VERY ASSHAT-Y. I DEFINITELY DON'T SEE ANY OBVIOUS CONNECTION BETWEEN THEM.
WELL, LOOKIT THAT. DAHLIA'S HERE AND SHE'S NOT DRAGON FOOD. IN FACT, SHE LOOKS READY FOR HER CLOSE-UP.
OHMIGOD. DID YOU JUST MAKE A SUNSET BOULEVARD JOKE?

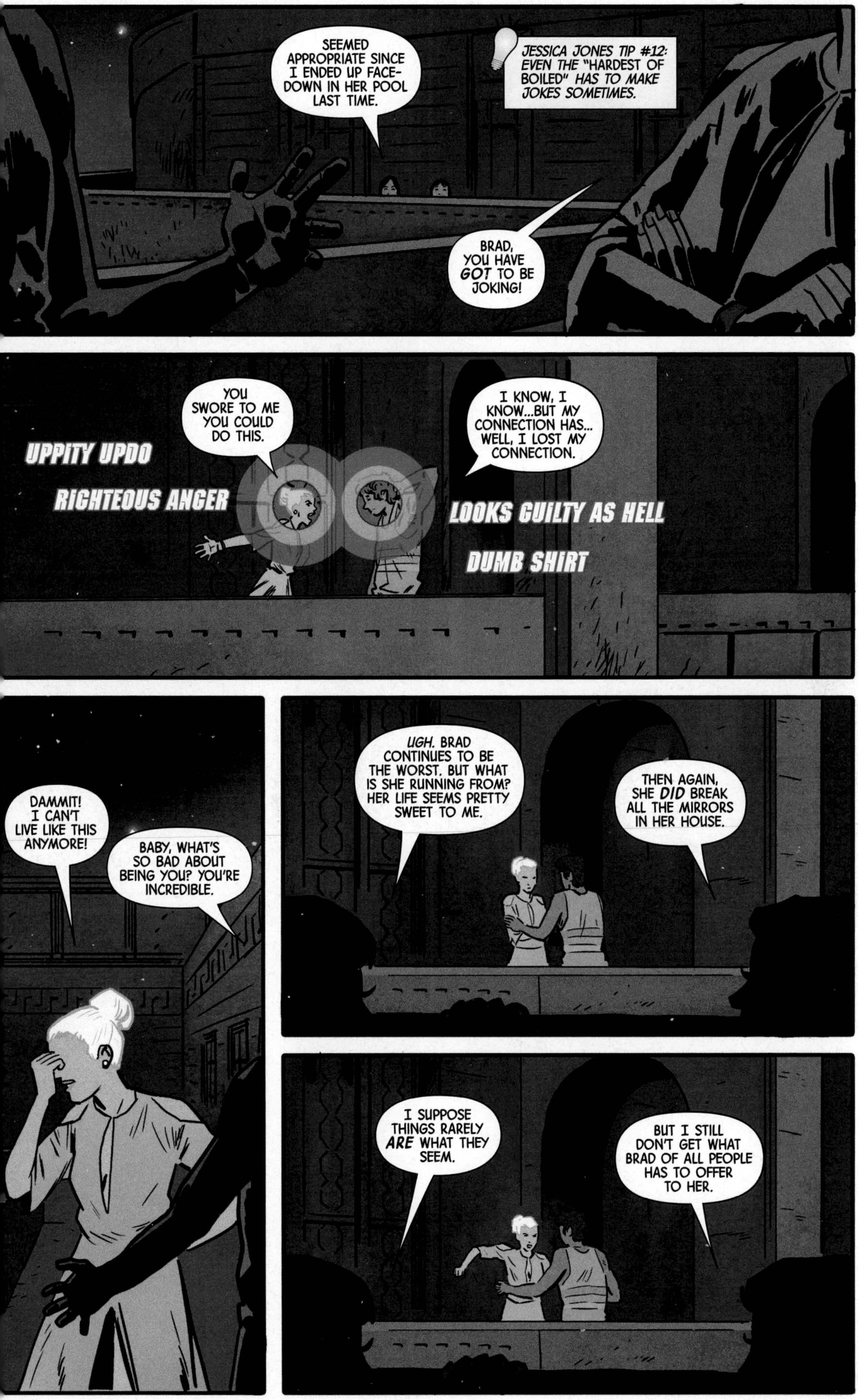
SEEMED APPROPRIATE SINCE I ENDED UP FACE-DOWN IN HER POOL LAST TIME.
JESSICA JONES TIP #12: EVEN THE "HARDEST OF BOILED" HAS TO MAKE JOKES SOMETIMES.
BRAD, YOU HAVE GOT TO BE JOKING!
YOU SWORE TO ME YOU COULD DO THIS.
I KNOW, I KNOW...BUT MY CONNECTION HAS... WELL, I LOST MY CONNECTION.
UPPITY UPDO
RIGHTEOUS ANGER
LOOKS GUILTY AS HELL
DUMB SHIRT
DAMMIT! I CAN'T LIVE LIKE THIS ANYMORE!
BABY, WHAT'S SO BAD ABOUT BEING YOU? YOU'RE INCREDIBLE.
UGH. BRAD CONTINUES TO BE THE WORST. BUT WHAT IS SHE RUNNING FROM? HER LIFE SEEMS PRETTY SWEET TO ME.
THEN AGAIN, SHE DID BREAK ALL THE MIRRORS IN HER HOUSE.
I SUPPOSE THINGS RARELY ARE WHAT THEY SEEM.
BUT I STILL DON'T GET WHAT BRAD OF ALL PEOPLE HAS TO OFFER TO HER.

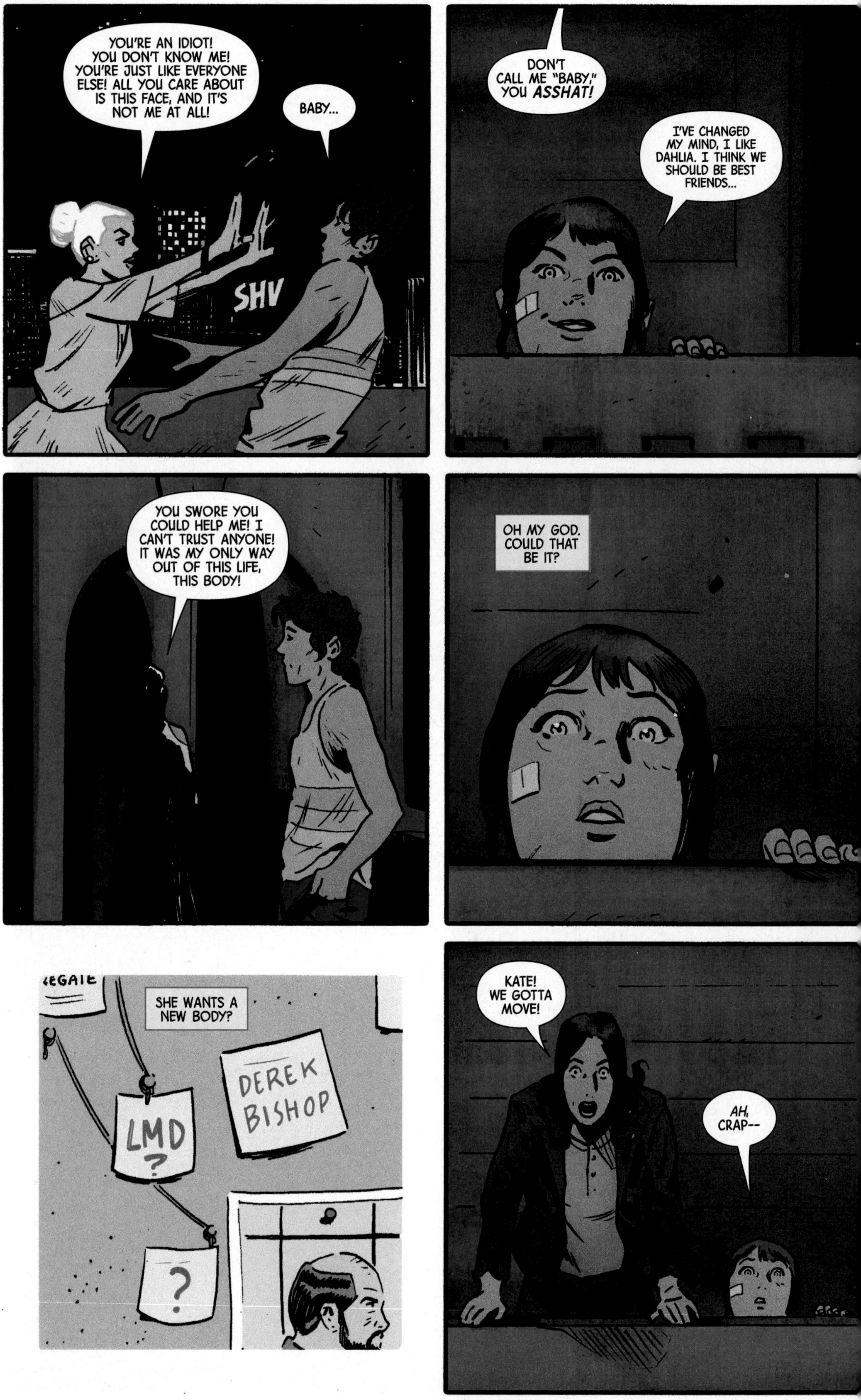
YOU'RE AN IDIOT! YOU DON'T KNOW ME! YOU'RE JUST LIKE EVERYONE ELSE! ALL YOU CARE ABOUT IS THIS FACE, AND IT'S NOT ME AT ALL!
BABY...
DON'T CALL ME "BABY," YOU ASSHAT!
I'VE CHANGED MY MIND, I LIKE DAHLIA. I THINK WE SHOULD BE BEST FRIENDS...
YOU SWORE YOU COULD HELP ME! I CAN'T TRUST ANYONE! IT WAS MY ONLY WAY OUT OF THIS LIFE, THIS BODY!
OH MY GOD. COULD THAT BE IT?
SHE WANTS A NEW BODY?
LMD ?
DEREK BISHOP
?
KATE! WE GOTTA MOVE!
AH, CRAP--

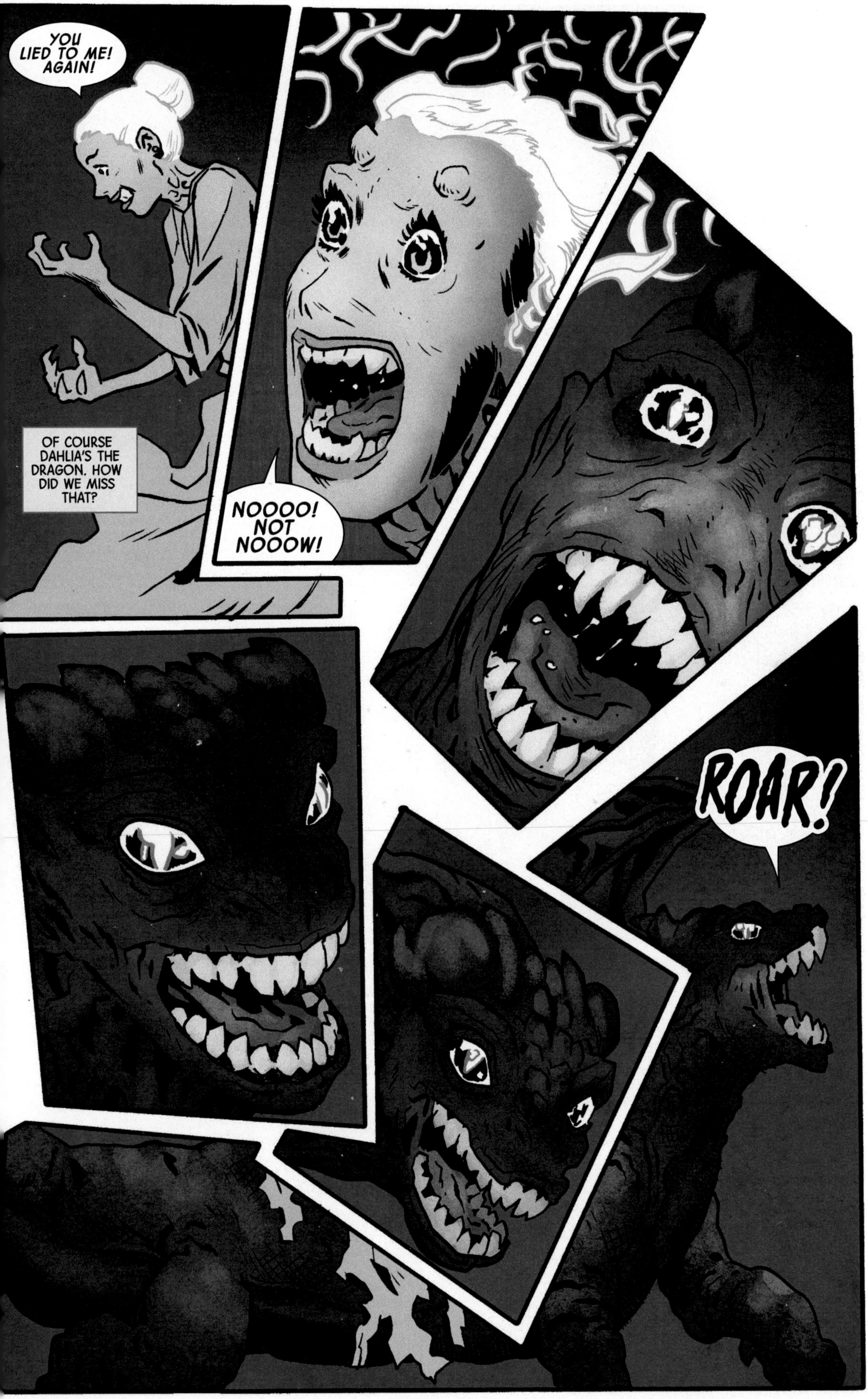
YOU LIED TO ME! AGAIN!
OF COURSE DAHLIA'S THE DRAGON. HOW DID WE MISS THAT?
NOOOO! NOT NOOOW!
ROAR!

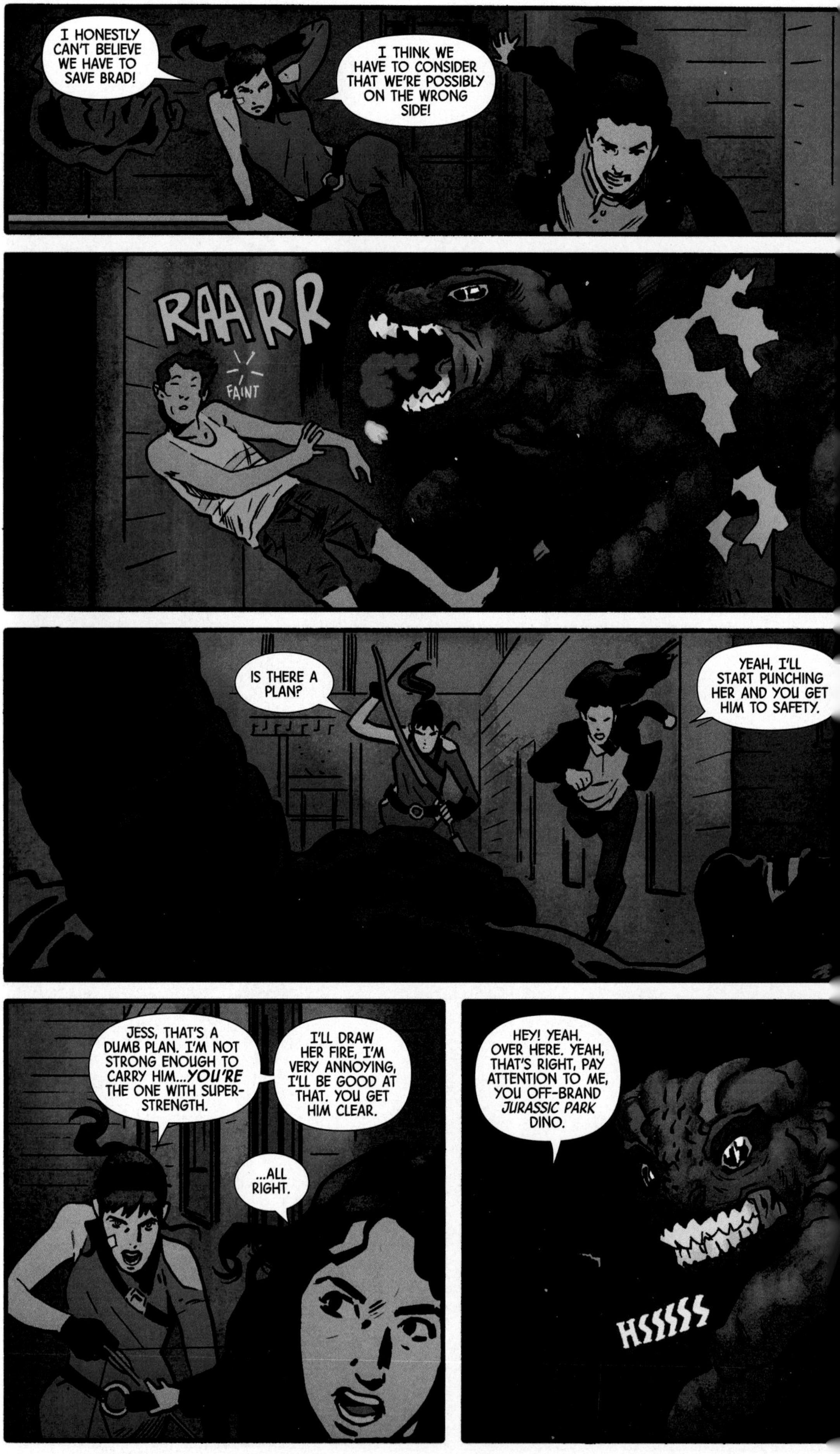
I HONESTLY CAN'T BELIEVE WE HAVE TO SAVE BRAD!
I THINK WE HAVE TO CONSIDER THAT WE'RE POSSIBLY ON THE WRONG SIDE!
RAARR
FAINT
IS THERE A PLAN?
YEAH, I'LL START PUNCHING HER AND YOU GET HIM TO SAFETY.
JESS, THAT'S A DUMB PLAN. I'M NOT STRONG ENOUGH TO CARRY HIM...*YOU'RE* THE ONE WITH SUPER-STRENGTH.
I'LL DRAW HER FIRE, I'M VERY ANNOYING, I'LL BE GOOD AT THAT. YOU GET HIM CLEAR.
...ALL RIGHT.
HEY! YEAH. OVER HERE. YEAH, THAT'S RIGHT, PAY ATTENTION TO ME, YOU OFF-BRAND *JURASSIC PARK* DINO.
HSSSSS

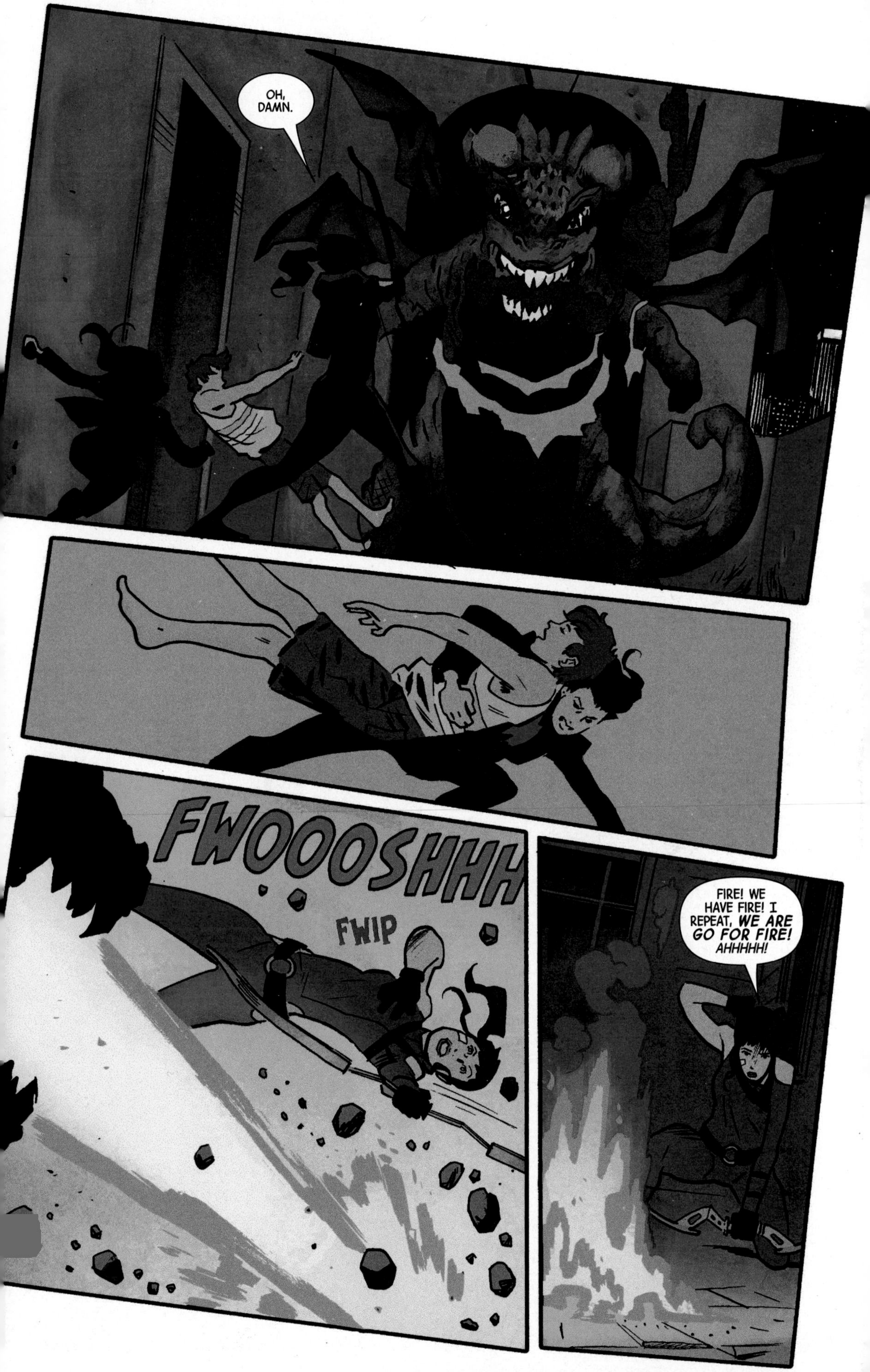
OH, DAMN.
FWOOOSHHH
FWIP
FIRE! WE HAVE FIRE! I REPEAT, WE ARE GO FOR FIRE! AHHHHH!

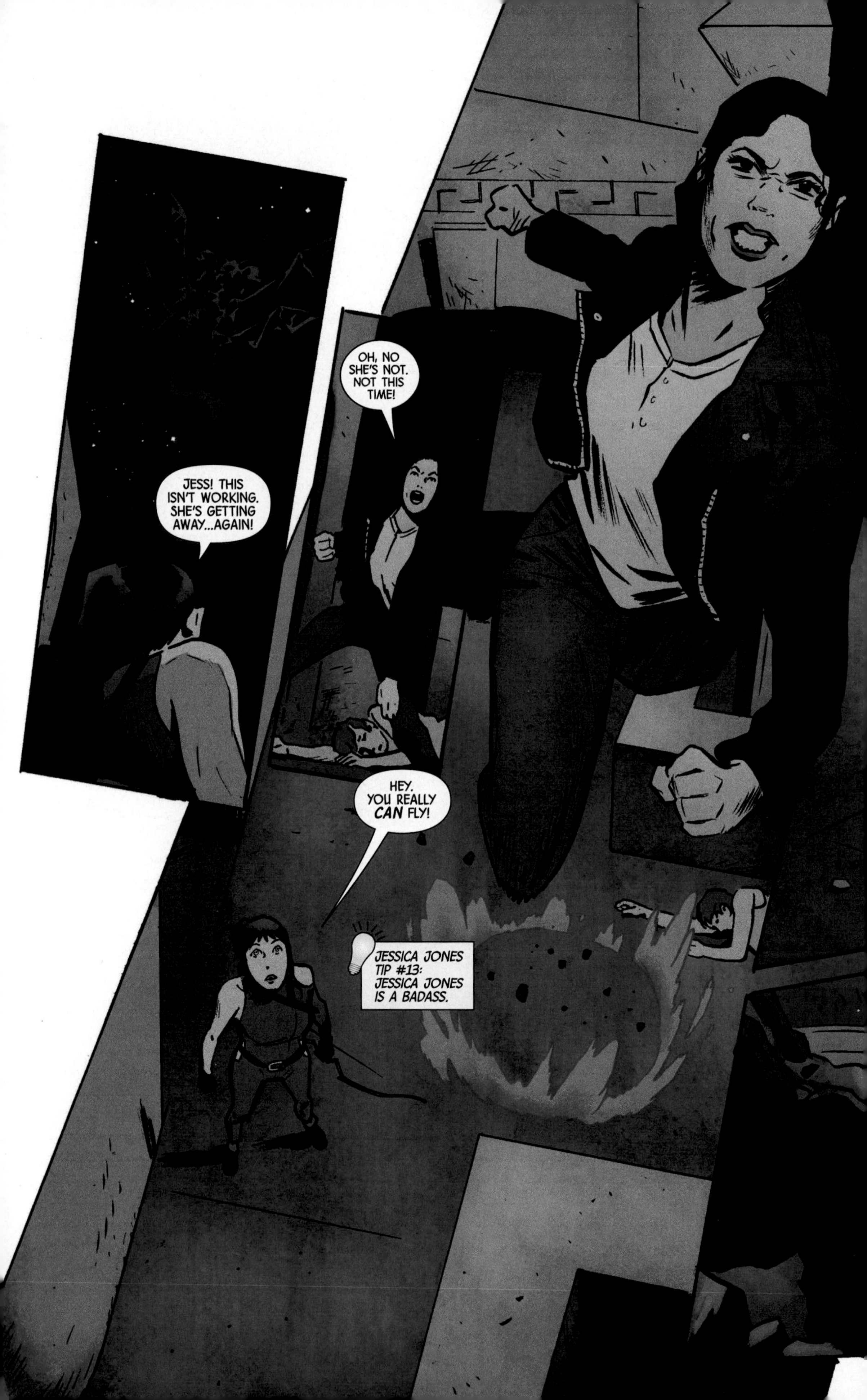
JESS! THIS ISN'T WORKING. SHE'S GETTING AWAY...AGAIN!
OH, NO SHE'S NOT. NOT THIS TIME!
HEY. YOU REALLY CAN FLY!
JESSICA JONES TIP #13: JESSICA JONES IS A BADASS.

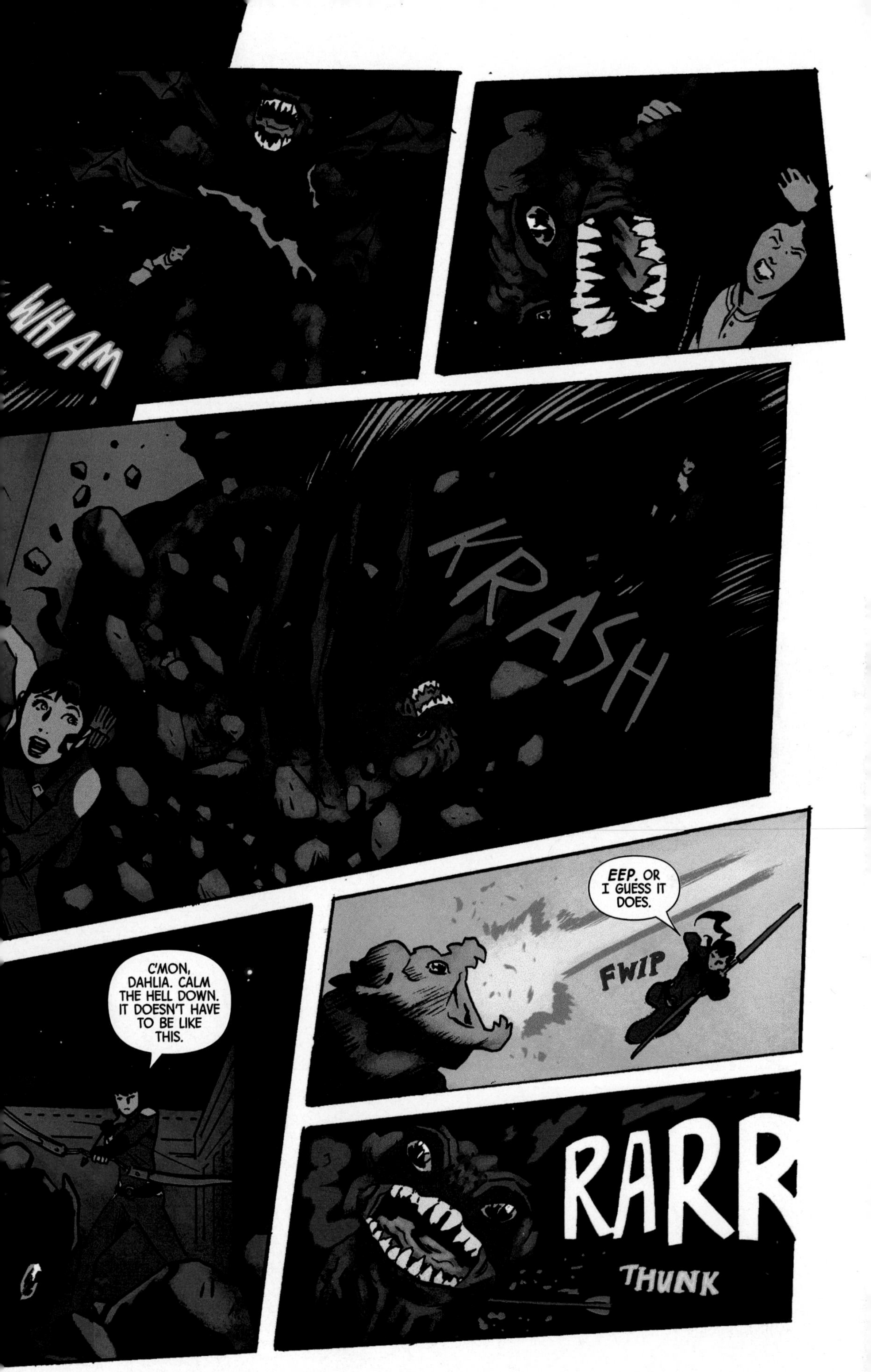
WHAM
KRASH
C'MON, DAHLIA. CALM THE HELL DOWN. IT DOESN'T HAVE TO BE LIKE THIS.
EEP. OR I GUESS IT DOES.
FWIP
RARR
THUNK

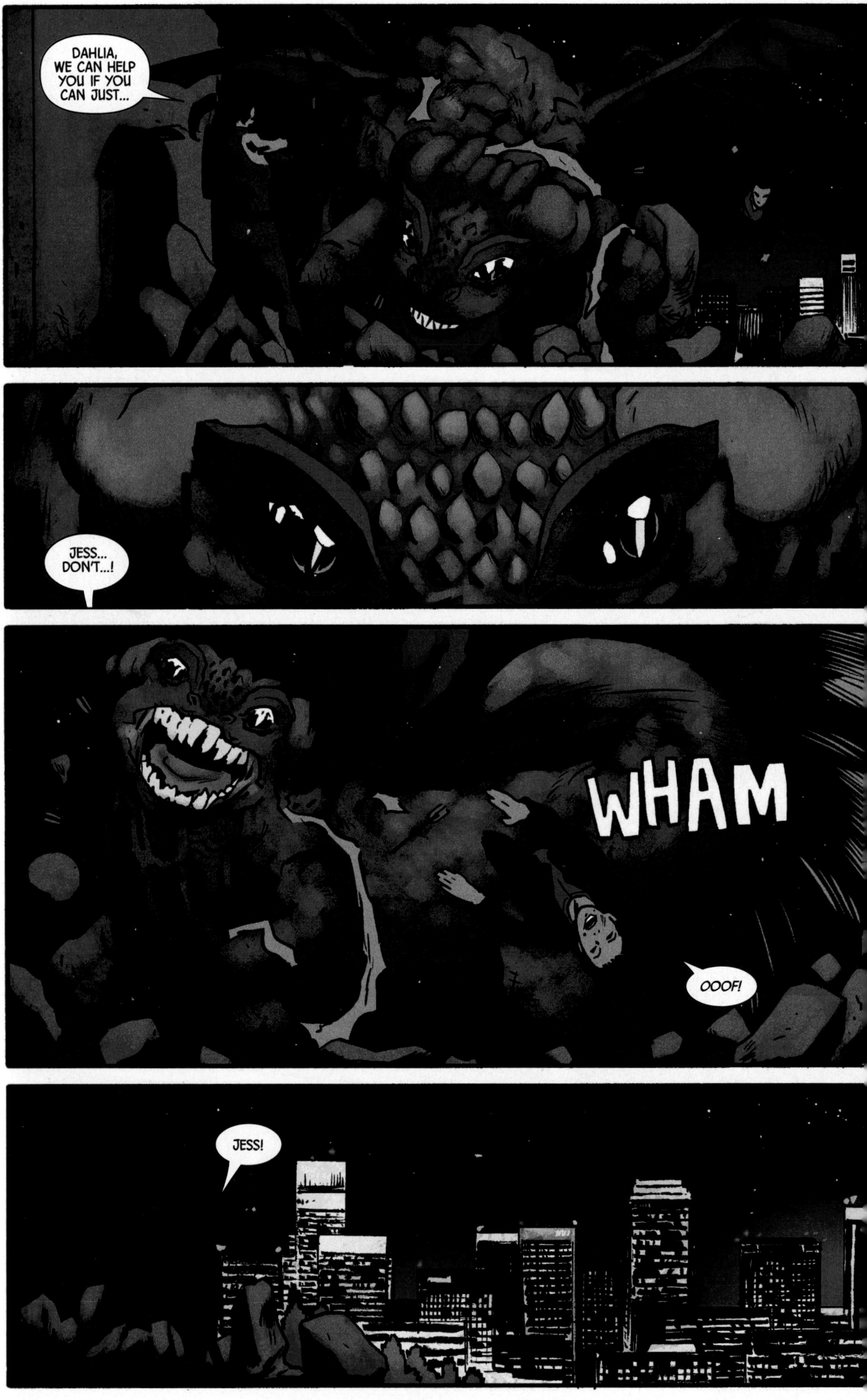
DAHLIA, WE CAN HELP YOU IF YOU CAN JUST...
JESS... DON'T...!
WHAM
OOOF!
JESS!

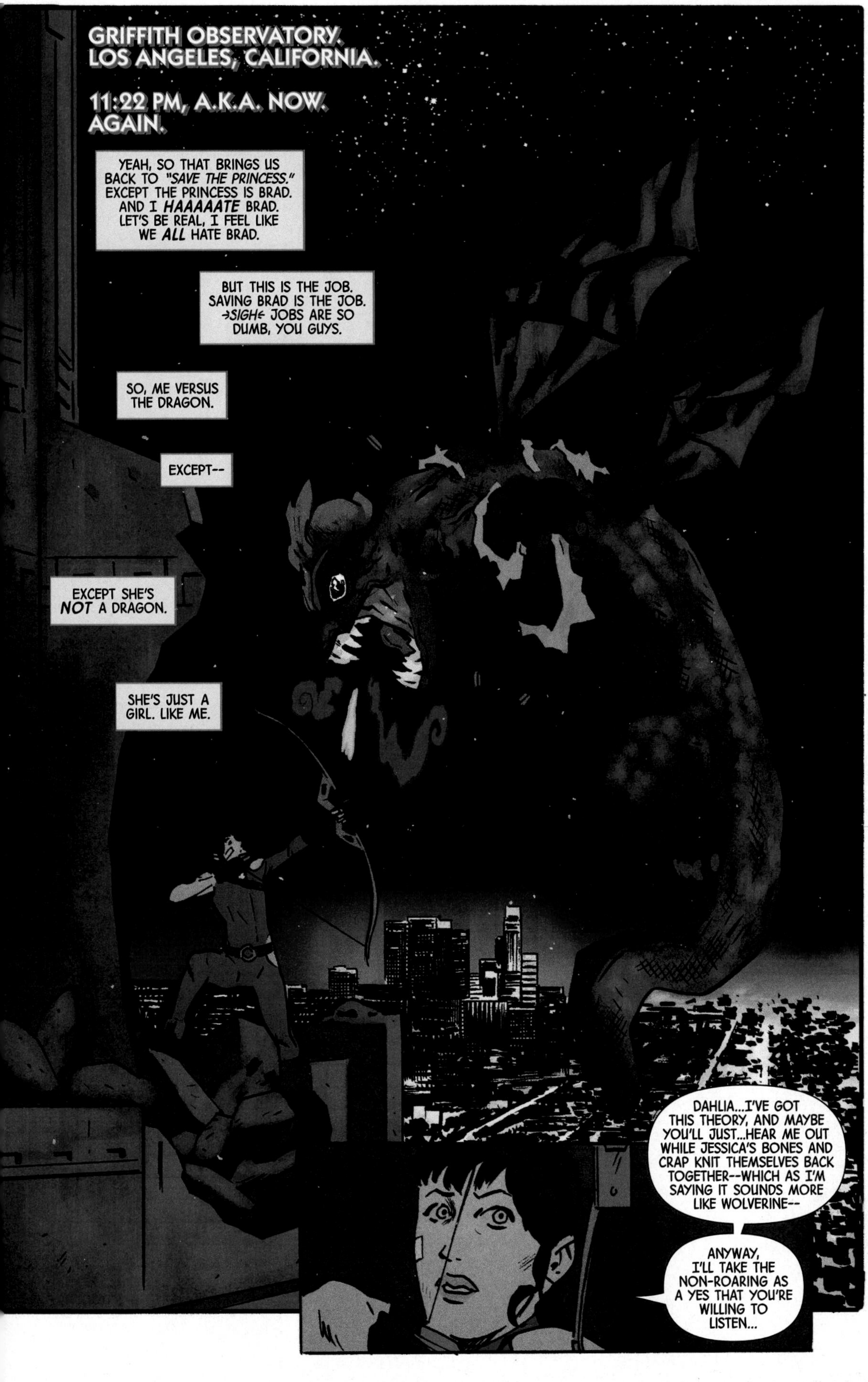
GRIFFITH OBSERVATORY.
LOS ANGELES, CALIFORNIA.
11:22 PM, A.K.A. NOW. AGAIN.
YEAH, SO THAT BRINGS US BACK TO "SAVE THE PRINCESS." EXCEPT THE PRINCESS IS BRAD. AND I HAAAAATE BRAD. LET'S BE REAL, I FEEL LIKE WE ALL HATE BRAD.
BUT THIS IS THE JOB. SAVING BRAD IS THE JOB. →SIGH← JOBS ARE SO DUMB, YOU GUYS.
SO, ME VERSUS THE DRAGON.
EXCEPT--
EXCEPT SHE'S NOT A DRAGON.
SHE'S JUST A GIRL. LIKE ME.
DAHLIA...I'VE GOT THIS THEORY, AND MAYBE YOU'LL JUST...HEAR ME OUT WHILE JESSICA'S BONES AND CRAP KNIT THEMSELVES BACK TOGETHER--WHICH AS I'M SAYING IT SOUNDS MORE LIKE WOLVERINE--
ANYWAY, I'LL TAKE THE NON-ROARING AS A YES THAT YOU'RE WILLING TO LISTEN...

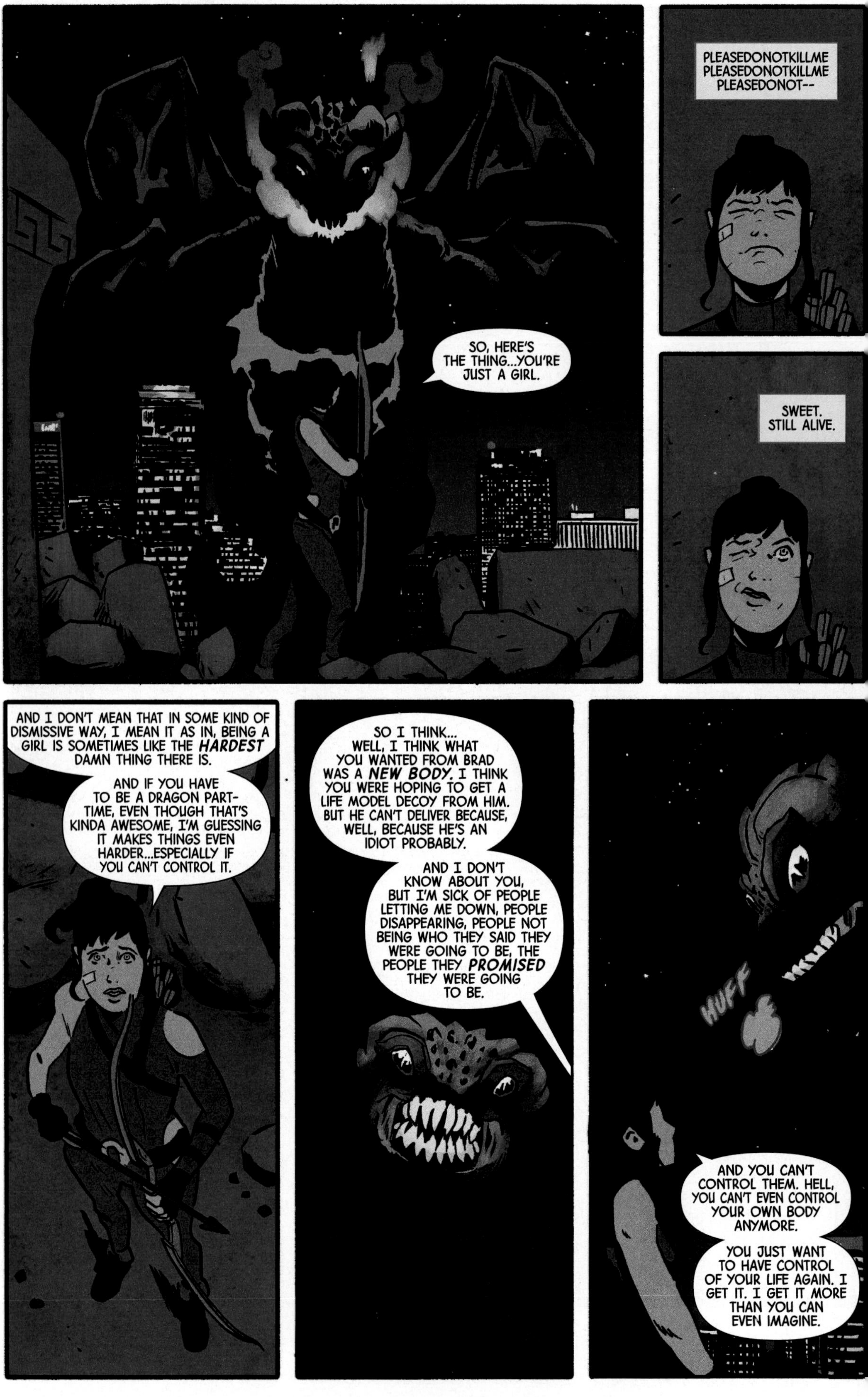
SO, HERE'S THE THING...YOU'RE JUST A GIRL.
PLEASEDONOTKILLME PLEASEDONOTKILLME PLEASEDONOT--
SWEET. STILL ALIVE.
AND I DON'T MEAN THAT IN SOME KIND OF DISMISSIVE WAY, I MEAN IT AS IN, BEING A GIRL IS SOMETIMES LIKE THE *HARDEST* DAMN THING THERE IS.
AND IF YOU HAVE TO BE A DRAGON PART-TIME, EVEN THOUGH THAT'S KINDA AWESOME, I'M GUESSING IT MAKES THINGS EVEN HARDER...ESPECIALLY IF YOU CAN'T CONTROL IT.
SO I THINK... WELL, I THINK WHAT YOU WANTED FROM BRAD WAS A *NEW BODY.* I THINK YOU WERE HOPING TO GET A LIFE MODEL DECOY FROM HIM. BUT HE CAN'T DELIVER BECAUSE, WELL, BECAUSE HE'S AN IDIOT PROBABLY.
AND I DON'T KNOW ABOUT YOU, BUT I'M SICK OF PEOPLE LETTING ME DOWN, PEOPLE DISAPPEARING, PEOPLE NOT BEING WHO THEY SAID THEY WERE GOING TO BE, THE PEOPLE THEY *PROMISED* THEY WERE GOING TO BE.
HUFF
AND YOU CAN'T CONTROL THEM. HELL, YOU CAN'T EVEN CONTROL YOUR OWN BODY ANYMORE.
YOU JUST WANT TO HAVE CONTROL OF YOUR LIFE AGAIN. I GET IT. I GET IT MORE THAN YOU CAN EVEN IMAGINE.

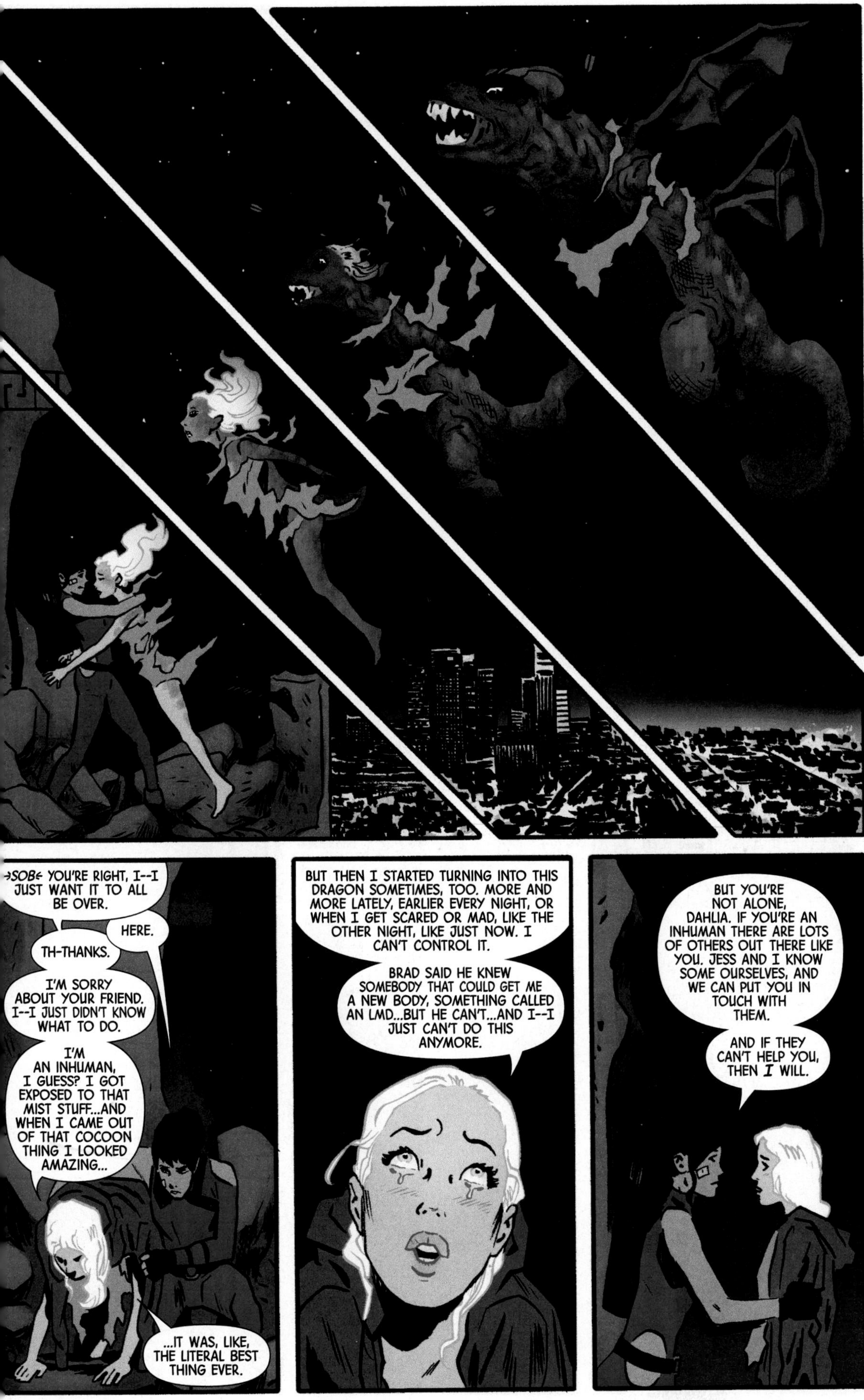

>SOB< YOU'RE RIGHT, I--I JUST WANT IT TO ALL BE OVER.
HERE.
TH-THANKS.
I'M SORRY ABOUT YOUR FRIEND. I--I JUST DIDN'T KNOW WHAT TO DO.
I'M AN INHUMAN, I GUESS? I GOT EXPOSED TO THAT MIST STUFF...AND WHEN I CAME OUT OF THAT COCOON THING I LOOKED AMAZING...
...IT WAS, LIKE, THE LITERAL BEST THING EVER.
BUT THEN I STARTED TURNING INTO THIS DRAGON SOMETIMES, TOO. MORE AND MORE LATELY, EARLIER EVERY NIGHT, OR WHEN I GET SCARED OR MAD, LIKE THE OTHER NIGHT, LIKE JUST NOW. I CAN'T CONTROL IT.
BRAD SAID HE KNEW SOMEBODY THAT COULD GET ME A NEW BODY, SOMETHING CALLED AN LMD...BUT HE CAN'T...AND I--I JUST CAN'T DO THIS ANYMORE.
BUT YOU'RE NOT ALONE, DAHLIA. IF YOU'RE AN INHUMAN THERE ARE LOTS OF OTHERS OUT THERE LIKE YOU. JESS AND I KNOW SOME OURSELVES, AND WE CAN PUT YOU IN TOUCH WITH THEM.
AND IF THEY CAN'T HELP YOU, THEN *I* WILL.

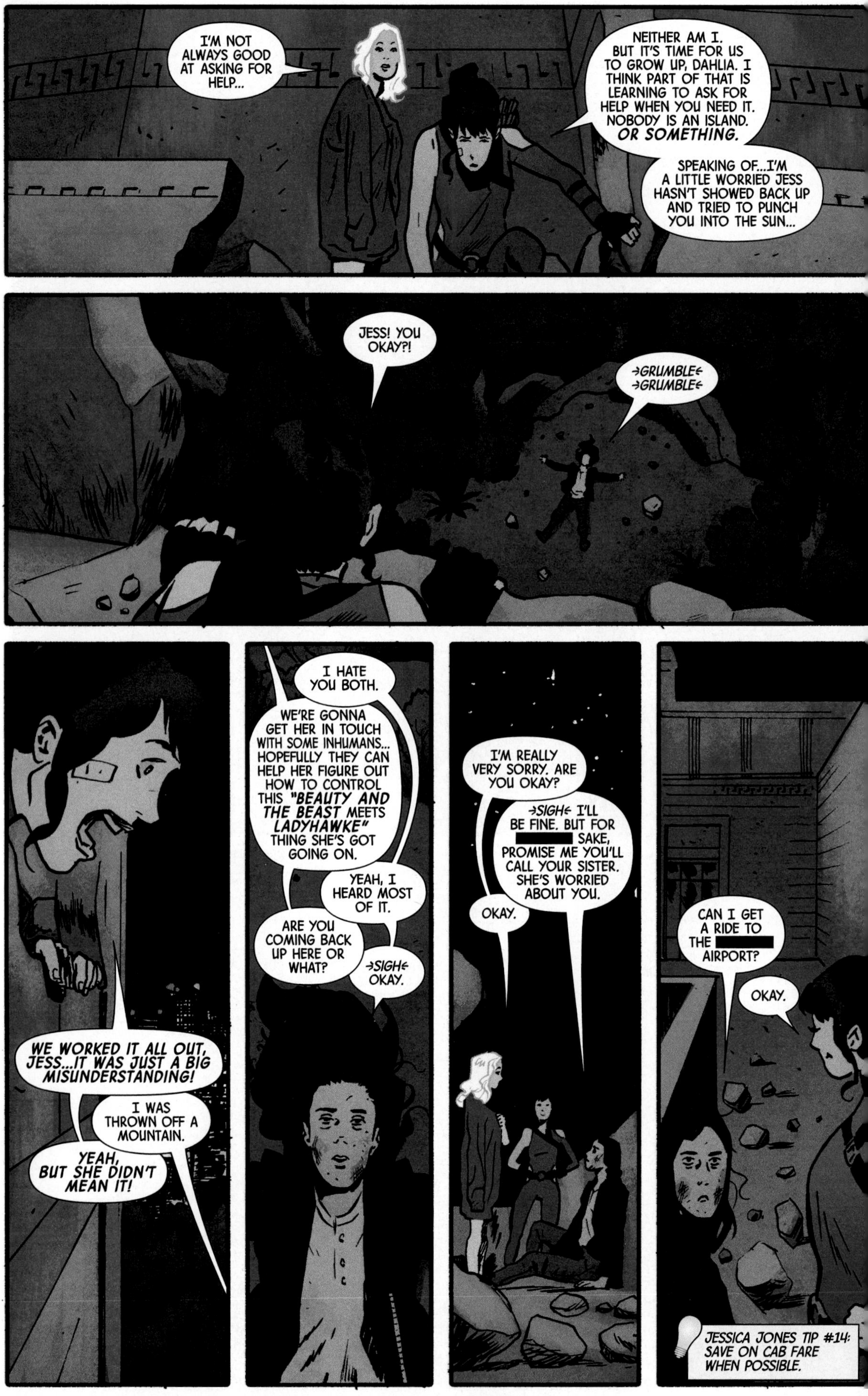
I'M NOT ALWAYS GOOD AT ASKING FOR HELP...
NEITHER AM I. BUT IT'S TIME FOR US TO GROW UP, DAHLIA. I THINK PART OF THAT IS LEARNING TO ASK FOR HELP WHEN YOU NEED IT. NOBODY IS AN ISLAND. OR SOMETHING.
SPEAKING OF...I'M A LITTLE WORRIED JESS HASN'T SHOWED BACK UP AND TRIED TO PUNCH YOU INTO THE SUN...
JESS! YOU OKAY?!
→GRUMBLE← →GRUMBLE←
WE WORKED IT ALL OUT, JESS...IT WAS JUST A BIG MISUNDERSTANDING!
I WAS THROWN OFF A MOUNTAIN.
YEAH, BUT SHE DIDN'T MEAN IT!
I HATE YOU BOTH.
WE'RE GONNA GET HER IN TOUCH WITH SOME INHUMANS... HOPEFULLY THEY CAN HELP HER FIGURE OUT HOW TO CONTROL THIS "BEAUTY AND THE BEAST MEETS LADYHAWKE" THING SHE'S GOT GOING ON.
YEAH, I HEARD MOST OF IT.
ARE YOU COMING BACK UP HERE OR WHAT?
→SIGH← OKAY.
I'M REALLY VERY SORRY. ARE YOU OKAY?
→SIGH← I'LL BE FINE. BUT FOR [redacted] SAKE, PROMISE ME YOU'LL CALL YOUR SISTER. SHE'S WORRIED ABOUT YOU.
OKAY.
CAN I GET A RIDE TO THE [redacted] AIRPORT?
OKAY.
JESSICA JONES TIP #14: SAVE ON CAB FARE WHEN POSSIBLE.

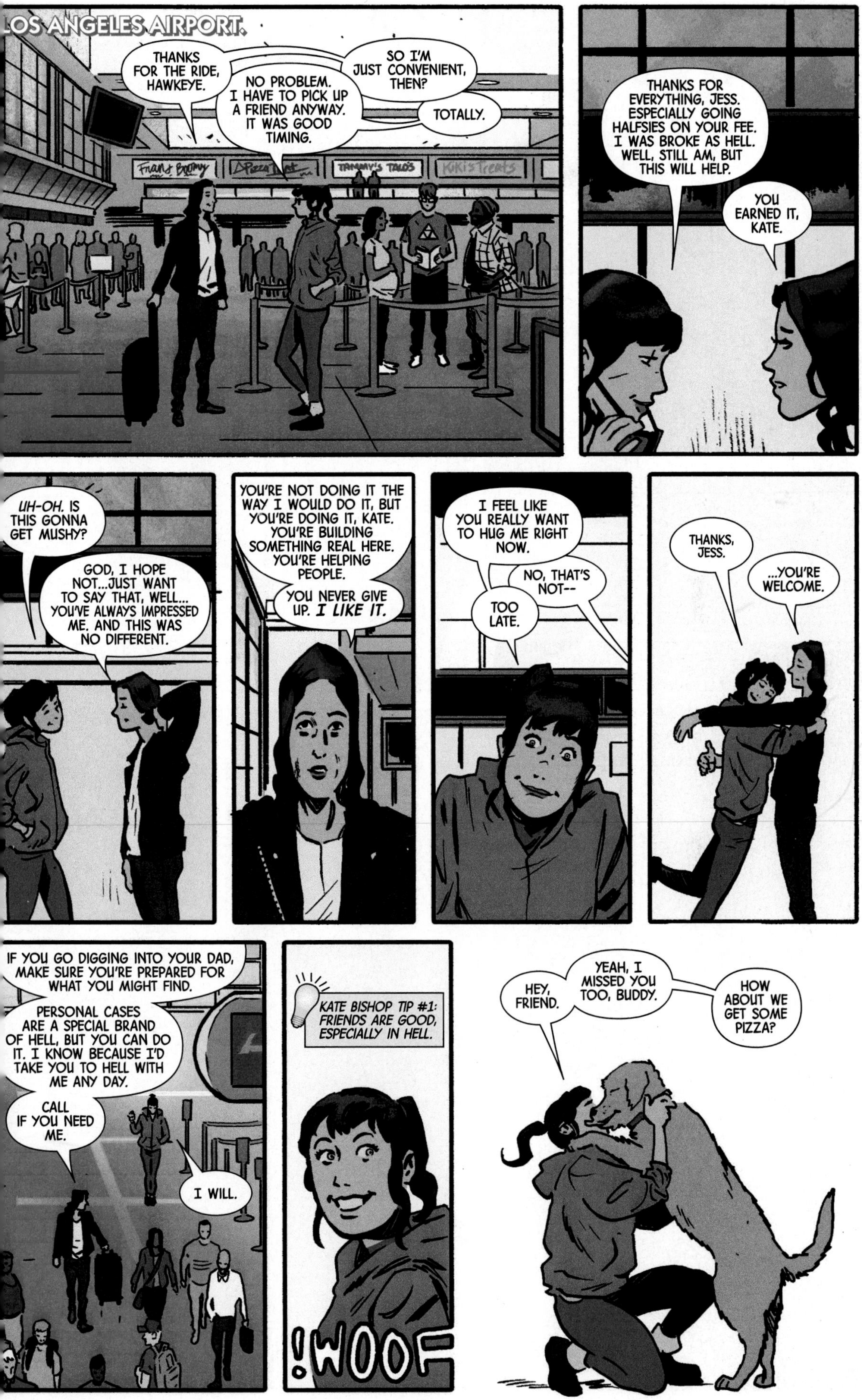

LOS ANGELES AIRPORT.
THANKS FOR THE RIDE, HAWKEYE.
NO PROBLEM. I HAVE TO PICK UP A FRIEND ANYWAY. IT WAS GOOD TIMING.
SO I'M JUST CONVENIENT, THEN?
TOTALLY.
TAMMY'S TACOS
THANKS FOR EVERYTHING, JESS. ESPECIALLY GOING HALFSIES ON YOUR FEE. I WAS BROKE AS HELL. WELL, STILL AM, BUT THIS WILL HELP.
YOU EARNED IT, KATE.
UH-OH. IS THIS GONNA GET MUSHY?
GOD, I HOPE NOT...JUST WANT TO SAY THAT, WELL... YOU'VE ALWAYS IMPRESSED ME. AND THIS WAS NO DIFFERENT.
YOU'RE NOT DOING IT THE WAY I WOULD DO IT, BUT YOU'RE DOING IT, KATE. YOU'RE BUILDING SOMETHING REAL HERE. YOU'RE HELPING PEOPLE.
YOU NEVER GIVE UP. I LIKE IT.
I FEEL LIKE YOU REALLY WANT TO HUG ME RIGHT NOW.
NO, THAT'S NOT--
TOO LATE.
THANKS, JESS.
...YOU'RE WELCOME.
IF YOU GO DIGGING INTO YOUR DAD, MAKE SURE YOU'RE PREPARED FOR WHAT YOU MIGHT FIND.
PERSONAL CASES ARE A SPECIAL BRAND OF HELL, BUT YOU CAN DO IT. I KNOW BECAUSE I'D TAKE YOU TO HELL WITH ME ANY DAY.
CALL IF YOU NEED ME.
I WILL.
KATE BISHOP TIP #1: FRIENDS ARE GOOD, ESPECIALLY IN HELL.
!WOOF
HEY, FRIEND.
YEAH, I MISSED YOU TOO, BUDDY.
HOW ABOUT WE GET SOME PIZZA?

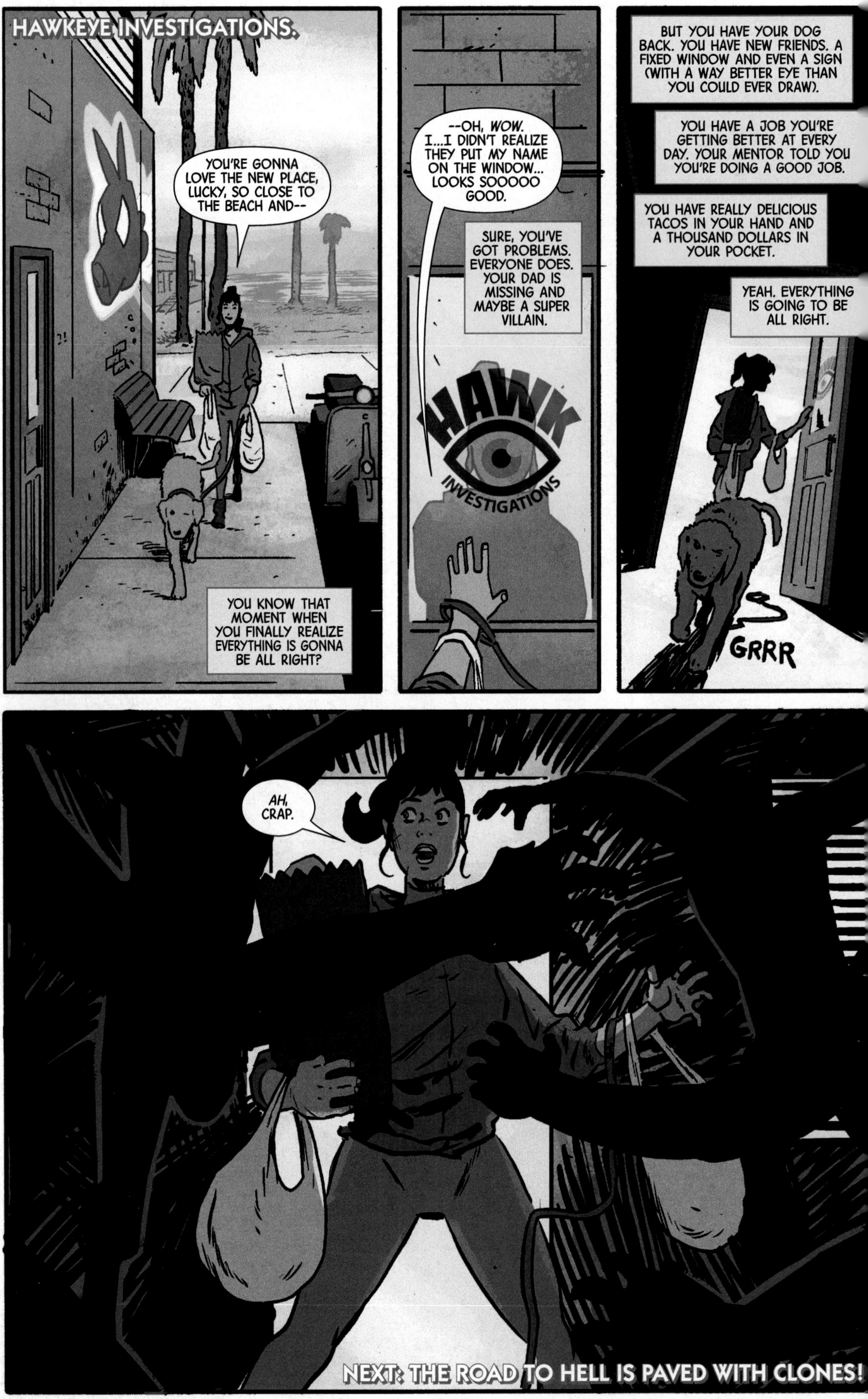
HAWKEYE INVESTIGATIONS.
YOU'RE GONNA LOVE THE NEW PLACE, LUCKY, SO CLOSE TO THE BEACH AND--
YOU KNOW THAT MOMENT WHEN YOU FINALLY REALIZE EVERYTHING IS GONNA BE ALL RIGHT?
--OH, WOW. I...I DIDN'T REALIZE THEY PUT MY NAME ON THE WINDOW... LOOKS SOOOOO GOOD.
SURE, YOU'VE GOT PROBLEMS. EVERYONE DOES. YOUR DAD IS MISSING AND MAYBE A SUPER VILLAIN.
HAWK INVESTIGATIONS
BUT YOU HAVE YOUR DOG BACK. YOU HAVE NEW FRIENDS. A FIXED WINDOW AND EVEN A SIGN (WITH A WAY BETTER EYE THAN YOU COULD EVER DRAW).
YOU HAVE A JOB YOU'RE GETTING BETTER AT EVERY DAY. YOUR MENTOR TOLD YOU YOU'RE DOING A GOOD JOB.
YOU HAVE REALLY DELICIOUS TACOS IN YOUR HAND AND A THOUSAND DOLLARS IN YOUR POCKET.
YEAH. EVERYTHING IS GOING TO BE ALL RIGHT.
GRRR
AH, CRAP.
NEXT: THE ROAD TO HELL IS PAVED WITH CLONES!

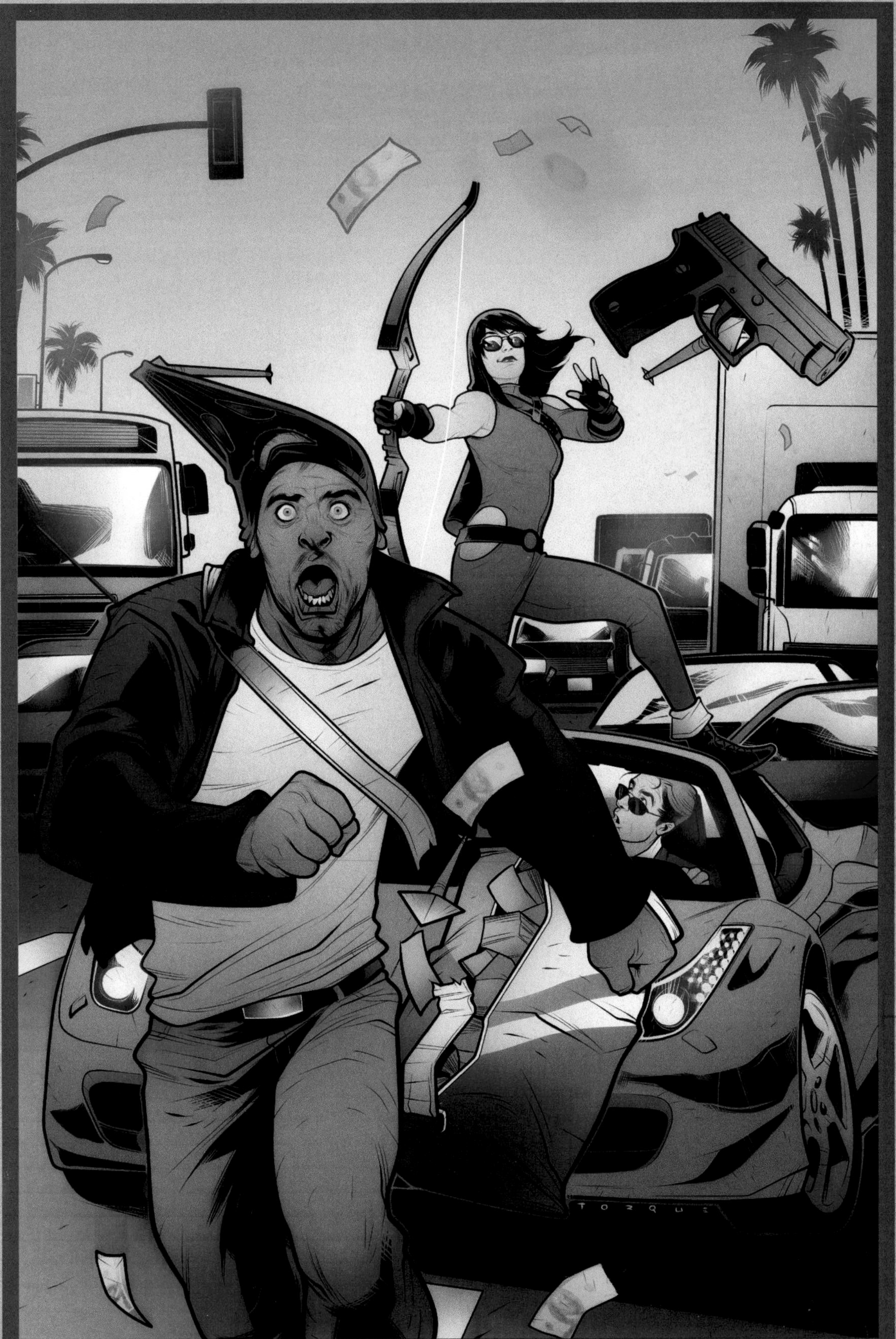
TORQUE

#3 variant by Elizabeth Torque

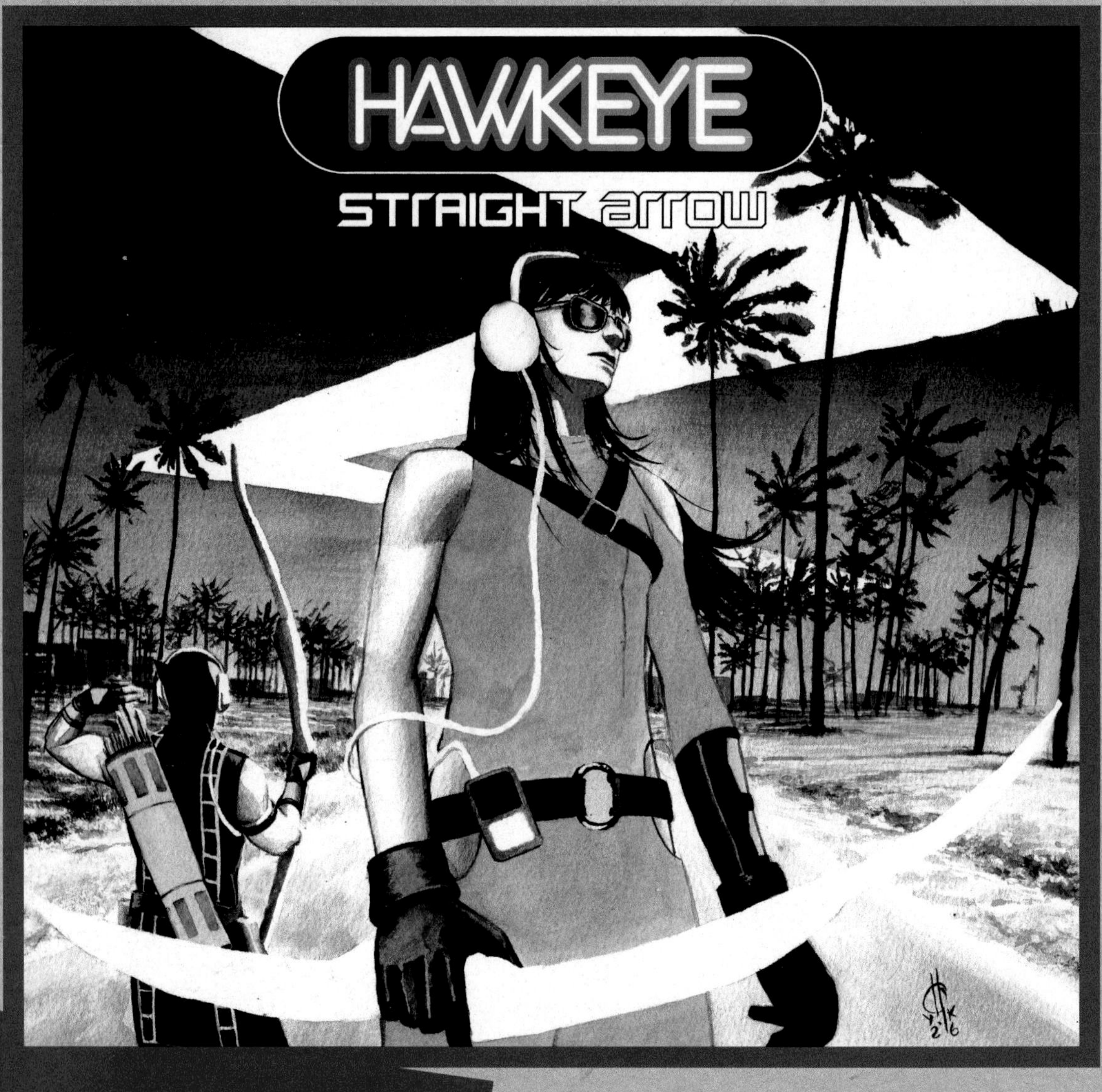
HAWKEYE
STRAIGHT arrow

#1 hip-hop variant
by Marco Rudy